Ice Bears and Kotick

Ice Bears and Kotick

Rowing on Top of the World

Peter Webb *Best wishes,*

Peter Webb

SEAFARER BOOKS

SHERIDAN HOUSE

S

© Peter Webb 2007

First published in the UK by
Seafarer Books
102 Redwald Road
Rendlesham
Woodbridge
Suffolk IP12 2TE
www.seafarerbooks.com

2nd impression 2009

And in the USA by
Sheridan House Inc.
145 Palisade Street
Dobbs Ferry
NY 10522
www.sheridanhouse.com

UK ISBN   978-1-906266-03-5
USA ISBN 978-1-57409-264-6

Library of Congress Cataloging-in-Publication Data

Webb, Peter, 1968-
Ice bears and Kotick : rowing on top of the world / Peter Webb.
p. cm.
ISBN 978-1-57409-264-6 (pbk. : alk. paper)
1. Webb, Peter, 1968—Travel—Norway—Spitsbergen Island. 2.
Webb, Peter, 1968—Travel—Arctic regions. 3. Spitsbergen Island
(Norway)—Description and travel. 4. Arctic regions—Description
and travel. 5. Rowing. I. Title.

G780.W33 2008
910.9163'24—dc22
2007040396

Edited by Hugh Brazier
Typesetting and design by Julie Rainford
Cover design by Louis Mackay
Drawings by Peter Webb
Photographs from the author's private collection

Printed in Finland by WS Bookwell OY

To my mother and father

CONTENTS

Foreword by Dr Monica Kristensen
Explanation and thanks

FOREWORD

It must be some sort of human instinct. Whenever we encounter an island, we immediately want to circumnavigate it. However lovely the beach in front of us is, we are curious to know if the one around the corner is better. Maybe it is only natural. Once you have seen an island from all angles, you know its geography. You are in control. The island is yours.

I met Peter Webb for the first time at the Hat and Feathers in Cambridge, close to the Scott Polar Research Institute, where I was working. He asked me to become a patron for his undergraduate geography expedition to Svalbard. In my mind patrons were ancient and extremely accomplished persons, and I felt that I was neither. We had spoken on the phone many times before we met. Every time I had forgotten who he was, and had to be reminded by a young, very polite voice:

'Nick has phoned you about me. I am going on an expedition to Svalbard. We would like you to be our patron.'

At last we met. A ridiculously young man stood up when I entered the pub. He insisted on paying for my drink. I was embarrassed, but he was adamant.

Lesson number one: Peter does not give in.

Peter's expedition to Svalbard went well, of course. And then I heard about the plan to sail and row a small boat around Spitsbergen. Since I had spent about two years in the village furthest north on the planet, the little mining town of Ny Ålesund, I felt that I knew something about the hardship involved in a circumnavigation of Spitsbergen. I also knew Wally Herbert and had heard for years about his many interrupted attempts to sail around Greenland.

Svalbard is, of course, much smaller than Greenland. But the forbidding nature is the same. The cold, the loneliness, the vast space without another human being. The sometimes bad weather. Not to mention the polar bears. I was worried. But most people I spoke to did not think that Peter and his friend would actually go ahead with the expedition.

Lesson number two: Peter does not give up.

I must have been in Antarctica, on one of many expeditions to that continent, when I heard that the two men were under way. Later I heard that they had actually made it. As the first boat ever, they had rowed and sailed around the whole island.

This is an amazing accomplishment. Although many had tried – with much publicity and hoopla – no one had done it before them. No one has done it since.

Lesson number three: Peter goes through with things.

This book is about how, what, where, and maybe a little bit about why, too. Do buy this book and read it. It is an old-fashioned account of a proper Arctic adventure performed in the best tradition of Cambridge exploring: competent, successful and modest. When Peter contacted me about writing a foreword to his story, I was delighted. Good for you, Peter – the trip and the book! The island is yours.

Dr Monica Kristensen

EXPLANATION AND THANKS

I feel bound to give two explanations to the potential reader. First, why did this story take sixteen years to write? Put simply, that is because I did it a number of times and other things happened. The second: why do I think this story is still worth telling? That is because the question 'what drives us?' is important and because the changing weather will melt most of the Arctic ice before very long. I offer this story as a window onto that wilderness. It is also my own small plea for action, one that I hope is no longer required.

It will help the reader to know that I have taken the liberty of using both Norwegian and English names, and sometimes the English version of the Norwegian name, depending on which I found most evocative. You should also know that some events have been re-ordered for the sake of the narrative. It's no secret which parts these were, and the narrative modifications are minor. The dates, times and distances that are reproduced at the back of the book with the detailed maps are all accurate.

If you read through to the end you'll see that I couldn't have made the journey without Shaggy, it would never have happened without Nick, and it was more fun that Katie was there too. So I want to give these three a special thank-you from deep down. Thanks also to the Governor's Office Head of Historic Sites, Per Kyrre Reymert, for helping with factual details (the remaining errors are my own) and to Åsmund Lien for allowing the reproduction of Oselvar Foundation information at the back of this book.

In England I want to thank all those who read or listened to drafts. You know who you are, many thanks. I want to mention and thank Tessa McWatt for showing me how to stitch a story together. And a big thank you to Patricia Eve of Seafarer Books for buying me lunch on a cold snowy day in Orford and for saying, 'I think you should be encouraged.' This book is the result. Thanks also to her team: Hugh, who did the editing, Julie, who did the typesetting, and Louis, who did the photo graphics. Finally, Sophes, thanks for being there for the real writing and for all the support. It was a lot, all of this, wasn't it?

Needless to say Shaggy tells his own story, and it is no surprise that he and I have different recollections of some situations. But we've been through too much together to worry about those differences. They are details and in the words of an old master, 'Life is what you remember it to be.' This is how I lived it.

Peter Webb
May 2007

Fair-
haven
Smeerenburg
Seven Glaciers
Kapp Mitra
Kongsfjord
Prins
Karls
Forland
Røsthulet
Raudfjord
Bjørnhamna
Laxbu
Sars'
tangen
Forlandsundet
Velkomsprynten
Woodfjord
Gråt-
huken
Wijdefjord
Rekvik
Hut
Hinlopen Strait
NORDAUSTLANDET
SPITSBERGEN
Ny Ålesund
Kapp Payer
Heleysundet
BARENTS-
ØYA
Freemansundet
Daudmannsodden
Isfjord
Longyearbyen
Isfjord Radio
Barentsburg
Orustosen
Camp Bell
Bellsund
Storfjord
Kapp Lee
Agardh-
bukta
EDGE-
ØYA
Kvalvågen
Isbjørnhamna
Hambergbukta
Hornsund
Isbukta
60 nautical miles
Stormbukta
100 kilometres
Sørkapp

And, tell me, wasn't that the best time, that time
when we were young at sea; young and had
nothing, on the sea that gives nothing, except hard
knocks – and sometimes a chance to feel your
strength

Joseph Conrad, *Youth*

1

The High Arctic

North of Norway lies the sea, the great grey restless sea, and beyond that lies the Arctic Ocean.

The blue-black waves turn in the wind and glacial foam crashes down on itself. Great whales rise from the deep to blow spray and suck air while fulmars dive on sickle wings to work upwind, then rise and swoop again. The heaving ocean breaks on the icebergs of the drifting pack ice and between the floes the water is calm, falling away into the black depths of the Nansen basin. A quantity of seal rest on the ice, tired after countless submarine miles. But they don't rest too well because of the wandering isbjørn, or ice bear, that hunts them throughout that white wilderness. From time to time the deep water and polar winds pull and drive the ice in contradictory directions. The floes groan and ride up onto each other, then explode in frost smoke and a sustained thunder clap. Shards of ice fall back into the salty ocean or as ridges on the ice floes themselves before an uneasy silence returns. It's no place for a rowboat.

The islands in that wilderness remained beyond the reach of mankind through most of our history. There were always legends of an island far to the north where the sun never set. Homer sang to the Ancient Greeks of the Aeaean island, 'where is the dwelling place of Dawn and her dancing grounds, and the land of the sun-rising', and similar myths were told by the Norsemen in early sagas. It seems impossible that the wandering Vikings never saw these lands of cold coasts and needle peaks while travelling their 'road of the whale'. But it was not until the turn of the seventeenth century that the island of Spitsbergen[1] in the archipelago of Svalbard was formally discovered, and it became a summer destination for the whaling fleets of Europe.

My own haphazard journey to Svalbard started in the years when global warming was no more than interesting science. One day, after a lesson spent drawing the physics of the greenhouse mechanism and reviewing a spiky graph of rising carbon dioxide with a teacher that I remember for old tweed and splayed toes, I joined a queue for chicken and mash in the school dining hall. By chance I found myself next to an athletic man with a weather-beaten face and razor-creased trousers. There was a small red dagger sewn onto his khaki jumper. A thousand teenagers were chatting, fighting for space and making fun. I was curious.

'What does the badge mean?'

He turned and looked at me with rock-steady eyes. His answers to that and my subsequent questions took me to the Admiralty Interview Board in Gosport, the commando course in Devon and arctic warfare training in north Norway. One short gap year later I'd learned to iron and salute, to ski and to shoot. I'd won the famous Royal Marines' Green Beret and I'd made a few very close friends.

Once at university all of that cooking and travelling in cold places meant that my application to join a geological expedition going to study the Arctic Shelf was successful. So while my fellow first-year students were enjoying the Cambridge May Balls and the last balmy days of summer term, I was vomiting in a polar gale en route for Bear Island and Spitsbergen.

After I'd recovered from the seasickness and made some friends among the island regulars, I discovered the cold clear air and honest hard work of the high latitudes. I came to love the boats and planes and journeys, the sledge dogs, the white whales, and the reindeer grazing on tundra moss. There was

---

[1] 'Spitsbergen is the only correct spelling; Spitzbergen is a relatively modern blunder. The name is Dutch, not German. The second S asserts and commemorates the nationality of the discoverer.'
– Sir Martin Conway, *No Man's Land*, 1906.

no end to the stories they told each other – of Arctic gales, anchors dragging among autumn icebergs and a Great Yarmouth expedition ship breaking up, of sledging partners coming to blows over the snuffing or blowing out of a candle, to snuff or blow was the question, and one about playing sub-aqua football *under* the sea ice. Both teams had to leave their diving weights on the surface and the game was played upside down. All this where the light had space, the colours were vivid, and it was wondrous cold.

Shortly before I was due to come home I stood on the beach in Ny Ålesund, the northernmost community, with the geologists and boatmen of the expedition. The low and dramatic outline of Kapp Mitra lay fifteen sea miles to the northwest and the sun was dipping down towards it. We were preparing to slip a much-loved wooden boat called *Salterella* and Nick, the logistics chief, was coiling line on the pebble beach.

I opened the wooden boatshed door and peered inside.

'Hey Nick,' I called, 'There's a boat in here already.'

He looked up and I opened the door some more. The hinges whined. He walked up the gently shelving shingle that was littered with mine works debris and seaweed. More light fell into the boatshed, and we could see better now. Nick and I stood side by side, surveying a new arrival. As a boat it was a calamity: flakes of paint clung to the bare wood of the plywood doghouse and the padlock which secured its hatch hung on a latch that had been fixed at an odd angle. The owners were nowhere to be seen. The other boatmen joined us.

'They went out in that?'

'They're crazy!'

'They're mad!'

The mechanic bent down.

'There's no oil on that prop-shaft,' he said.

The crotch of his trousers was well down between his thighs and the waistband was low on his bum. He had plenty of oil for the prop shaft, on the denim of his jeans. He took a swing at the propeller and it rang out.

'I bet those boards leak like a sieve,' he said.

'That cabin top looks like a fridge.'

'Bloody ugly,' said another.

'Bloody rude using our boatshed,' said Nick.

Going to sea in this calamity of a boat seemed ambitious at any latitude. In the Arctic Ocean it was madness. But these people, whoever they were, had done it. I was vaguely aware of a question deep inside and as I stood there it breached the surface of my consciousness. If it's possible to go out in that, then how far could a good boat go? And what if the crew were strong and skilful and dedicated? My thoughts trailed off and my eyes lost their focus. Then I looked up to Kapp Mitra on the horizon.

Salterella *and Kapp Mitra*

The coast of Spitsbergen stretched out to the north, lined by glaciers tumbling into the water. In good weather and with sufficient respect it would be safe to travel past them in a small boat. Then the coast turned to the east and continued near the edge of the drifting pack, cut by fjords. From there it turned south into the Hinlopen Strait, famous for cold and mist and the katabatic[2] winds that come rushing down from the ice cap. From the stories that is a terrible place.

Perhaps a small boat and a fit crew could reach Hinlopen, depending on the weather, and the ice. Where to from there?

---

[2] A katabatic wind, from the Greek word *katabatikos*, meaning 'going downhill', is a wind driven by cold heavier air that blows down an incline such as a hill, a mountain or a glacier.

Where would you go if there were no limits? If you wanted to go all the way? Down to the southern tip of the island, and then back north again? My head rocked a little as I realised that 'all the way' meant right back to where I was standing on the beach outside Salterella Boatshed: a full circumnavigation.

I hardly slept in the days that followed, all the time thinking: Is it possible? Yes, it probably is. Can I do it? Maybe, if I'm good and a little lucky. And am I brave enough to find out? That one was difficult – but with the right preparation I believed that I would be. While these questions preoccupied me, they also seemed ridiculous, so I kept them to myself.

Three days later the washing-up was finished and the buckets of dishwater had been poured away. There was fresh tea and the team sat around writing and chatting. The mechanic was reading a well-thumbed paperback by Stephen King. The conversation paused. Outside, an iceberg stood stranded by the ebb tide in King's Fjord,[3] glowing white in the midnight sun. The silence stretched out. Having kept my silence for three days I felt bound to speak.

'Do, you, think, it's, … possible …' I lost my nerve, then spoke in a rush, 'to take an open boat around Spitsbergen?'

'What, you mean right round?'

'You mean all the way?'

'I don't know. How far is it?' We stood up and crowded around the map on the wall. It would be at least a thousand kilometres.

'You'd need to put in food depots.'

'How many would you put?'

'At least three: here and here, and here,' I said, choosing headlands at random. I might as well have been standing back and throwing darts.

'Or maybe there, it's a better beach,' one of the boatmen said.

That night, as the sun turned into the northern part of the sky, I lay awake – elated, because none of the experienced boatmen had thought it a mad idea.

The following day I met a young Dutch girl, Heleen. She'd

---

[3] Kongsfjorden.

19

spent two seasons on boats among the islands of Svalbard and I asked her if she thought the journey was possible. She glanced at me quickly and looked away.

'Yes, but I wouldn't go with you.'

'Has anybody done it before?'

'No, I don't think so.'

'Has anybody tried?'

'Oh yes, a trapper sailed out north one time with the idea of going around. He came back six hours later.'

'Why?'

'The wind started to blow, and he was scared witless!'

She laughed and her eyes sparkled. The scar on her temple creased in two.

When I asked around, I discovered that many people had tried the journey and failed, most recently a French sea-kayak champion in two successive attempts. The circumnavigation that I had thought my own idea was in fact a popular challenge, and this made me love the idea more. Breaking a new wake in the Arctic Ocean would be like cutting fresh tracks in virgin snow, and if I were the first then it would become, in some sense, mine forever. That would be something.

I kept with the idea for some weeks and it still seemed good, so I built it like a mountain and made it my dream.

2

Departure

B ack in the cold light of an English autumn the scale of the challenge dawned on me. On the face of it, to sail and row around Spitsbergen in an open boat was impossible. The island is the size of Scotland,[4] seven-tenths glacier, and depending on the wind and current it was often surrounded by the drifting pack and wildlife of the Arctic Ocean. The summer season, between the break-up of the sea ice in late spring and the onset of darkness in early autumn, was a short one, and the wind was unpredictable. So it would be necessary to travel fast in each and every weather window.

If you tried such a journey you could expect your hands to blister and your feet to freeze. The discs of your spine might rupture, your stomach would grow sick of reconstituted rations and the high latitude sunlight might burn your face into strips of chestnut leather. That's if your boat was not smashed by the icebergs, overturned by waves, split open on rocks by a rip tide, or blown off-shore by katabatics first.

While I did want to follow my dream and cut the first wake around the island, I did not want to rush into any of these dangerous and less comfortable things.

The following summer I had to make a geological map for my degree course, and while this prevented me from attempting a circumnavigation, it did give me the chance to

---

[4] Strictly, it is the size of the northern portion of Scotland if it were cut along the Caledonian canal.

return to Spitsbergen and learn how to organise an expedition of my own. For scientific reasons I chose an area near Isfjord Radio Station, an outpost at the southern mouth of Ice Fjord.[5] The station and beacon was originally built in the 1930s to help coal ships avoid the rocks in the all-too-common bad ice conditions and poor weather. At that time it was the island's communications centre and only link with the outside world.

While I was out there, crawling along stream beds and over outcrops, measuring the dip and strike of bedding planes with my inclinometer and recording and drawing them in my notebook, I would often look out to sea. I imagined a seaworthy boat and a fit crew focused on making the distance. And I would think, is it possible? Yes it must be. Can I do it? I think I can. How would you pull a heavy boat up through the surf, or out onto ice? And I decided it would have to be a lightweight hull, or there would have to be an ice anchor of some kind. And a pulley block … perhaps an ice screw would do the trick. And I would wish that I was out at sea.

Then one day, low under the coastal horizon, there was a wooden boat driven by a small white sail. It was made of pine; three seventeen-foot planks on each side rising to a pointed stem and stern. The wood was warm in colour, like amber, and the bow cut the waves like the boat felt at home in them. There were two sailors, and they turned to land. One of them moved forwards ready to jump into the surf. They beached and the one in the boat pulled up the rudder, which hung from hooks on the stern. They lifted her out through the surf, just the two of them. The hull had a deep V cross-section, good simple rowlocks and a solid thwart to step the mast in. The sailors introduced themselves as carpenters from Norway.

They were coming back from rebuilding a hut destroyed by bears further around the island. After some polite questions, I asked them if the boat might be for sale. Yes, they said, in fact it already was. We discussed a price, which I quickly agreed to pay. Shortly before the end of the field season, I arranged for a short-term cash loan from friends of Heleen, who was on a tour ship that year, and went to pick up the

---

[5] Isfjorden.

boat from near the airport where the carpenters had left it. Then I sailed it back to the Radio Station and with the help of the station crew I hung it in the roof of the boatshed.

Now that I had a plan and a boat, I needed crew. So I described what the journey might be like to a friend from Royal Marine days. It would be long and cold and hazardous but it would be beautiful too. I told him about the clear air, the freedom of the ice, about the polar bears hunting harp seal on the ice floes. And that we would be the first to cut a wake right around the island in such a boat.

'But what happens if we're shipwrecked?'

'We take climbing equipment and hike to Longyearbyen.'

'But what happens if we're miles offshore?

'We hang onto the wreckage, swim to the beach, and then walk out.'

'Yeah, right, we'll freeze.'

'We'll have dry suits.'

'And if the wreckage sinks?'

'There'll be buoyancy barrels, so it won't,' I said.

'Just like the *Titanic*?'

He raised his eyebrows and nodded upwards at me with his chin. I could see what he was thinking, 'safe return doubtful', like Shackleton all of those years ago.[6] But despite his initial astonishment my friend continued to listen, because we'd travelled and suffered together before. We'd both learned to ski in squeaky-cold snow, watched as the northern aurora swept the stars and mountains with curtains of purple and red. We'd both suffered the pain of 'heartbreak lane' near Exeter and were accustomed to digging inside ourselves, looking for strength we did not know existed. And we both remembered a field on the edge of Dartmoor where we stood in the rain and won our Green Berets on the same cold afternoon.

---

[6] Ernest Shackleton famously travelled nearly 1000 km through Antarctic sea ice and 1500 km across the Southern Ocean in 1914–16 when his ship *Endurance* was crushed by ice and sank. Despite what he had said in the famous advertisement ('Men wanted: For hazardous journey. Small wages, bitter cold, long months of complete darkness, constant danger, safe return doubtful. Honour and recognition in case of success') he led every one of his 27 men back to safety.

My friend sensed that I was afraid of what might happen and he could see the idea was crazy. But he loved the prospect of this ridiculous journey. His name was Shaggy and he decided to come.

* * *

Once his decision was made it was irreversible and we looked at times and distances and made plans for food and logistic support. If I had any doubts about the wisdom of the undertaking I had to put them to one side, because the project picked up a momentum of its own. I discussed the idea with a professor who had spent many summers in Spitsbergen.

'Make sure you take a rifle,' said the professor, 'for the bears.'

'Extraordinary strength,' he said. 'Once saw one attacking a seal. It was a big adult seal but the bear knocked that seal's head clean off. It went flying through the air, landed yards away. Yes, take a good heavy rifle.'

There was no doubt that we would do that, but the rifle was just one of many things we had to find. We might have taken one of the new satellite phones, but they were heavy like a brick and well beyond our student budgets. Neither did we look for a GPS because in those days it was exclusively US Defense Department technology. We did however seek approval and charitable status from the University Explorers Club. So on a grey November morning in 1990 I went to find Shaggy in his basement flat.

Dim misty light filtered through the window in the pavement above and I could see just enough to tread around his magazines and lecture notes. There were beer cans and climbing equipment on the floor. The smell of old tobacco and spilt alcohol hung to the curtains and rose from the carpet. I reached for his bedside table, flicked the light and shook the duvet. There was a wriggle and a black mop of hair appeared. Shaggy did not have a black mop of hair.

'Hello.'

'Oh, hello.'

'Good morning.'

The black mop disappeared, then the duvet moved again and Shaggy looked up from the far side.

'Morning Pete.'

He rolled out of bed onto the floor. He pulled on a crumpled shirt and threw a tie around his neck, then pulled on his smartest V-neck sweater, which clung uncomfortably to his angular torso. Next he squeezed toothpaste, rinsed and stepped towards the door.

'First impressions, right, Shags?' I said.

'Absolutely,' he replied, flattening his tousled hair.

It was a short walk from his flat to the Department of Geography and while we stepped in time he explained to me that the black bob of hair belonged to a fresher called Anna. He pulled his tie to a more comfortable position, and twenty minutes later we were sitting in a board room. There was a panel of dons and a dark oak table. The eldest of the four was the first to speak.

'So, why circumnavigate this island, Spitsbergen, in an open boat?' That was easy.

'For fun,' I said, 'for adventurous reasons, and because it's a First.'

'What do you mean by first?'

'It will be the first circumnavigation of Spitsbergen in an un-powered, open boat. That'll make it a record.'

'I see, and do you have any other reason? Is there a scientific angle?'

'Umm, nope, none at all,' I said, knowing that students sometimes use natural science projects to justify adventure holidays, and that he might be trying to screen us out if that were the case. The old don nodded and I think I even saw a smile. Then another question came from the youngest one. He had a beak-shaped nose.

'Do you feel that you have the right to shoot a bear in its own habitat?'

This was difficult. It depends, I was thinking. Do we have the right to trespass in their natural habitat? The answer had to be delicate.

I hesitated and Shaggy cut in.

'Well, if it was you or him of course you'd shoot it.'

I winced, but from that angle the answer was simple and there was nothing more to say. The beak raised his eyebrows and did not respond. Then the one on the end asked about medical provisions and our physical condition. The answers were straightforward. We stood and walked out. Three days later they told us we'd been successful. So from then on we approached sponsors with the credibility of the University's formal approval and the small tax advantage of having charitable status. The material difference the tax advantage made was zero because we'd elected to pay the cash costs ourselves. But their approval did encourage potential supporters-in-kind and it was good for our confidence.

Thus armed with charitable status, Shaggy went to speak to the adjutant at the Royal Marines depot, and I called the supporters of my previous year's mapping expedition. Many of them were happy to support this 'fun trip' as well. They helped with radios, blue watertight cargo barrels and sailing equipment. The brother of a friend who worked in a sail loft stitched a balloon jib from green and yellow fabric. My mother bought a pair of fisherman's waders as an out-of-season birthday present. Then one day Shaggy returned from the Royal Marines training depot with a car-load of the latest Arctic ration packs which had brand new boil-in-the-foil main meals as well old favourites like 'Biscuits, Fruit AB' (Garibaldis) and 'Biscuits, Brown' which are the modern equivalent of ship's biscuits, square and tough. He also had miles of sticking plaster and pots of cream from the sick bay. Anna helped unload it and we packed it all into blue cargo barrels in his basement flat.

By now we had to hurry, because of the need to send the barrels north months ahead, and because the chocolate rations were disappearing on the nights that Shaggy's climbing friends met and went out to scale the ancient libraries and not-so-dreaming spires of Cambridge. While the chocolate disappeared my Granny prepared secret packs of snacks and travel games to put in the top of each ten-day food barrel.

* * *

Shortly before the Dutch supply ship called at Aberdeen, its only stop in the United Kingdom en route from Holland to the Arctic, we typed up the cargo manifest. Then we sealed the cargo barrels and loaded them onto a flat-bed lorry bound for Scotland.

With the sea freight dispatched I breathed a long sigh and addressed an urgent need to study for my final exams. I hid away in my study and was working through my Part Two files when the telephone rang.

'Hallo, hallo? Is that Peter Vebb? This is Ko de Kort. What can be left behind?'

'Hello, that's who? What do you mean, left behind?'

'It's Ko de Kort, from the MS *Waterproef*, from the Dutch supply ship. I'm in Aberdeen. We do not have room to take all of your sea freight. What can we leave behind?'

I was deep in study and my mind was full of slow-motion fluid dynamics and the two hundred seismic listening stations around the world which pinpoint the epicentre of every earthquake. I was thinking strike-slip, strike-thrust, p-wave and shear wave and I was trying to get my head around the intricate geophysical equations which define the behaviour of the rigid crust that lies over the earth's fluid core and mantle.

'Oh hello Ko, let me think, errh, yes, you have to hang on.'

It was a leap from the maths of plate tectonics to the cargo manifest, which was buried in paper on a shelf nearby. What's he thinking? How can he ask this? What can we leave behind? What have we got? A barrel with clothes, a tent and sleeping bags; we have climbing equipment, tools for boat repair, sails, fuel, and six ten-day food barrels to keep us alive for the short two months when sailing at that latitude is possible. We've packed the minimum to make the journey because the boat's tiny and we have to shift it all with our own hard muscle.

'No, Ko, there's nothing that you can leave behind, we need it all.'

'We have to leave it half behind, tell me what can we leave?'

'No, you can't, we need it all. We can't make the journey without.'

'Well, I am sorry. I have to leave half behind.'

'But you can't, you can't stop us going like this.'

'I have no choice, Mr Vebb. I will leave half behind.'

He hung up and I put the receiver down, rested my head in my hands, looked at the telephone, and closed my eyes. I shouldn't be thinking about this. I should be studying. The journey's impossible, it's all failed. Why am I putting so much into this?

Why I was putting so much into the circumnavigation idea was a good question, and the answer was not at all clear to me. It was true that the idea inspired me. I felt driven. It was my dream. And I wanted to show that the journey was possible with simple equipment, with careful judgement and the power of the wind and our own bare hands. And I loved the High Arctic with its freedom and simplicity. But that was not all. If I was honest with myself, the truth was that I thought the journey might save me.

I was twenty-two and I'd climbed a mountain, loved and been loved, suffered and met with some success. Next I would graduate and move to London; find a job, catch the tube, get a mortgage and buy a flat. Then I would move to the country, buy a house and catch the train. Then I would retire and die. My life reached out as if I had already lived it and I could think of nothing worse. I almost preferred to die.

Rather than live a life I could already see I wanted to explore, find my limits, push them, and make a success. The risk of death didn't scare me because risking death is what young men do. An uncle on my mother's side died young in the Alps and my paternal grandfather had been shot down in the war. I didn't care about the emotional damage that comes with the bereavement of loss because I had never lived it. I was young and brave and selfish. If I followed this dream it would save me from that grey London life. It was as simple as that.

I looked at the telephone. The A4 ring-file on plate tectonics lay open before me and a cup of thin black coffee was cooling in a mug lined with student grime. The telephone receiver lay on its cradle and the Dutchman Ko de Kort was in Aberdeen loading just half of the carefully prepared sea freight onto the supply ship.

What should I do? Go to Aberdeen? I couldn't face the effort or give more time. I was far behind the other students with revision and could not afford the loss of three days' study on a train travelling from Cambridge to Aberdeen and back again. The telephone rang and the weight in my ribcage fell further.

'Hello, Peter? Do you know what Ko de Kort wants to do? He wants to leave your stuff behind.' I smiled. It was Heleen, beautiful, fair-haired, blue-eyed Heleen, with a scar by her left eye, who'd helped me find the money to buy the boat. She been promoted to bosun and was working on the supply ship for one more year.

'Yes, yes. He told me. Is there anything you can do?'

'You don't know how hard we've been working.'

From the tone of her voice I believed it. She and her boyfriend and the deckhands had spent two hours shifting cargo below decks in order to make room for my ten blue barrels.

'Don't worry, it's going to be OK, it's all on board now.'

'D'you mean that? Thanks, oh thank you. You're a star.' I wanted to hug her but all I could do was smile enthusiastically into the handset.

'That's OK. You owe me.' I could hear her smile.

'Thank you, thanks. You don't know.'

'That's OK. Good luck with the trip. And take care.'

'I will. I'll see you in Svalbard.'

'I'll see you there.'

I hung up the receiver and a smile bunched in my cheeks. I clenched my fist and stabbed down with my elbow. Then I made a hot cup of stronger coffee and returned to geophysics.

* * *

Final exams came and went and Arctic daydreams kept me company as I sat the geophysics paper in the Senate House. Summer dresses, sticky fruit and fizzy white wine came to the lawns of Cambridge and both Shaggy and I rowed in the May Bumps, a relentless rowing competition that was serious in the top divisions but not at our level because we both rowed in our respective College 'joke boats'. Our aim was to spend a few days on the river and enjoy the cocktail parties afterwards. The four bumps my own crew made (this was a great success) augured well for the challenge ahead. But we could not stay for all of the parties because the short Arctic summer had started.

So while our friends partied on the lawns and talked about the best years of their lives just past, imagining the world that lay at their feet, we packed up our student belongings and made preparations to fly north.

One discussion that we still had to resolve was whether to take a life raft. Shaggy had originally been happy to go along on the understanding that the cargo barrels, secured to the hull, would provide the buoyancy required to keep us afloat should the boat be wrecked. And his mother had been happy with him undertaking the expedition on the understanding that Spitsbergen was a 'small island just off Norway'. When, shortly before our departure, she opened an atlas and saw just how far north Spitsbergen is, and to be honest it's a very long way from Norway too, she was more than a little shocked. After an earnest conversation with her husband, she phoned her son with the urgent news that he had to take a life raft.

How far north it is

I was set against taking anything we did not absolutely need. A life raft would be big and heavy and only marginally more useful at keeping us above the water than all of the buoyant wreckage I anticipated being available should the boat break up. We had a provision for every eventuality: an impressive range of glues and small hand tools for shipwreck, dry suits and lifejackets in case we went in the water, climbing equipment should we need to walk home across the ice cap and glaciers inland. A life raft was bigger than all of this equipment put together and I felt we could do as well without it. We discussed and discussed and we agreed that the life raft was unnecessary.

Shaggy would speak to his mother.

After a final dinner party with friends at my parents' house, I packed between three and seven in the morning in a bedroom that was littered with folders, books, pictures, shoes, a collection of hockey sticks in various states of disrepair, a kettle and some coffee mugs. Shaggy had called to say that he would take a walkman and a plastic bag, but that he had no cassettes. So just before I walked out of the door, I threw three at random into the top of my bulging canvas kitbag and knotted the drawstring. I stumbled down the stairs under the weight of it, wondering whether I should have taken time to choose the cassettes more carefully, and whether three was enough.

My mother dropped me at the airport. Shaggy was already there with Anna, who had driven him down, and when I met them I was dismayed to find that he had a bizarre black package in a yellow plastic-canvas carrying case. He lifted and moved it with difficulty; it was both bulky and heavy.

'What the hell's that?'

'Oh it's an, ummm, life raft.'

'But I thought we agreed?'

Quite clearly we had not, and I was quietly happy when the ground staff told us that the life raft could not go. We had left check-in to the last minute, and while they seemed to have turned a blind eye to my comprehensive pack of distress explosives, Shaggy was stopped on account of the canister of compressed gas in the life raft. Despite arguments that came direct from the heart, Shaggy could not persuade them to take it, and the minutes ticked by.

'Let's leave it behind,' I said shifting my weight.

'No, let's just see. You mean it's the compressed air inside the canister that's a problem, not the canister itself?'

By now Shaggy was talking to *all* of the check-in staff and three security officials because we were the last remaining passengers. From their interest it was clear that this did not happen every day at Terminal Four.

Then Shaggy was talking to one security guard in particular who he'd discovered was an ex-Navy diver, and fifteen minutes before departure time they disappeared outside. After some tinkering they released a plume of carbon dioxide 'fifty feet into the taxi rank' and onto the windscreen of an oncoming maintenance van. The driver's quick reactions prevented a pile-up and they came back smiling.

Half an hour later we were airborne. The hastily repacked life raft, with a now empty canister, was stacked in the hold. We would try and re-fill the canister with gas in Longyearbyen, or failing that, buy a foot-pump. That was the plan anyway.

Hours later we crossed the Arctic Circle at thirty-nine thousand feet, and as we descended icebergs lay in the black restless water of the Barents Sea. Then the needle peaks of west Spitsbergen and the other islands reached up towards us. My nose was stuck to the aircraft porthole and my fringe was plastered down my forehead.

'Look Shags. It's Svalbard.'

'Man. That looks cold. D'you really think we can?'

3

Isfjord Radio Station

We stepped down from the aircraft and towards the
Longyearbyen airport buildings. The smell of earth
and ice came with a stab of euphoria because beneath the
quiet grey clouds, the air was astonishingly clear. Black scree
and snow ramps tumbled down from between the ramparts
above the hillsides and there were snow drifts along the
runway. The cold air cut into our travelling clothes as we
walked across the tarmac.

The arrivals hall was small and there was lino on the
floor. While we waited for the cabin baggage I had time to
think about how to make it to the Radio Station, where most
of the sea freight should be. We had no passage booked and
therefore would be looking to take a ride on whatever boat
or helicopter was going that way. Shaggy was handling a
slim book with the local birds and animals at a news-stand.

'So, which of these do you think we'll see?' He turned it
over and over.

'I think I'll buy it,' he said. 'It'll be fun to tick them off.'

The luggage arrived on a small trolley and the life raft,
distress explosives and radios were all there. I wanted to
check in at the Governor's office and then collect the rifle
that the local hardware store had ordered for us. Shaggy
wanted to recharge the gas canister for the life raft, but it
was already late and the offices and shops were closing, so
all that would have to wait for tomorrow. For now we
needed somewhere to sleep.

A single-storey hotel had just opened near the airport, the

first hotel in town, and after asking the price of a room and finding the cost prohibitive, we settled down on the stony ground under the eaves of the hotel building. We were out of the wind so we'd be warm enough in our three-season bags and semi-permeable bivouac bags, and the hotel staff didn't seem to mind.

Now that we were on the island itself the detailed maps of the coast had come alive. Each inlet was more important. We opened them one by one and did not dare talk about the far side of the island in case we never made it. In the fjord below us we could see the beach from the map. This one was dark like the coal under the mountain. We tried to picture the beaches where the supply ship *Waterproof* would leave the food depots in their blue plastic barrels.

I thought of questions, one after another. We needed the answers. Had the sea freight arrived safely at the Radio Station? Would all the food depots be in the right place? What was the ice like this year? How would we make it to the Radio Station? What was Shaggy going to drink his tea out of, because he'd forgotten to pack his large plastic mug? The sea freight should be there and the five food depots should be in place around the island, if not yet then very soon. We would look for a mug in the hardware store. The hours and the questions and the plans made my eyes heavy but the daylight kept us awake. Finally we slept two hours while the sun turned through the north, high above the horizon. It broke though the clouds in the east in the early hours of the following day.

I sat up. Blue and red huts and houses littered the valley floor, and the derelict remains of an aerial tramway clung to the hillside, it had once carried coal down to the dock. Shaggy was barely dozing, and while we waited for the world to wake up he made tea on his petrol cooker and then had trouble drinking from the metal rim of his cooking pot. I opened my expedition book, chosen for its weight and page count, *The Lord of the Rings*, and while the inhabitants of Longyearbyen climbed from their beds and did whatever they did every morning I read the first pages about a hobbit that lived at Bag End. After a second brew of tea he'd inherited a special ring. It was nearly seven o'clock.

The hardware store was a large hut of wooden boards at the end of its own gravel track near the harbour. Above the door hung a yellow trade sign and written in black it said 'YAMAHA' for the outboard engines and snow-scooters that they sold. It opened at eight, and the rifle that I'd ordered earlier in the year was there waiting for us.

It was a good, simple rifle with heavy seven-six-two shells and a manual bolt that was unlikely to jam. I worked the action and packed the shells in a day sack. We didn't expect to need many. In theory just a few would be enough for one polar bear: a couple of warning shots and one or two for real, but I bought six boxes of twelve because I did not want – under any circumstances – to run out. The store owner gave me the certificate of ownership. It was good for one year.

We looked at the footwear. The canvas mukluks had inch-thick soles and then two inches of felt. We tried them on and walked about, and in that warm shop the heat filled us up to our knees, then all the way to our hair roots and fingertips. I tried to imagine the task of keeping the insulation dry in a small wet boat. It might be impossible to dry the brine out of the sodden felt. Then we looked at the price, our credit cards were already maxed out, and the mukluks cost as much as the rifle which we'd just bought with money we did not have. So we left the shop without them, hoping that thick socks and rubber boots would keep our feet warm.

At the dockside there was a tour ship preparing to leave. The captain said they would be dropping a field party on the north shore of Ice Fjord and then head south for Hornsund. They could stop at the Radio Station because it was on their way and he was prepared to take us there. He wanted to sail later that afternoon. But there was still the canister for the life raft. I was happy to forget it; Shaggy was not. I said leave it; he said we at least needed the foot pump. I couldn't argue with that without convincing him to leave the whole life raft behind, and there was no time for that. So we decided to split up.

I would go with the tour ship to prepare the boat and unpack the sea freight while Shaggy stayed behind to sort out the gas cylinder or the foot pump and do whatever the hell he wanted to do with the life raft. So I heaved my rucksack onto my back, slung the rifle case over my shoulder and threw the heavy kitbag across the top. My knees felt the weight and I walked up the gangplank.

The deckhands pulled the manila hawsers aboard as the tour ship edged away from the dock. The grumble of the engine vibrated from below decks and the screes of Adventfjord soon opened onto the flat-topped hills along the southern edge of Isfjord. In the distance, along the northern edge, high serrated rock ridges were cut by glaciers reaching down to the water. The ship sped towards them.

I went up to the bridge to ask the captain for tidal information. He did not have any tidal charts for the islands but he was curious at my question. With reluctance I told him why I was asking – because I wanted to take a small boat around the island. The captain became anxious. You want to do what? And how small is the boat? When I gave my answers his eyes flashed with conviction as he tried to stop me attempting suicide in the pack ice.

Did I know about the unpredictable gales? The tide rips? And the fog that descends without warning? Did I know that a thin wooden hull would never survive the impact if it struck an ice floe? That death would follow immersion in minutes?

He was the first Arctic seaman to say this idea of a circumnavigation was unworkable and stupid. If I'd heard this view two years before I might not even have started planning the journey. But I had not. I'd chosen my road without the benefit of his opinion and I was already some way down it. When my resolve held he made certain I knew how to send a mayday.

'Never forget to send your position!' he said. His head was shaking.

His fear rattled me, and that night I slept just a few hours on a couch on the mess deck. I was mostly staring at death with wide-awake eyes. It would be my fault, this death, not Shaggy's. It would be my fault and the fault of my stupid dream. In the solitude of midnight my sanity was shot and the threat of madness hovered like a cloud. I thought about trying

Norwegian sailing boat *Kotick* ▶

▼ An old friend, Shaggy

◀ Supply Ship MS *Waterproef*

Isfjord Radio Station ▶

◄ In action
at the oars

► Sailing
in the
snow

▲ *Kotick* under sail

◄ Field repairs

▼ Katie and Grøtos in Ny Ålesund

◄ Ready and shipshape again

 Thanks, goodbye and out

◄ Midnight visitor

Sleepy walrus ►

▶ Walrus awakes

▲ We made
great distance

▶ High pressure
over the Pole–
settled weather
at last

◀ Getting out of a tight corner

▼ Fifteen minutes to move these

▼ Many kilometres to land – what next?

▲
Hot soup from
meltwater

►
Polar bear
patrol

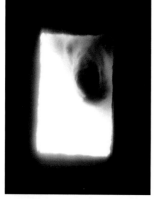

▲ Good morning

▲ Bear at the window

▲ Photographed by tourists

◀ Cooking under way

▼ Ice cliffs

▲ Asleep in *Kotick*

Then the wind
stopped ▶

Valhallfonna
from afar
▼

▶
Cliffs and
pinnacles

▲ Bergs from the ice cap

◄ A strong smell of fish

► Swimming towards Siberia

◀ Welcome arrival of post

▲ Waterskiing

▼ Katabatic wind

▼ Freezing spray

▼ By compass in the fog

◀ Eighteen
kilometres
across Ice Bay
– we nearly
died out there

Svalbard reindeer ▶

◀ Barnacle geese

▶
Polish
research
station

▲ Long paddle through the night

◀ Unloading for the last time

Some stories to tell

a different route, maybe sailing around the inside of Spitsbergen to the end of each great fjord. But that was not pushing the limit, there would be no pioneering circumnavigation in that. I rocked from side to side and closed my eyes. The cloud of madness enveloped me, the mountains and the water went spinning around in a fog and there, in that cloud, I slept.

When I woke up I found a bar of chocolate.

'It's for you.' The galley maid smiled as she put out breakfast. She was young and attractive, maybe this was her summer holiday job.

'You looked so sad, asleep on your own,' she said and smiled again. I smiled back and thanked her.

At breakfast I sat next to the captain. He was surprised to discover how much of the archipelago I knew from the geological work I'd done in small boats over the previous two summers. He relaxed and told me it was his first season north of the Arctic Circle. A wash of relief brightened my smile and the dark cloud of madness blew away. I ate the holiday girl's bar of chocolate with my second cup of coffee. It had nougat inside.

* * *

After buying a foot-pump, Shaggy hitched a lift on a helicopter going to the Russian coalmine at Barentsburg, which was near to the Radio Station. He sent a message via the Station Chief with a number for me to call, so I called and spoke to him against the noise of a dining hall full of Russian miners.

'I might not make it,' he said. 'They say there are no boats to Isfjord Radio, I might have to walk around, it may take a week, that's what they're telling me.'

'Just wait there, Shags,' I was speaking loud and clear into the handset, 'and if a boat leaves make sure you're on it.' I was making plans to walk around the coast to pick him up – it was far less than a week's walk – but I didn't have to worry because of his usual luck. The next day there was an unexpected boat to the Radio Station and he made sure he was on it.

When news came that a ship was anchoring in the bay, the

Station Chief, the Engineer and I walked out towards the small dock. The Engineer was a tall whippet of a man with angular cheeks that were coloured by weather or alcohol. He was striding out in front because we might need the crane. The Station Chief followed. He was slower, with kind eyes, loose jowls and a comfortable belly. I walked along behind, thinking that it would have been men just like these that welcomed the Canadian and Norwegian commandos during the last war.

This warm welcome was the same for all, for field scientists, tour ships and the occasional round-the-island sailor. I remembered the Chief and station crew from the previous year, and I felt a debt for their hospitality and common sense. Both years they'd allowed me to sleep in an outhouse known as the 'barracks', and had been happy that I store the carpenters' boat here over the winter. I was thankful for all of that.

I followed both of them across the stones and tundra moss, watching for the eider ducks nesting around the outbuildings, then down the concrete steps through the low cliffs to the concrete dock with rusty bollards.

The ship from Barentsburg was there in the bay, with a tender alongside and a figure climbing down into it. The water was calm because it was sheltered from the swell. There were two in the boat and the low roar of an outboard came to us over the slap of water on the old tyres at our feet. Inland the scarp slope of the Linnéfjella ridge cut down to the coastal plain and there was the blue-white glow of a glacier in the upland valley behind it. We waited and the ship's tender grew towards us. Shaggy was in the bow, looking, smiling. He held his hand up and waved when he was close.

'I got a foot pump,' he said. 'It should do.' That was good because it was lighter than the gas canister. It wouldn't be much use to blow up the life raft in a panic. But if we went down slowly then it would work just fine. He threw a line and the Engineer caught it.

'Hello,' said the Station Chief as Shaggy climbed up. They shook hands. The ship's crew shouted up in Norwegian and the Engineer smiled then shrugged. The crewman threw his hand up into the air and over his shoulder, laughed, and took the line that the engineer threw back down. The crewman nodded goodbye, then he looked down and the outboard roared. The tender sped off, leaving white water behind.

'Do you want to see the boat?' The Chief's eyes glinted. Shaggy nodded and the Chief led us to the shed where the Engineer and I had lowered the carpenters' boat from the rafters that morning.

'It's called an Oselvar, built at Os on the mainland near Bergen,' I said, and I picked up the spars that were lying to one side. The four oars were cut with a right-angled section to pivot on the rowlock posts, and a spliced strop of line kept each one in place. The oar handles were rough-carved to fit a palm and we tried to guess where the blisters would come first.

With the Engineer's help we put her in the water for a practice run and she rolled from side to side, slapping down to port and starboard in a way that alarmed me. Without cargo she sat high on the small waves and they tossed her around like a cork. We threaded the oars through the strops of line spliced to the rowlock posts and paddled out into the bay. First one of us dipped the oars, then the other. One of us took one stroke to correct the direction, and then the other.

The Station Chief laughed at us from the dock.

'It's a long way around the island!' he shouted as we tried to agree what to do.

There was a hole in the front thwart which was the mast step, and while Shaggy kept her steady with the oars I lifted the mast to vertical and secured the shrouds to eyes on the gunwale. Then I pulled up the snow-white sail and pinned it out with the pinewood yard-arm. It was loose-footed and flapping. It felt comfortable having no boom and I pulled on the mainsheet so the small sail bowed into a curve, brimming with the breeze. The Oselvar butted into the waves, cut them and left a stream of bubbles turning in the water.

'That feels better,' I said and we sailed two long tacks across the bay before lifting the boat out and going up to the barracks to check the sea freight. With the cargo manifest in hand we opened the barrels one by one. Was it all there? Was anything damaged? Did the chocolate supplies get through? As far as we could see everything was in order.

The next priority was to practise a capsize, so we would know how to pull the boat upright, bail her out and get going again if this should ever happen for real. We would also learn how to pack the boat in a way that would make a capsize survivable.

First we tied two empty barrels into the boat, then we pulled on the dry suits. It was difficult to pull the tough rubberised canvas over the bulky clothes on our arms and legs, and the black rubber cuff that sealed around the neck was almost too tight to pull over our heads. It stuck in our eye sockets and above the jaw bone. And once we had our head and limbs in place there was the zip which ran across the back from shoulder blade to shoulder blade. It was impossible for each of us to zip up our own, so we both had to help each other make the final seal, that done, we pushed the boat down the beach again, and rowed out into the bay.

I stood up and the two of us leaned on the same gunwale until glacial water came spilling into the boat. We leaned some more and the gunwale went under so that a wall of ice-water tumbled in. The boat tipped some more and we shouted 'Whooaah,' as we fell forward and the boat rolled upside down.

The shock of it made me suck for air. Shaggy was making a double-time breast stroke and trying to keep his head far above the water. To my dismay the buoyancy barrels slipped out of their slings and floated away, so we spent a few very cold minutes swimming back and forth and pulling the boat upright, throwing the water out with a bucket and then rowing after the cargo barrels. With everything back in the boat we hauled her up the beach and looked at each other and the boat in disappointment.

Shaggy, proud of his recently acquired engineering degree, fetched the tool bag and took a close and personal interest in identifying strong points in the hull, and after brief consultation he drilled a number of holes with his brand new multi-tool. That done, and with the straps crossed and re-crossed over the barrels and ratcheted tight, it seemed they could only escape if the hull itself disintegrated. Nonetheless he secured our two air-filled roller bags under the thwarts, just in case.

Meanwhile I painted the name I'd chosen, *Kotick*, in black paint on the gunwale, and the next time we capsized her, *Kotick* floated high out of the water until we pulled her up again.

'You see, Shags, no need for a life raft.' It was only half a joke, and while his mouth smiled, his eyes did not. He still wanted to take it and I didn't push further because of the very small chance that we break the boat, end up in the water and face a cold wet death together. Then he might turn to me and say, 'I told you so', and curse me with his dying eye.

I couldn't die like that. Besides, without the gas canister the life raft didn't weigh so much, and – as he had demonstrated by sitting on it – 'Look, it makes a great seat.'

Now that we had faith in the buoyancy of the boat and our ability to survive a capsize, we set to sorting through and choosing the rest of our equipment. There was space in the boat for two cargo barrels, a large one in the bow, of one hundred and twenty litres, and a small one in the stern of sixty litres. Every item had to justify its weight and the space it occupied. We started with the essentials: oars, sails, mast, rifle, distress flares, waders, fuel, fresh water, roll-mats, and a sponge for mopping water out of the bilge. We laid these to one side. Then we unpacked the rest of the sea-freight and started to choose and prepare those items that we would take. To survive and complete this great island adventure the preparations would have to be absolutely right.

Shaggy was a whirlwind of activity. He surrounded himself in mountains of kit and wrapped everything in masking tape and plastic bags to make it waterproof. I worked more methodically from carefully thought-out lists for everything from boat repairs to escaping out overland. My mind was full of questions. Do we need this? Will something else do? What happens when? What happens if? I tried endlessly to make the trade-off between saving weight and being ready for all events while he was busy waterproofing everything from socks to spare stationery. I spent hours making lists and piles of equipment and then he would mix up the piles and lose the lists. This hampered progress, but we both became very familiar with the equipment that we had.

In the large watertight cargo barrel we put the camping equipment, dry clothes and sleeping bags; we also squeezed in the maps, books and spare film. It would be one of the few truly dry places and so we also put in the reserve ammunition, spare distress explosives and the walkman. The small watertight barrel was already packed with enough food for ten days, and it was identical to the food depots that the Dutch supply ship would leave around the island.

I prepared the rucksack for boat repairs. Tools and glues, sandpaper, a sailmaker's needle and cork, wood screws, cleats, shackles, a hacksaw and blades, long-nosed pliers and a clamp. I wanted to include a broad-faced screwdriver, but Shaggy convinced me his multi-tool would do instead. I tried to persuade him that my geological hammer would be worth taking for boat repairs. The reality was that after two summer seasons working as a field geologist I felt naked without it. We called all of this, and the bag it was in, the 'bosun's bergan'.[7]

Meanwhile Shaggy packed a rucksack filled with the minimum kit required for escaping overland should we wreck the boat: an ice hammer, crampons, medi-pack, food, spare ammunition, a tent sheet, cooker, dry socks and climbing rope. We both took great care checking this because we did not want, under any circumstances, to be rescued. We called it the 'escape bergan'.

We put spare food and fuel, and the bosun's bergan, in the bow next to the anchor. Next to the food barrel in the stern we fitted waterproof kitbags with clothes, oilskins, dry suits and lifejackets; we called them the 'voyage bags'. We tied 'rummage bags', with useful bits and pieces like masking tape, penknives, sweets, thermos flasks and a handheld VHF radio, to grab lines below the thwarts. There was a waterproof map case tied to a bench seat and the bilge pump and bucket were secured in the foot well where we could reach them

---

[7] 'Bergan' is the Royal Marines' word for a rucksack.

easily for bailing out water that came into the hull.

Finally, we tied down the oars and spars and in this fashion everything was secured and waterproofed and buoyant so if we went over fully laden we should be able to bring her up again. That was the theory anyway. The one non-buoyant item was the rifle. That would sink. So we covered it in oil, wrapped it up in plastic, and tied it to one of the buoyancy bags under the thwart. *Kotick* was ready.

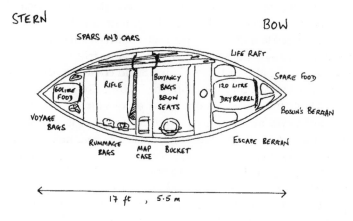

Plan view of Kotick

* * *

A tour ship arrived to visit Isfjord Radio. The passengers came ashore, buffeted by the wind, and walked around the outbuildings accompanied by their rifle-bearing tour guide. *Kotick* was waiting on the beach. I was down there too and one of the boatmen took an interest. I asked him about the state of the open water.

'You could go out in that, but I would not,' he said.

I looked into the wind coming out of the northwest. It was twenty-one kilometres across Isfjord. The clear air made it seem closer than that, but to work against this wind was impossible. I winced.

* * *

One week later Shaggy and I were perched on the sofa in the Radio Station, deep in discomfort. We smelled the cow hide of the sofa and our socks rested on a hairy rug while we watched the wind flying out of a wide-open sky. There was a polar bear skin fixed to the wall and scattered all over the fjord there were whitecaps. Cold clear gusts swirled around the Radio Station and buffeted the huge panes of glass. *Kotick* was upside down on the beach, and we had taken the carefully packed barrels and bags and stored them in the barracks.

The Norwegian chef was called Gustav. He was surprisingly short and what he lacked in height he made up for in friendliness. He had quick eyes and a shiny-white-teeth smile, and most days he would invite us for fresh coffee and chocolate cake at four thirty. So we could come into the warm, check the forecast and talk with the Station Chief about ships. The whole crew was usually there, except for the one on the radio console. But today we were alone because the Station crew was tidying and cleaning, making preparations for the arrival of the Governor.

'What happens if it blows all month?' said Shaggy.

'No, it won't, it can't,' I replied, but the conviction that I wanted in my voice was not there due to the ribbons of high white cloud scratched across the blue sky. They were obstinate in their persistence, beautiful and frustrating, driven by the jet stream, and forecasting yet more wind. There was no way we could reach Dead Man's Point in this, and the headwind was showing no signs of dying down.

'Don't worry; the weather changes every three days,' I'd said when it started blowing. That was more days ago than three. Shaggy pointed this out, again, and then stood and perused the bookshelves, as he did every time we came. As usual he found the books were all in Norwegian so he sat down again.

He picked up the small hardback he'd bought in Longyearbyen airport, *Birds and Mammals of Svalbard*. On the cover there was green tundra and a flock of eider under a blue windless sky. It fell naturally open at the page entitled *Ursus maritimus*.

'So, what's the biggest polar bear?'

'Huge, at least to here ...' I indicated chest-high, 'and as far as the wall, nearly a ton. And incredible athletes.'

'That's a small one,' I said, nodding at the bear skin on the wall.

'It says here, seven hundred kilos.'

'As big as a small car, and nearly as fast,' I said.

'Can you stop that with a bullet? I doubt it somehow.'

'You've got go for the eyes I guess.' My tone was flippant. I smiled.

'Best it doesn't charge then.' He smiled too.

'D'you reckon we'll see one?'

'If we ever leave,' I said, pursing my lips and raising my eyebrows. 'They'll be near the ice, on the north coast, and the east.'

'No need for a rifle between here and the barracks then?'

Shaggy wanted to repack the escape rucksack and run a tank of fuel through his petrol cooker. So he stepped across the rug onto the shiny floor and skidded off in his socks. He pulled on his trainers at the doorway, and stepped into the heat-lock before letting himself into the wind.

I remained sitting on the sofa with the *Birds and Mammals* book. Shaggy had started marking the pages. Fulmar, kittiwake and glaucous gull all had a blue tick and next to eider duck there was tick and a scribble in spidery writing: 'Kapp Linné, Isfjord Radio Station, sitting on eggs (lots)'.

As I sat there the wind juddered against the window frames and the thud, thud, thud of it increased. The chef Gustav emerged from the kitchen and stood in his high-heeled clogs on a box by the window.

'The Governor is early,' he said. 'That is usual.'

I stood up to go because the Station crew were banging doors and calling to each other. I wanted to be out of their way but I was caught by a large gathering in the heat-lock. They introduced me to the Governor.

'So you want to go to the north coast in a small boat?' he asked in his flat Norwegian accent.

'Yes, that's right, I'm from England.'

'And how far do you want to go?'

'Oh I'd like to see how far we can get. We've got depots.'

'Oh yes, where?

'There's one at Smeerenburg, and at Rekvik, then Edge Island.'

'That's most of the way around. Do you have a distress beacon?'

I nodded.

'And have you done a lot of rowing before?' he wanted to know.

'Ummm.' Compared to the challenge of the journey ahead, the truthful answer would be no, but I didn't want to say that. I knew that we were fit and I thought we could learn to row long hours quickly enough, but I didn't want to say that either because we might seem unprepared. Thinking quickly, the only response that came to mind was, 'Cambridge is a very famous rowing university.'

I smiled and he seemed happy with that. So I smiled some more, but with relief because there would be no more questions. And because he had not objected to me wanting to attempt this journey. Now I could go out there and take the risks with care, one by one, quietly and concentrating as they came.

*   *   *

In the days that followed, June turned to July, and while we waited for the wind we unpacked and packed the barrels, the escape bergan and the voyage bags in order to adjust and check details. We both disassembled and assembled the rifle, mindful that intimate knowledge and deft handling might save us in the face of a polar bear charge. Then we sat around in the barracks and on the cow-hide sofa in the Radio Station, brushing the stiff bristles of the polar bear skin that was nailed to the wall, or perusing the library of Norwegian books.

Now this challenge was too big and too close so I broke it down into steps: the boat was prepared, we were prepared. Next we had to cross the fjord. Then there would be another step, and if I made all the steps, one after the other, around the island, then they would become a great thing.

In quiet moments alone my mind turned in on itself, as it

had on the ship. My thoughts revolved around images of ice breaking wood, swimming in a whirlpool of frozen water, the strength of the bears, the oblivion of fog and the power of a high sea. It was often that I couldn't sleep.

'What 'you writing?' I called across to Shaggy from my sleeping bag. He looked up.

'What, this?'

'Yes, that, go on, what is it?'

'It's three a.m. I'm still up. Pete's in bed. I'm not used to the light yet. I wish I could be with you. I'm scared.'

'That to Anna?'

He nodded and I raised my eyebrows, asking him to continue.

'I read Pete's diary. He's nervous and glad that I am too. I'm nervous and glad that he is. Does that make sense?'

'You read my diary? You nosy bastard.'

'Well, I'm effectively reading you mine.'

I was relieved that Shaggy was scared, because it made me think that my own fear was justified. I wasn't going mad after all. And I was happy because the fear united us. But most important of all I knew that his fear would curb his courage, which sometimes bordered on the insane.

* * *

We were anxious to leave and scared to leave, and after we'd packed and repacked all we could, we both filled our time reading or playing the harmonica.

We looked for birds to tick in the *Birds and Mammals* book and found a sanderling: 'a small wader which is often seen running rapidly in the tidal zone. The sexes are identical ...' It was not as exciting as a polar bear.

We talked about climbing a nearby mountain. I thought it was a good-looking mountain and that there might be a view from the top but Shaggy wanted to climb the tallest or none at all. It wasn't the tallest and I didn't want to go alone so I curled up on the sofa. In my heavy expedition book the wizard put the hobbit's ring in the fire and in the chapter-breaks I took my harmonica and my lips learned their way around the Royal Marines March made famous by an advertisement for bubble bath.

Then one day we went for coffee and chocolate cake and Gustav was smiling. He said the forecast was that the wind would drop, and the next day it did. So, on the ninth of July, we carried *Kotick* down the beach and tied her alongside the tyres in the small dock. We carried the barrels, voyage bags and bergans down to the water's edge and checked them one last time before we tied them down in the boat.

'Here, take this, I brought it for you.' Gustav handed down a two-kilo pack of *geitost*. He'd discovered that we liked the toffee flavour of the goats' cheese, and I stacked it as ballast next to the two packs he'd already given us. *Kotick* sank lower in the water.

'Take care,' said the Station Chief.

'I am actually very envious,' said the Engineer. 'I sailed them when I was young, those boats will never surprise you.'

'Enjoy the cheese,' said Gustav.

'Thanks, thank you,' I said, and, 'Goodbye then.'

* * *

The taste of farewell chocolate cake lingered in my mouth and my arms and chest were sweaty from carrying our equipment down to the small dock. My hands were cold and salty from the wet ropes.

Shaggy untied the lines from the rusty bollards on the dock and climbed down. The equipment we'd spent so long talking about, and making lists of, and packing and repacking, half of which had nearly been left in Aberdeen, was all tied down in *Kotick* just as we wanted. The life raft was on the port side under the thin canvas spray cover and the geological hammer was back in the barracks awaiting my return.

The sea was grey and the colours were flat because of the low cloud. Holding the old tyres and rusty chains, I looked at Shaggy. Our eyes locked, he nodded, and I pushed off. The gap of water between *Kotick* and the dock grew wider and wider. It was dark and clear and very, very cold.

4

Kotick the white seal

The storm shall not wake thee, nor shark overtake thee,
Asleep in the arms of the slow-swinging seas!

Rudyard Kipling, Seal lullaby

As I pushed off from the old tyres in the small dock I did not try to guess how long it would take to cover the twenty-one kilometres to Dead Man's Point.[8] I did not care because I was in the adventure and the air was wonderfully cold.

I was more than a little afraid. So, instead of looking ahead with times and distances, I concentrated on the pressure of my knees on the wooden thwart, my toes on the floorboards, the oar that I held in both hands pushing on the water and balancing the boat. Distance, the first thing we needed was some distance, after that I would think about the twenty-one kilometres. And then, very much later, hopefully not at all, I would think about the dreadful prospect of coming back *without* having made it to Dead Man's Point.

Kotick seemed much steadier now that she was loaded down into the water by all of our food, camping equipment and the kilograms of toffee-coloured *geitost*. She no longer sat on the water but in it, and the freeboard between the

---

[8] It was named by Norwegian hunters after a comrade who perished there. The Norwegian name is Daudmannsodden.

glacial waterline and the gunwale seemed to have disappeared to just twelve inches.

The Station Chief, Gustav and the Engineer were watching so we took care to thread the oars through the strops on the rowlock posts without tipping the boat. Shaggy coiled the stern warp and I re-tied the mast so that it stayed snug against the gunwale. We wanted a smooth start, hoping that we could cross this fjord, hoping most of all that we could cover distance towards the unthinkable thousand kilometres around the island. Without distance there could be no dream made real. And we would have to explain the failure.

I watched Shaggy dip his blades into the water and followed his lead. I squeezed the handles in my palms and made swirling water around the blades. We lifted our oars and stroked and stroked again. The pine of the oar creaked against the rowlock post and the boat drove into the low waves so that the water slapped against the pine planks and the gap of water between us and the dock stretched open. The Station crew waved. We both tried to raise a hand to wave back but the oars dropped and caught in the water so we grabbed them and realised that we could not wave back. Instead we grinned and stroked again.

'Keep the ensign on the dock,' I said.

The stern with its red flag on the wooden pole was moving across the scene behind us as the boat veered off course. We both tugged harder with our right hands on the next stroke. The flag pole stopped moving and drifted back the other way. One more tug with the left and *Kotick* straightened and pattered towards the open water. Then we rocked a little and a cold breeze played on my right cheek. The shelter of the bay was behind us and we were committed to each other, the warm pine of *Kotick* and the solitude of greys in the open water of Ice Fjord.

'Do you reckon we can sail?' said Shaggy. I was thinking the same.

'Yes, let's try,' I said.

I left my oars and laid them across the boat, and buried my head in the sail bag looking for the jib and sheet. Once I'd found them, while Shaggy continued pulling, I knelt on the thwart and swung the mast up, careful with the balance, and brought it down into the step through the thwart where I had been sitting. Then I secured the shrouds and tied the jib halyard to the sail. I tugged and the pulley at the mast head was smooth, the jib went up and the wind pulled it into a curve. Sitting down in the bow, I looked out beyond the sail brimming with the breeze. It pulled us gently in the direction we were travelling and a confidence stirred the ache in my chest and I even felt a little warmer.

I remembered we had not waved, and turned, but back at the Radio Station the crew were walking up the steps through the low cliff above the bay. I raised my hand high above my head and swung it from side to side. They continued, heads down, stepping up, and I imagined that their minds were set on chocolate cake. It was wonderful chocolate cake that was not for me.

I turned and unbundled the mainsail and passed the sheet to Shaggy. He leaned forward over his resting oars and threaded it through a pulley block in the stern. I ran the sheet over his shoulder and tugged the halyard so the mainsail ran smoothly up and fell over Shaggy's head. He eased forward, pulled back and put the mainsheet in his mouth so he could take up the oars again with both hands. I pinned the mainsail out with the yard arm so that it too curved with the wind.

Both of us tried to anticipate what the other might do. We moved carefully, glancing at each other often, and very soon I had clambered over him and was sitting in the stern with the rudder bar in my hands and both sails pulling. Shaggy lifted his blades clear of the water and rested on them at 'easy oar' so the drips fell. The sheets, the shrouds and the mast in its step tugged *Kotick* along and the bubbles and turning water ran out behind us just as quickly.

'No need for these then,' he said, and shipped the oars. I told him where to tie them down because I wanted to keep the boat tidy and it was safer if everything was tied down. He tied them down so we were ship shape and moving. That was good.

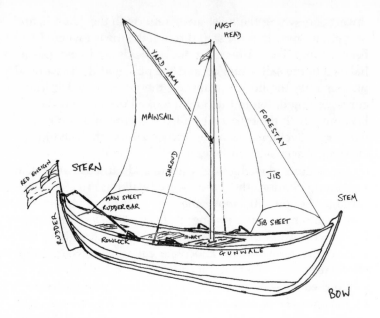

Sail plan of Kotick

The wind was in the southwest and at five degrees Celsius it felt warm and wet, drifting in from the Barents Sea where the Gulf Stream finished its long drift to the top of the world from across the North Atlantic. The wind was almost favourable and *Kotick* butted into the waves and rocked with the swell, but she did not point to windward of the headland where we wanted to go. That was bad, because we would have to sail and then row two sides of a long triangle.

I pinned the sheets as far as they would come without spoiling the curves that deflected the light wind backwards, and pushed and pulled the rudder bar to fill the sails and steer as far upwind as possible. Two woollen tell-tales streamed from the shrouds and as I pushed and pulled they came towards the line of the boat, the bow came up towards Dead Man's Point, but always, just as there was clear water between it and the high prow, the leading edge of the sails would sag and flip, the boat slowed down, and I had to turn away to fill the sails and move the boat again.

The rocks of Dead Man's Point lay twenty kilometres

distant like a charcoal brushstroke between the greys of the sea and the sky of Ice Fjord.

I steered *Kotick* up towards the outermost rocks, which lay in wait, beckoning, teasing, from their vantage point defended by six days of high wind. And every time the bow cleared the headland the sails sagged and the way fell off. There was just ten degrees between the course we could hold and the course I wanted but in the twenty kilometres of the crossing we would lose a lot of water.

'Looks like we'll have to row at the far end.'

'Let's get over there first.'

'That's a shame.'

I was not so bothered about the need to row for a few hours at the far side of the fjord, but I was disappointed that *Kotick* couldn't sail close to the wind. If the wind shifted and blew against us we would not be able to sail to the far shore at all. And we would always have to be careful setting out into unfavourable wind and adverse tides. What if we were caught and swept away? There was no rescue boat. I puffed my cheeks and blew out. I shrugged and shook my head. That was a problem for later.

By now we'd been out one hour and the masts above the Radio Station were shrinking on the headland. The black rocks of the low cliff were dull brown. It was a relief to be moving, and suddenly the world was simple, uncluttered by the need to respond to questions and demands. The sails were set, the wind was almost fair, the equipment was packed and secure. The bow was slapping against the waves in the open water and *Kotick* rolled with the swell that drifted in from the Gulf Stream.

There was time to think and time to feel cold.

'Where's the tobacco?' said Shaggy.

'In one of the rummage bags, I think.'

'How about you roll a cigarette?'

'No, you try.'

'OK, but tell me how.'

'Lick your fingers slightly, pinch above the tobacco, not the tobacco itself, and roll.' I tried to help his clumsy fingers coax the brown hairy knot of tobacco into a paper tube made from the cigarette paper that he cupped in his lap. His big fingers squashed the tobacco and crumpled the paper.

'Try warming your hands up. Lick them, but not too wet.'

He twitched his neck.

'No, you try.'

He handed it to me and took the rudder bar. We changed places, and I wondered if that was his intention all along. I smoothed out the crumpled papers and demonstrated how to roll two cigarettes, thinking that Shaggy would learn with time and that I needed to be patient. I lit them and they glowed hot in the palms of our hands, two solitary points of heat in all of that cold open water.

Kotick creaked and swung with the Gulf Stream waves, as comfortable as a seal bobbing in the water, and we pulled on the cigarettes.

Black-backed white-breasted common guillemots with fine white eyebrows circled and hit the waves. There was a small flock of Brünnich's, and scraggy little auks paddled by; they were stocky with a short neck and short bill. Every so often a bird scurried across the black water, with webbed feet kicking away from *Kotick's* bow as she came down on them. Shaggy got me to name the birds and made a mental note so he could tick them the next time the *Birds and Mammals* book came out of the dry barrel. Then with the roll-ups dying in our hands he opened the thermos flask and we drank hot tea that steamed in the wet air.

'Ah, tea. The King of Drinks,' he said and gulped.

'Have another piece of *geitost*.'

We rocked in *Kotick* as if in a hammock and the birds bobbed in the water – then we were past them, alone again on the expanse of water, and the mast creaked in the forward thwart. An orange flash came flapping from under the bow, there was a broad pink-striped beak and a yellow beauty spot in the crack of its smile, red-rimmed spectacles and two flicks of black eyeliner.

'Hey, it's a puffin.'

Shaggy pushed and pulled on the rudder bar and a coal ship steamed out of the fjord, miles ahead. They could never have seen us. I imagined a warm bridge with fresh coffee in warm porcelain cups. If they had seen us at this distance they might have mistaken us for driftwood. A ring seal bobbed up and surveyed the pine planks that cradled us and the snow-white sails tugged us north. The hours stretched.

'So why *Kotick*?' said Shaggy, rhyming 'Ko-' with 'snow', as I did.

'White seal in the *Jungle Book*,' I said. 'It's a name I like.'

'I didn't know there was a white seal in the *Jungle Book*.'

'Oh, there is. He saves the seal colonies from bloodthirsty hunters and leads them to an island deep in the Arctic,' I told him. 'I read it up here two years ago.' And I'd decided then that *Kotick* was a good name for a boat that I hoped would take me somewhere special like the unknown island in Rudyard Kipling's story, a place where 'Kotick knew by the feel of the water, which never deceives a true Sea Catch, that no men had ever come there'. It was strange how this was working out, but I didn't say that. If we made this journey it might be the perfect name.

Shaggy steered as close to the wind as possible and I kept an eye on the gusts in the water and still we could not point to windward of the headland. Dead Man's Point grew darker but no bigger. The steel-grey water pattered on the thin pine hull that was feeling like it was a part of the sea and our bums froze. So I pulled the kip mats from our pile of equipment under the thin canvas spray cover and we sat on them.

They were warmer to sit on than damp wood.

There was a ship far out to sea.

'Is that the same one?'

The masts of the Radio Station were low on the horizon and then they disappeared in a bank of mist that drifted in from the open sea. In the hours that followed I watched for the wind in the mist. There was time for reflection. And I started with more questions and answers. Is this possible? Now it seems it might be. Is it right that we try? We should. Will it save me or kill me? I don't want to die. Who has been here before? There were two men, they'd both been 'out there' and they never came back. They haunted me in my hours of musing while I watched the breeze on the water and the strike of it on our sails.

John Cooper was a distant uncle. An alpinist and a mathematician, he enjoyed astronomy and he played the violin. He grew up with his sister in Belfast and he graduated from Christ's College, Cambridge. That same summer he fell from a shoulder of the Matterhorn in the days when it was still a great adventure. His obituary in the 1960 Cambridge Climbing magazine reports:

> John was killed ... while in a party attempting the Zmutt ridge ... [he] was filled with a profound love for the mountains, a passion akin to the deep emotions which have inspired great climbers ... Words cannot convey the bewilderment of seeing a life so rich ended so abruptly.

Now he lies in Zermatt near the Swiss–Italian border. My godfather, his cousin, visits the grave from time to time. There were two on the rope and they always said he was the careful one. Granny remembers his rucksack arriving in the front room afterwards.

'Unpacking that was quite something,' she would say.

'That death destroyed his father.'

John's violin music survived and now it's mine. I play those soft yellow pages of Irish jigs and reels – the Blackthorn Stick, Jackson's Favourite, Rollicking Irishman and a Western Lilt – and in moments of reflection they take me to a family home that was never the same. And the wrong end of a climbing rope. As *Kotick* rocked with the sea I picked out the Irish Washerwoman on my harmonica. I always wondered how he fell.

The other one, who had also been out there and never returned, was nicknamed 'Gino'. He was famous: Gino Watkins, the Arctic pioneer, a Cambridge graduate with a love of cold places. He'd learned how to build sledges and kayaks and embraced the Eskimo ways. But he was hunting seal too close to a Greenland ice cliff when it crashed down around him. The rush of water was too much and he froze in the water where nobody found him. His Memorial Foundation had given me money for last year's mapping expedition. He was a hero for me. I always wondered how he drowned.

Kotick rocked us and the water slapped the hull. I made peace with their ghosts. What were you like? I thought, wishing that I knew. Knowing that I might go like them.

Two hours later the air was cooler than before. I checked my watch. It was midnight. Our noses were running and our feet were cold but the far shore was closer. I realised it was the closest point of safety and I was suddenly relieved with the almost-certainty that we would not have to return to the Radio Station with early explanations of failure. Then I was sure. Dead Man's Point was strong and real; no longer a brushstroke on a canvas of greys but wet rock, sweeps of pebble beach and breaking water.

The white canvas sails tugged us into the bay and the sound of white water was in our ears. I smelled the foam in the air, clean brine washing over stones, and the faint tang of crustaceans.

Shaggy untied his oars and looped the strops of rope around them, and when I had swung the mast down from its step in the forward thwart I did the same and we paddled into the quartering sea. With cold feet and stiff hands, with waterproofs constricting and impeding the free movement of our backs and arms, and with the light rain brushing our hoods, we rowed in earnest for the first time. There was no rhythm or comfort but the wind was light and we barrelled our way around the rocks and towards the promontory.

Rowing in time with each other should be easy like walking but it is not. And even if it were, walking in time with somebody else can be troublesome if the other has a different stride.

Shaggy's back went to and fro in front of me and I watched the blade of his oar dig deep and jump out of the water, slow in the water, fast through the air, quite the opposite of what I wanted to do, which was sweep fast and shallow and recover with time. So keeping the rhythm was difficult but this did not bother me because of the novelty of making distance and because we had to find a way through the rocks of Dead Man's Point.

We both kept looking over our shoulders and picking the way and we had to agree where to go and then where on the horizon we should see the flag pole which was lashed to

Kotick's stern post. Our shoulders and chest warmed up, and despite the rain on our hands my palms warmed up too. The wood was warm in my boiled wool mittens and the rough grain fitted easily. *Kotick* rolled and swung from rock to rock and our oars jumped in time from puddle to puddle of swirling water. Shaggy put his oars down and took out his waterproof camera for a snapshot.

'Got to get one: In Action At The Oars,' he said, so I pulled my hood back and stretched my cheeks into a smile.

It took us about two hours to row along the beaches and through the rocks off the promontory. To be honest we felt a little ridiculous paddling along so far from everywhere and anybody else. One storm petrel agreed, judging from his quizzical expression. He followed us, looping and sweeping on the waves with the dark feathers over one eye raised in a cartoon cocked eyebrow. He was still with us when we reached the breaking water at the end of Daudmannsodden.

Despite the heat of exertion and the sweat inside our shirts, our toes and ankles were cooling down towards an irreversible numbness. Shaggy opened the thermos flask and steam tumbled from its opening but the tea was no more than tepid. It was long past the time when sensible campers would beach, pitch a tent and climb into dry sleeping bags to relieve their fatigue.

That was our choice: to camp or continue. The wind was coming up in our favour and it seemed a shame to waste it after waiting for headwinds to die for so long. So with the world of men far behind, and many hours of wakefulness behind us already, we moved outside of ourselves. We rounded the headland and set the sails. The wind kept on increasing and it blew us up Forlandsundet like a snowflake before a storm.

Kotick flew. She surfed down the waves with water crashing out from under her bow and rode the occasional breaker. The three of us, *Kotick*, Shaggy and I, put kilometres of water under the bow and the ghosts of John and Gino trailed far behind. I was cold and hungry but the progress was a drug, we were out there, going outside the limit before the real journey had started. The progress was fantastic and the euphoria carried us. But it was too early to be real; we were still training for long-distance success, and it was hard to hold against the cold.

Hours later, at three in the morning, it was still light like day but our biological rhythm was telling us to sleep. My concentration lapsed; I was cold. Damp was creeping down my neck and up the inside of my sleeves. I put on all my clothes and sitting on a kip mat pulled the drawstrings tight. I had to ignore the feet for their cold. Meanwhile we kept the boat sailing and changed the sails for the wind. We kept enough sail to keep her moving fast through the water but not so much that she would lurch into the waves and take it onboard.

The rain which fell from the warm southwesterly was incessant and our noses dripped incessantly too. We started by wiping them with our cuffs but soon gave up because our hands and sleeves were as wet as everything else. Shaggy had a long tongue but I never knew how long until he used it to wipe his nose. He did this secretly at first but in a boat the size of *Kotick* there could be no secrets. I saw it go right up his nose, just like a cow. That seemed very useful.

I watched him and his tongue and the hours passed. With all of his experience in difficult places, an ascent of the north face of the Dru and windsurfing around Coll from nearby Tiree, I had expected him to arrive in the Arctic and already behave like an old hand. But he did not. The cold sea and eternal light were new to him, and his eyes explored the terrain, the animals and the weather. He looked at me.

'I thought you said it never rains.'

'Well, it doesn't, usually. This is, unusual,' I replied.

A pause stretched into minutes, nearly an hour. The rain was running down his face and the drips were falling from his nose. He was bewildered by the surroundings, he was bewildered by me.

He took time and considered, and then he spoke.

'When I get cold and wet and miserable I think, God I'm cold and wet and miserable, I wish I wasn't here. I wish I was a vegetable.'

We both smiled and he licked the drips from his nostrils

without effort. I had already rubbed mine raw with the sodden sleeve of my jacket but I didn't tell him I was jealous of his tongue. It did, in fact, hardly ever rain in Svalbard except for here on the west coast, and if it did it was a light drizzle. But as luck would have it heavy rain fell for nearly twelve hours.[9]

After another hour we changed to the small jib because the balloon jib was whipping and cracking, threatening to split. *Kotick* rocked easily again and we ran on into the clag. Only the lower scree slopes of the mountainsides were visible on either side of Forlandsundet and that horizontal sliver of ice and rock was hidden sometimes by driven mist. I caught forty minutes' dreaming and tried to pretend to myself that I'd been asleep. Meanwhile the wind died so I hoisted the balloon jib back up and we sped on again. Not for long was the wind calm. It soon strengthened and freed off to the south, making the balloon jib whip and crack again, out of control, and when it did fill we heeled so the glacial brine came tumbling over the gunwale. I picked up the bilge pump and stroked the water out again over the leeside gunwale, and then I mopped up what was left under the floorboards with the sponge.

The line Shaggy had chosen had brought us close to the coast again. I took the next watch and over the next two hours we worked back out into the open. I was happier in the deep water because, like most keelboat sailors, I preferred the open sea. Out in the wind and the water most boats will survive anything. It's only when they hit the land that they do worrying things like break up. Shaggy was of a different view, and as a windsurfer he liked to be close enough to swim ashore. So as we took two-hour turns with the rudder bar we made four-hour-long zigzags up the coast.

When Shaggy took the helm in the early hours of the morning we were well out in the open. I suspect he had already decided we should go in because he turned for the cover of the outer island, Prince Charles Foreland,[10] and soon

---

[9] Svalbard is commonly categorised as an Arctic desert, with 7–8 inches of rain per year.

[10] The Norwegian name is Prins Karls Forland, named after Charles I of Great

he was persuading me that we should make a camp on the north of the Dawespynten spit. Judging from the contour lines on the map, this was a long shingle promontory which would protect the beach from the swell that was now running from the south.

Beyond lay the Narrows, and the *Arctic Pilot*, the guidebook with details of the landfalls and local ice and currents, warned us to be wary of the shallow ground and the tide race.

I wanted to approach the tide race fresh and in fine weather. Judging from the map, the Dawespynten spit seemed to be the last bolt hole where we could camp and eat and rest. Now that we were close I wanted to know what the tide rip looked like. What was the exact time of high tide? Would we be safe going with a rising tide or would it be better at slack water? What kind of chop would this southerly kick up if the current was running against it? All of these questions helped me agree with Shaggy that we should aim for that beach. But it was a waste of so much good wind and I was reluctant to stop.

After two more comical zigzags, from and to the shoreline, we landed and unfolded our stiff limbs on the beach of the Foreland, a long desolate uninhabited island. It was ten kilometres back to the main island of Spitsbergen. As my feet crunched in the pebble beach the blood ran back into them.

We hauled the kit and *Kotick* up the beach and made a gritty campsite above the high-tide seaweed. The rain was still falling as we pitched the tent. Shaggy pulled his petrol cooker from its carry bag and pumped it for pressure. He lit a solid fuel tablet under the fuel line while I filled a cooking pot with fresh water. Then he opened the throttle and white naphtha smoked and caught. It burned yellow, then blue, and gave a throaty roar. He placed the tin of water.

I was rummaging in the food barrel out in the rain.

'Lancashire hotpot? How about that?' I called out. He

Britain and Ireland (1600–49). It was also called Isle of Kijn by the Dutch for a time, after a sailor who tried to 'climb a high hill but missed his footing and broke his neck'.

grunted so I threw two foil bags to him and climbed back into the tent. He submerged the bags in the water in the pot. He covered the pot with a lid and we waited for the water to boil. The lid started jumping and tapping as puffs of steam and the smell of white naphtha blew into the tent-liner. After ten minutes Shaggy turned down the heat and tore along the top of the bags. We ate them with spoons while they warmed the hand we held them in and called it 'breakfast' because it was eight in the morning. We licked the spoons and there was no other washing up.

My diary was carefully packed away so I decided to leave it. I lay down next to Shaggy, who had gone out like a candle, disheartened because he quite logically assumed that the further north we went the worse the weather would become. I listened to the wind cracking in the tent sheet and the light drumming of the rain. I sipped my tea. He was right. It was the king of drinks.

My feet were dry inside the down tent boots and the warmth was coming back to them. I felt good because we had made distance. It was proof that we could make good distance and in quite a blow. The eighty kilometres between us and the Radio Station meant that the nay-sayers no longer could. My sleeping bag was warm.

I finished my tea and fell asleep to the sound of the rain, and then woke up eight hours later, forced outside by a full bladder. Shaggy slept on with half of his tea still in the measuring jug he had bought in Longyearbyen. It was wise of him to drink only half the cup because he slept full through. I drifted back into my own thoughts and half slept, dreaming of the dancing dawn and needle peaks, and the miles and miles of cold coast that lay ahead.

5

Northernmost coal mine

I rolled in my bag and lifted my hips so I could curl into an 'S' but the small of my back was obstructed. The fabric of the tent liner cooled my nose and an orange glow played on my eyelids. I opened them and light scattered inside the tent from the vent hole and danced with the fluttering of the flysheet. Shaggy was behind me but something was missing. I listened to the wind. It was gentle and I realised, of course, no rain.

I rolled over. Shaggy was propped up on his elbows reading.

'Hello, hello,' he said. My feet were warm in my tent boots.

'Morning, you sleep well?' I said.

I unzipped my sleeping bag then the tent liner and wriggled on my elbows so I could see out to the expanse of water and distant mountains. The stones were round and cold and the high-tide seaweed was drying in the sun. There was a way to go to Ny Ålesund.

'Beautiful day,' I said and remembered this island, Prins Karls Forland, was miles from the mainland and entirely empty. If bad weather kept us here there was nowhere that we could walk to.

'I know,' he said, his nose in the Norwegian Polar Institute *Arctic Pilot*, our nautical guidebook. His concentration was deep. Foam broke on the pebbles and, over the Sound, snow-caps scratched the blue sky and ice tumbled down in the broad valleys. There was black moraine in curving lines on the glaciers creeping down between the craggy mountains.

'What does it say?' I asked. He was silent, and I looked out again. Cat's-paws were scuffing the water. Shaggy turned back a page.

'It says the tide runs in the Narrows at four knots, which is faster than we can row. It says it can wash you onto the rocks.' He turned over a page.

'It says the beacon is liable to damage from pack ice.' He looked up. 'It sounds like a nightmare, I'm glad we stopped,' he said.

Then I remembered me not wanting to stop because of the wind. I remembered the Narrows and the wide crossing back to the main island and the thirty kilometres up King's Fjord to Ny Ålesund. The cat's-paws drifted off across the sound.

'The wind's changed.'

I remembered we had nine days' food, and when you did the maths it was clear we couldn't afford many days waiting for a following wind.

'Best we have breakfast then,' he said and pulled the petrol cooker from under the flysheet to the bell-end of the tent. He pumped it for pressure and submerged two foil bags that said 'beans and sausages' along the top edge. He covered it with a lid.

'I still think it was a good thing we stopped.'

He was thinking about the wind. That was a good thing.

'It's a long way to Ny Ålesund,' I replied

'Yes exactly. I was going to say, let's not go there, let's go straight on. If we make it across Kings Fjord today, it's not like we need to pick up the depot, and it's miles up the fjord.'

He was right, in a way, but for me Ny Ålesund was the true start point of this journey, because that's where the idea had come to me. My dream had been to start and finish at Salterella Boatshed, that very same spot, around the island and back to it again. Fate had conspired that I start at Isfjord Radio Station and I was OK with that, but to make the journey without visiting Ny Ålesund would have been like not making the journey at all.

'We don't need the depot, yet, but it would be better to get it, and you'll love Ny Ålesund,' I told him, feeling that my pilgrimage to the boatshed was best left unmentioned.

'It's *miles* up the fjord,' he said, turning to a page with a map and starting to measure with his thumb. 'It'll take us nearly a hundred kilometres out of our way, we should just go straight on.'

'But you'll love it,' I said, 'and there might be post.'

I knew he was hoping for a letter from Anna.

'It's just an old coal mine, right?'

'Naah, it's great,' I said. 'There's a whole bunch of people.'

Aside from the fun I'd had there before, and my desire to visit the beach where I'd wanted to start the journey, I wanted to see Nick and Katie, who had both been part of the team on my first visit to the islands. They'd helped with the planning discussions for this journey from the outset. And to see them in the far North was never the same as seeing them in England. I also wanted to see and talk with the others in Ny Ålesund because they would understand the value of this journey, that it was worth doing for its own sake, unlike so many people back home. But these were selfish reasons, and for Shaggy the trip up King's Fjord was a waste of time on a trip that was turning out to be less fun and more uncomfortable than he'd expected. We'd been unlucky with the rain.

It bothered me that he just wanted to make it around the island and go home.

'And there might be a football match, it's the northernmost football pitch in the world,' I tried to cajole him some more, 'and there'll be fresh food and a hot shower in the Coal Company mess.'

The King's Bay Coal Company administration is all that remains of the coal operation set up by seal hunters looking for fuel in the First World War. The mines themselves are mass graves. One hundred miners worked fourteen-hour days through the dark Arctic winter until there was a series of explosions. In the aftershocks of the final accident in 1962 the Norwegian government of the day fell.

'There are folk studying mad things like sunsets and tundra moss.'

'Bloody long way to go for a hot shower,' he said.

'And above all,' I said, 'they have great parties.'

'Is there a telephone?' he said, and finished his beans. 'If there's a telephone it might be worth going.'

As we packed the blue barrels, the escape bergan and the bosun's bergan into the hull and secured the rifle beneath the seat, a light swell arrived. We pushed off and the surface of the sound was liquid glass breathing with the long waves, but before we had taken one hundred strokes a draught scuffed it and short waves came. They made *Kotick* dip down first to one side and then the other. The delicate balance of a narrow hull driven through clean water by the muscle in our shoulders, arms and backs was thrown off kilter, the blades caught the water and the wind blowing off the line of the hull made it swerve away.

'Pull straight, Shags, straight, it's always turning.'

'I am. You pull straight,' he said. And we concentrated on keeping the flag pole on the same piece of horizon.

We discovered, again, that we rowed differently. I tried to drop the oar into the water to catch it with the blade barely covered, and pulled through to a hard finish, just as a university oarsman flat-mate had told me. Then I popped it out to leave swirling water and came back with time to the next catch. Shaggy dug the oar in, pulled deep and hard until it would go no further, then yanked it back to the surface and sent the boat tumbling.

'Lug' then 'chuck' went Shaggy's stroke as he strained at his oars. 'Lug-chuck, Lug-chuck,' and my own measured strokes flipped out or stuck painfully deep.

'For chri'sake,' I muttered, under by breath, then, out loud, 'Fast in the water, slow recovery.'

'No, you can't pull hard that way.' He pulled again.

'You have to, Shags, it's the only way we'll go the distance.'

'When I pull hard the oar goes deep. It's better that way.'

'That's bollocks. At least recover slowly.'

I tried to explain to him: it was the best way to row, he would find it easier that way, we had to do it properly, together, otherwise we'd never go the distance. Shaggy's neck twitched both ways. He was determined to pull long and deep with every stroke. His blades dipped, they went 'lug', then 'chuck' as he tore them from the water. Mine hit the waves and stuck deep as *Kotick* barrelled over the swell. Before ten minutes, pain cut the tendons in my arms and there was sweat in my shirt.

'Man,' I called, 'and we could have been sailing.'

'It was right to stop.' He said, 'We were tired and we'd been going a long time, and the wind was getting stronger.'

We pulled another stroke not quite in time. He continued –

'And we didn't know if we could beach further north and we didn't know about the rocks and the current might have been too strong.'

We pulled another stroke.

'And we were cold, wet, without sleep. And too far out.'

We pulled another stroke.

'And I kind of lost my nerve.'

'Uhh-huh?' I jumped at him, finally.

Then I winced as my blades caught in a wave and I pulled them free.

'It's smart to know when to quit.' He was retreating to philosophy.

I agreed inwardly, that it had been right to stop and camp instead of continue with the following wind, but did not say so. I preferred to watch him suffer as the ache of muscle fatigue settled in my shoulders. We both knew in those next hours of rowing and pain that we could have travelled at twice the speed if we'd been sailing with last night's favourable wind. He lunged forwards and caught the next wave early. I had to catch out of time to keep up.

'This isn't working, Shags.' I took two slow breaths. 'Can I set the time?'

To set the rhythm I had to sit in the back of the boat so we changed seats, me believing that I could show him how to row, that if he watched me stroke then he would copy and learn.

'Ready?'

I lifted my blade from the water and tilted forwards on the bench seat, I extended my arms so the two handles of the oars moved in a measured way, I dropped them and caught the water, hoping that Shaggy would do the same. I pulled and tilted back, and stroked again and felt the hull wobble. One of Shaggy's blades came flying out of the water, scattering icy spray that soaked my cheek and filled my ear canal.

'Hey!' I shouted, and shook the iced water from my face.

'Fast in the water. Slow recovery,' I said urgently. But it was no use. He rowed the way he rowed, which was slow in the water and fast in the air.

It was like trying to walk in time, or three-legged, with different strides. Every time *Kotick* lurched into a wave she stopped and every time she rolled our blades popped out of the water on the upside, or going forward blades would catch on the downside. In the next thousand kilometres our rhythm could only improve, so I decided to keep quiet. As we rowed in silence we both thought about the kilometres that we'd lost and the following wind that had blown all night while we slept.

'We were tired and the wind was too strong,' echoed Shaggy, again. I agreed but I did not say. As he ran through his reasons again his voice was strained. He was pleading. I watched him suffer as we rowed, and we rowed, and as we rowed he suffered more than I. There were eider duck in the water.

'I wish I was an eider duck,' said Shaggy, 'never cold, you can stop when you want and you'd be around the island in less than a week.'

We paddled along the pebble beach, sheltering from the northerly waves by tucking into each cove formed by spits of moraine reaching out from the glacier snouts. The Dawespynten spit behind us grew hazy and sank lower into the water. After an hour and a half we had covered six kilometres and the land behind wedged out into a horizontal line. The next stroke it had gone.

'Cool, I've never done that before,' he said.

* * *

We did find an uncomfortable rhythm, and over the next four hours the shooting in my tendons dispersed into an aching in my muscles. My head became empty and my chest turned cold. We had tea and biscuits in the middle of a bay and drifted in circles before rowing again. The fatigue quickly returned, and in the next hours the blisters came.

The pebbles and seaweed on the beach passed along my right arm and in all of that time we watched countless spits disappear over the horizon. It seemed strange that the wide flat sound had such curved water and that so many headlands sank into the sea behind us. I wanted to feel sugar in my mouth but we'd already eaten the chocolate ration.

At the Sarstangen Narrows the startling clarity of the air allowed us to see snow caps one hundred and sixty kilometres to the south and we could not go any further towards Ny Ålesund because the tide was running against us. So we aimed at the beach and after the boat crunched on the gravel we carried the equipment up the shingle to the high-tide seaweed.

I emptied the water from the hull and we stood at either end. Shaggy was bigger and taller and I was grateful that he could reach a rib low in the bow, where we tied the anchor warp, to use as a handhold. I could only reach the rib if I bent my back into a weak position, and lifting like that scared me because out here I depended so much on being resilient and strong. I could not injure my back. So I was quietly thanking Shaggy and his strength as we lifted the two-hundred-pound hull and walked up the beach.

We walked off along the line of driftwood and as my weight worked through the pads of my feet they filled with blood and warmth and sensation. At the beacon we watched the angry water tumbling south across the overfalls. There was no chance of making into a tide like that. Standing waves danced close to the beach and a dark strand of seaweed made pirouettes. A snow shower blew flakes into my hair and I pulled up my hood.

'I'm glad we're not out there.'

According to the map, the mountains above the Radio Station were one hundred kilometres distant. The air was so clear that they were just a little hazy. At twelve noon the agitated water started receding. We snacked and had some hours to wait for the tide to turn, so we unrolled the kip mats and lay down. I put my hands behind my head. My eyes closed easily and I dreamed with the motion of the boat. The next snow shower was an hour upwind, there was absolute calm. The sun was shining through a break in the snow clouds.

A kittiwake flew over and the slipstream whistled. It reminded me of a quiet evening on Bear Island two years before, and I knew I'd returned to the Svalbard that I loved. It was the good memories that came, not the cold fingers or frozen feet or aching muscles.

I was missing my geological hammer; its absence made me feel like a tourist. I wanted to walk knowingly to that nearby outcrop and crack a chip of dark limestone, or would it be granite? The minerals in the fractured surface would tell me; the angles of the crystals and whether they scratched with a knife.[11] But there again, maybe mine was just idle curiosity. I was enjoying not having to take all of those notes.

'Pete, what are these sticks?' Shaggy was walking towards me.

He'd been looking for birds to tick in the *Birds and Mammals* book and he came back holding two wooden pegs and a wooden spike that had been carved so as to fit together.

Fox trap

'Ah, cool, it's a fox trap. There's another bit somewhere,' I said, and showed him how one peg fitted into a slot cut in the

---

[11] Quartz is harder than both steel and calcite; it also has a different crystal symmetry.

other, and how a depression cut in the long wooden spike held the two pegs together.

'Then you rest the wooden frame on top,' I said, 'and pile stones. You stick a piece of seal fat on the spike, and when the fox grabs it, crunch. The rocks break his neck.'

'Bummer for the fox, what's the use in that?'

'The pelts sell as coats and hood-fur for spindrift.'

We set the trap and nudged the spike with a stick and the frame with the rocks fell, crunch, onto it. Then we went looking for a self-shoot, which the trappers used for killing bears in the days the trappers were allowed to hunt. The curious bear approaches a vertical pole pulled from the Siberian driftwood and finds a box with a piece of seal. He grabs the flesh and blubber with his teeth and it pulls a string to the trigger of a revolver. A bullet hits him between the eyes. We found a box with two holes in one end, one for the string and one for the bullet.

'Cool,' said Shaggy. 'Poor bear.'

Then I wrapped my hands up with sticking plaster to protect the blisters. The ebb tide was almost spent and the water in the sound was smooth again. I would have been happy to wait for some of the tide to come back to help us but Shaggy was anxious to be moving so we pushed the boat off and nosed around into the shallow water. My hands burned when I gripped the oars again. I moved them slowly until the pain became dull.

* * *

Crossing the open water back to the mainland was long and monotonous and hard. Whereas before we had been skimming along next to cliffs and pebble beaches, watching the driftwood and seaweed and the spits of land disappear over the horizon, now we had twenty-five kilometres of open water and once we were a couple of kilometres offshore it seemed that we hardly moved at all. Sure, the tide carried us north, but the crossing was so wide we felt suspended in space and time between the two coasts.

We pulled at the oars to make noise and motion for

ourselves and only for ourselves. Our shoulders and arms were hot so we stripped to the waist. That was more comfortable until the sun burned our pale skin.

We did talk for some hours, about this and that, about previous trips and about the time we had spent in the Corps. About the dangers of the Eiger, a climb Shaggy had considered but avoided on account of the number of climbers and the quantity of falling rock. I told him about the rocks of Svalbard and we talked about friends and what would happen next. We talked about food, about parties and about girls.

Shaggy and Anna shared their own particular flavour of madness and a love of mountains. It did not take long for them to become friends, and to share a bed from time to time. In the talk that filled the gaps between the oar strokes Anna kept recurring. He told me there was a complication, she had a long-distance French boyfriend, and that surprised me. But it seemed to fit with their casual happiness. Anna had the post box of the Dutch supply ship *Waterproef* that would put in our depots, so she might write to him. He was hoping that she would respond to the letters that he'd written from the Radio Station.

'Do you think there will be post in Ny Ålesund?' he said.

'Like I said, it's possible.'

Our words became sporadic and stopped. My mind had been working double for months, for years, with finals, summer fun, preparing for this journey, and moving on from College. Now there was just empty space and light that made my eyes water. The boundless purity was dazzling, my thoughts unwound like a coiled spring, and the release of it washed through me.

We'd been through a lot in that year in the Royal Marines, then a climbing expedition to Mount Ararat in Kurdistan, and the nights of raki roulette.[12] Quietly musing, I re-lived my three years at Clare and gigs in the jazz bar in the crypt, the

---

[12] Raki is a high-proof aniseed-flavoured liqueur popular in eastern Turkey. It is similar to several kinds of alcoholic beverages available in the Mediterranean and parts of the Balkans.

hockey and beer afterwards and long vacations in Svalbard. There was a job that I might take, and hopes of Antarctica before that.

I thought about the mechanic with the greasy jeans, the geologist we'd nicknamed Genghis Khan. I thought about logistics Nick, who thought he'd kissed Katie in secret.

Eventually the ache of my wrists and muscles and the dull pain in my hands took over. The small of my back grew stiff and in the end, most of all, the agony of butt cheeks rocking to and fro on the wooden thwarts burned into the pain nerves in my head. They were pounded raw. This was no dream.

After that even the pain was boring. Each hour dragged out into the next, slower than the last, and we developed strategies to cope with the boredom. I liked to count the number of strokes we took in a minute to see how our rate went up and down. So while the sea and *Kotick* were suspended between the mountains I would count the imaginary kilometres, one every fifteen minutes, as the seconds ticked on my watch face. When I could do that no longer I withdrew into a daydream state and tried to keep the sweep of the rhythm. My brain drifted in a pool of aspic.

Shaggy didn't want to settle. He focused on the destination. And when his impatience at the lack of progress defeated him he started counting. He counted over and over, one number for each stroke, and then lost concentration and his count. So he would start over, and again, until he made it through to four hundred and some. Then he lost count and returned to one.

As we went north the far coastline tantalised us by turning away. After many more hours and countless hundreds under Shaggy's breath, we rounded the headland at the mouth of King's Fjord and a puff of wind blew a snow shower from behind us. I was still stripped to the waist and the snow flakes pricked my back before turning wet, and I pulled on my shirt.

Then the snow fell thick and fast. It was cold and wet on my hands and neck, and my fingers struggled with the rope that secured the mast to the bench seats in a horizontal position. I swung it up to catch this puff of wind, and the shrouds and halyards tangled. At another time it would have been comic but I was angry and I swore clear and loud into the wind. I turned and saw Shaggy grin before he looked away. His smile annoyed me. I was suddenly hot and wanted to break an oar over him then pitch him over the side.

When the sail was up the wind died but we were too tired to row again so we drifted in circles until the water ruffled. Then we ghosted with this latest breeze across the fjord. It was so cold that the snowflakes floated on the black water. By my watch it was midnight again.

A drum beat grew from deep within: Di-dah, di-dah. Di-dah, di-dah, and I hummed. Where was it from? I could not tell. The more it snows, di-dah di-dah, the more it snows. I tried to fathom it. The more it snows, the more it goes, there's a rhyme, the more it goes, tiddly pom, on snowing.

A A Milne. And nobody knows, tiddly pom, how cold my toes, tiddly pom. That's it. How cold my toes, tiddly pom, are growing. Or did they belong to Winnie the Pooh? His toes were never this cold.

The grim concrete coal tower and two golf-balls at Ny Ålesund grew out of the greyness. The snow showers continued to blow through and settle on the water before melting with the salt. Then there were the coloured huts and the small dock and the boatsheds. Then Salterella Boatshed and the beach I remembered, and then I felt pride and fatigue in great and equal measure.

* * *

I don't remember how we chose the place to land. I don't remember beaching *Kotick*. I remember laying her just above the high tide line with the painter running up through the driftwood to a post beyond the beach embankment. There were other boats and there was a concrete mooring block stained with the rust of the ring set in it, but we didn't fix her there. We tied her alone and free of the other boats and piled our kit under the eaves of Salterella Boatshed. I looked back along the fjord and out to sea. The snow clouds obscured Kapp Mitra. Then I turned and we grabbed our voyage bags and walked beneath the screeching terns to the Coal Company office.

It was very late now, and Nick and Katie were finished with late-night tea in the dining hall. Nick looked at me with empty eyes. I smiled and nodded. Katie looked at me with similar hollow eyes. I nodded some more, several times. There was a stuffed polar bear by the window. None of them were smiling, something was wrong. Then Katie burst out –

'Oh my God, it's Pete!'

Nick was suddenly cheerful.

'My, my Pedro, how good to see you,' he said and pumped my hand. Katie kissed me without leaning in.

'Goodness you look awful!' she said, and went for hot chocolate.

After chocolate we found bliss in a warm shower. Then they gave us whisky to warm us up, and a Swedish girl with a spare room handed us the keys to her hut so that while the snow banked up on the window ledges we slept. Late the following morning Katie woke us with sandwiches, boiled eggs and hot coffee in a thermos. When I chewed the ham and gulped the hot fluid I began to feel human again.

The wind was strong, too strong, and a team of French kayakers had just arrived by ship. They stood forlornly on the foreshore. One of their tents had blown away. Shaggy was quite happy to tell them that yes, we'd arrived in that tiny boat, and that yes, the weather was always like this. I was with him, and it felt like we'd scored a small victory.

There was no post in Ny Ålesund so Shaggy made friends with a German with a fax machine and he called Cairo, where Anna was spending the summer. But he only managed to wake up the principal of the Language Institute, who explained it was midnight in Egypt.

I slipped away to Salterella Boatshed. Two duck skimmed across the water. The calamity of a boat that inspired this dream was nowhere to be seen, and I remembered how comfortable *Salterella* had been lying at anchor in the bay. The silhouette of Kapp Mitra stood like an upturned anvil, beckoning from across the water amidst the snow clouds. This was the real start of my journey.

We had covered a vast distance in those two long legs, eighty kilometres to the campsite and sixty kilometres to this beach. If we could continue in such a way then we had the circumnavigation within our grasp. There was still the ice and the mist and the wind of the north coast, and the bears and the fear of Hinlopen. But if we could make a hundred kilometres every three days then we had the food and the time that we needed for the thousand kilometres ahead. What might go wrong? What was waiting? We could worry about that later; so far, so good.

It was fun, this, dreaming with my eyes open. I sat down on the driftwood and seaweed and wondered where all this would take me. Somewhere over the rainbow? It seemed ridiculous to think that now. A cold watery death? That did not seem so likely after our good start. If we kept our heads, and our luck, and this progress, then we would make it. That would be news. But would it turn my life? How would it do that? Then I suffered an attack of doubt.

Will it be worth it? I thought, and I started thinking too much.

What's it all about? I thought, as I walked back to the hut.

* * *

With the snow storm, a Russian trawler arrived at the coal jetty. The Norwegians came to meet them and bought boxes of prawns which they carried to the Coal Company kitchen. They invited the Russians to bring vodka, and the Norwegian store keeper drove around town on a four-wheel bike inviting the town to a party.

It was a party for the summer, for the island, a party for life. We started with prawns and aquavit and finished with pepper vodka. A Welsh field guide strummed a guitar and we all helped find a tune that we thought we all knew. It was 'Wild Rover' and we sang the chorus six times. By then we'd all finally learned the words so we sang it again.

'So many fun people, I never expected!' said Shaggy.

He laid two broom sticks on the floor and raised one hand above his head. He gathered our eyes, raised the other hand, then set to the guitar chords, skipping over the sticks faster and faster. His legs flew out and his arms pumped in time with this random sword dance. He howled and we clapped. Then we all danced with each other and the stuffed polar bear.

6

The walrus and the carpenter

While I was talking about our plans for the north coast with the energy of beer and dancing with the stuffed polar bear, a gale burst into King's Fjord from the Barents Sea and whipped the water into great rolling waves that smashed up the shingle. The breakers crashed and ran far beyond the high-tide seaweed and reached *Kotick*. Helped by the high spring tide they broke into her and carried her across to the concrete mooring block. The waves swamped her with brine and pebbles and crashed her into that mooring block.

I found *Kotick* the following morning. My heart lurched in my ribs and my knees crashed onto the shingle beside her. I put my fingers into the bare wood where the concrete block had scoured a four-inch hole in the planks, my nose was close to it and I could smell spray and brine. Nick was there and I looked at the sky. I shouldn't have been thinking this was so easy, before the party, the night before.

'No,' I cried. 'I don't believe it.' He knelt down beside me.

'What a stupid place to put a mooring block,' he said with assurance and quiet control. I didn't know if the damage was structural, nor whether I could I repair it. The disappointment I had in myself was overwhelming, but Nick's calmness reassured me. He'd started life as a carpenter and a boatman.

'It'll be alright, Peter. She'll be OK.'

His weather-beaten hands were feeling the planks inside and out, as if he was a doctor and *Kotick* the patient. The plank was cut but not all the way through. The hull had been thrown down on one side and the rowlock posts on the low side were twisted and cracked. He pushed one and it swung freely on the last screw that held it. He gripped and tried the gunwale and found it was sound.

'She'll be OK,' he said again. 'Have you got a hammer?'

'No, but I've got pliers with a broad head, they should do,' I said, wishing for my geological hammer.

I dug around inside the bosun's bergan and pulled out the astonishing variety of glues and pastes that was inside. With the different fillers, wood glue, sandpaper, *et cetera*, there was epoxy glue and glass matting, which might work. While I was laying it out on the beach Shaggy arrived, and after a brief chat we decided that the glass matting would be best.

It was designed to fill holes and cover cracks in kayaks, and would stick to woodwork too, but the wood had to be completely dry to take the adhesive. We needed some shelter for *Kotick*. So I went to the Norwegian boatman in the Coal Company mess – he was one of the party organisers – and asked if I could borrow his boatshed. He'd enjoyed our stories the night before and he smiled, of course that would be fine. So we carried *Kotick* inside their boatshed and arranged the tools and repair equipment around her overturned hull.

While Shaggy scraped down to hard wood, dried it with his petrol cooker and mixed the epoxy, I went around town asking for long wood screws for the rowlock posts. I discovered that the German with the fax machine had a wonderful range, and he brought the whole selection down to the boatshed so that we could choose the best ones together. I chose a drill bit and sited new holes and drilled them out to the correct depth with the manual drill that Nick had lent me. Screws would be better than nails, we'd decided.

Wood shavings fell onto the cold gravel floor and the tang of the epoxy solvent filled the air. It hit the back of my nostrils, and my head and chest seemed to lose their weight. I enjoyed the sensation of lightness until I breathed fresh air and my body was heavy again. As we knelt there the door latch clicked and it swung open.

Light and cold air fell into the boatshed and there was a short wiry man with a pre-war holdall. He stepped in, and there was strength in the agility of his legs.

'Hello Brian,' I said, rocking up from my knees onto my feet. I held out my hand, and I introduced him to Shaggy.

'This is Brian, Brian Harland, he runs the Cambridge Spitsbergen Expeditions. I was up here with him, two years ago.'

'Well, hello, hello.' Shaggy seemed respectfully bemused.

'And, so how is the field season, Brian?' I asked him, not quite sure.

'Oh, good, we're not going so far this year,' he replied.

Brian first arrived in Ny Ålesund in 1952, though that was not his intention at the time. He had set off from Longyearbyen, as he had been doing for a number of years, in a small 'Strandebaumer' open boat powered by an outboard engine, with enough stores and equipment for a geological field season on the north coast. There was a storm and it forced him up King's Fjord to the coal mine, where he found shelter and bought himself, for the first time, a waterproof jacket. What he found was the settlement that would become his summer base for the next forty years.

With all those years in the field Brian had acquired a legendary endurance, and there were stories that he'd once skied off the Ny Friesland ice cap with a broken ankle, a journey that took three days. Now there was a curve in his once-broad shoulders, whiskers in his ears and a tendency towards the cantankerous. But today he was nothing but friendly. In his holdall he had a thermos flask and two mugs.

'Would you like a cup of coffee?' he said. He knew the value of scalding coffee. My back was stiff and my hands were cold.

'Yes please,' we said with enthusiasm.

One year, after the mining operations were stopped, he had taken an old hut in Ny Ålesund which was known as 'Mexico', and installed bunks and a dining table, rifles for bears, a store of rations, spare coats and a fine range of sea-boots. When the sailor–mountaineer Tilman passed through in 1974 he reported meeting Brian and giving him flour, dried eggs and potatoes in exchange for 'ten boxes of Lifeboat biscuit and a ration box'. The way Tilman told the story, Brian's team 'seemed to be having a hard time, living entirely on pre-packed twelve-man-day ration boxes … since their arrival they had not eaten bread …'[13] Those twelve-man-day ration packs were the staple of half-a-century of expeditionary geologists. One of the games that we had played in idle lunch times was to take a pack of biscuits and try to remember what we had been doing on the 'use before' date, which was usually long gone.

Brian's Cambridge Spitsbergen Expeditions grew into the 'Cambridge Arctic Shelf Programme' and it was that organisation that had first taken me to Spitsbergen as a field assistant. His conviction that undergraduates should dedicate time to fieldwork had helped attract me to the subject, and I liked that he encouraged students to explain observations rather than refer to theories, presumably because that is how the real advances are made.

As a geologist on the world stage he'd advocated some of the major theories long before they were widely accepted, such as continental drift, which explains how land masses and the ocean floor move over the eons, throwing up mountains and volcanoes, and opening trenches in the oceanic deep. He'd worked on correlating the chronological sequence of geological events to such a degree that he was known by some as 'Timescale Harland'. And it was his interest in the rocks formed by glacial deposits, by the processes that he saw all around him in Svalbard, which led him to pull information from all over the world and find evidence for an extreme Ice Age. This work was developed by others into a theory that the entire earth had once been covered in ice.[14]

Now, feeling the onset of the years, he was making his last observations of the rocks that make these magnificent needle

---

[13] H W Tilman, *Triumph and Tribulation*, 1978.

[14] Snowball Earth theory, according to which the extreme Ice Age was 600 million years ago

peaks, before he sat down in Cambridge to collect the work of his life. He was pulling together a comprehensive and definitive full stop to his richly academic and adventurous life, *The Geology of Svalbard*.[15]

As we sipped the coffee he took a maritime traveller's interest in the way we were making the boat repairs. He'd always supported students with a future outside of academic geology, and I suppose he was interested to know where mine was taking me. After he'd looked at our glues and the rowlock repair we did not talk of much. We finished the coffee quickly, before it cooled. Then he put the cups back into the holdall and said he would wash them back at the hut.

'Good luck with it,' he said. 'And take care on the north coast.'

'Thanks, and good luck with the season,' I said, and he was gone.

* * *

With all of the favours and visits and smiles we received, we assumed the hopes of the town. It seemed they wanted the details of our plans so they could live the journey with us, and many said they would love to have come at least part of the way. As a result I felt a duty to live it for them as well as I could, to make a good journey and come back smiling. This extra responsibility made me uneasy because the gale had shown how easy it was for things to go wrong.

Even without mistakes and bad luck there was still the drift ice and polar bears, the gales and fog in Hinlopen Strait, the need to keep moving from one food depot to the next. And the unimaginable distance. So far we'd completed just a fraction of the journey: one hundred and forty kilometres out of at least a thousand and then some.

If only we had carried *Kotick* a little higher up the beach.

I finished drilling and picked up the screwdriver. The

---

[15] Brian Harland published the results of his Spitsbergen fieldwork, alongside that of many others, in the Geological Society Memoir *The Geology of Svalbard* in 1997. He died in 2003.

rowlock posts would be weaker after this repair. We had to be more careful. I turned the last wood screw down into the hole I had tapped, and Shaggy put his finger on the epoxy surface that he'd been working on. It had been tacky and now it was hard. I gripped the rowlock post and pushed and pulled. It wiggled, and the gunwale beneath it moved too. That was a good sign.

'It's probably stronger than it was before.'

'Seems alright. If the weather's good we'll go in the morning.'

We spent the rest of the day doing things slowly, and Shaggy spent some time with the arctic terns, which are rugged little birds that migrate vast distances, some to Antarctica and back. They have a forked swallow tail, sharp claws and a beak as keen as any knife. If you stray close to one of their speckled eggs lying on the tundra then with no warning the bird dives with a blood-curdling screech and attempts to cut you with its claws and beak. One solution is to wear a hat but they streak your jacket in white and it dribbles inside your collar. After receiving a couple of direct hits Shaggy took the flag pole from *Kotick* and carried it around so that the terns aimed at the ensign and their shit fell wide.

Arctic tern, about to dive

The following morning before Shaggy packed the *Birds and Mammals* book safely away in the dry barrel he ticked the pages of the birds we'd seen in Ny Ålesund. There were pinkfeet and brent and barnacle geese. We'd seen two long-tailed duck in the bay near the boatshed and an ivory gull that skulked around the seal carcasses out by the dog kennels. Then the snow bunting that chirruped at breakfast time and a grey phalarope with its rusty neck and breast that we suspected was nesting in the wet moss near the beach. And he ticked the suicidal arctic tern.

Nick introduced me to the captain of the Norwegian survey ship MS *Lance*, which planned to sail to the east coast. Nick wanted them to know that we might be there too and for them to be familiar with *Kotick* because it would make organising a search much easier. Not that he said that, but that's what was in my mind, and probably in his too. The bridge of that ship was cavernous. There was room for plenty of *Koticks* inside. But the ship was going to be on the east coast for just one week and I expected that they would be there long before Shaggy and I arrived, if we ever did.

As we ventured north into the unknown, Nick would keep track of our progress. In countless Arctic and Antarctic seasons he had seen plenty of field parties meet with success and failure. He knew me and what I could and could not do, and he would have a fair idea of the combination of weather and bad luck that would mean that something had gone seriously wrong for us.

The idea was that we would ask anybody we met to send a radio message or postcard to Nick: 'Peter and Shaggy say hello from far away on such and such a date. They have so many days' food, and all is well,' or words to that effect. Then if we had not shown up at the end of the season Nick would follow the trail of messages and know where to start looking.

Before we set out Nick made sure that we had a broad-faced screwdriver for boat repairs (I said we would make do with Shaggy's multi-tool), and he gave me a pair of leak-free rubber boots. Then Shaggy and I climbed into the boat and set off from the beach where I had realised that 'all the way' was no further than around the island. After waving to the farewell party on the shingle we rested at the oars and erected the mast. The small sails filled and we reached downwind towards Kapp Mitra and the open sea.

* * *

With the sails full, small waves in the fjord tapped out a light drumbeat on the pine cutwater while a stream of bubbles trailed out from the stern post towards the group of colourful jackets and anoraks on the beach. *Kotick* sailed heavier, weighed down by the expectations of our friends and our expectation that because we *could* make great distance therefore we *should*. I looked back again. There were fewer well-wishers than last time, and they were shrinking with the distance. They were still waving from time to time when the radio hissed into life.

'*Kotick, Kotick, Kotick*, this is Ny Ålesund, over.'

'Ny Ålesund, this is *Kotick*, everything's fine, over.'

'Good luck Pedro, take care on the north coast, over.'

'Thanks Nick, thanks for everything. We're gonna switch off now, best save the power. Over.'

'OK, roger and good luck, out.'

'Thanks for everything, out.'

It was an inadequate farewell. But I preferred to switch the set off and be alone with Shaggy and *Kotick* and the sea. I was afraid that we'd only come so far and so fast because we'd had the luck of beginners. Could we repeat our earlier success?

* * *

Under the scarp slope of Kapp Mitra the breeze died. Despite the lack of wind there were steep and choppy waves in the mouth of the fjord. Shaggy took the sails and mast down, wrapped the shrouds and halyards around them and tied it all down, snug next to the gunwale. We both lifted our oars and rubbed the damaged rowlocks. The repairs looked good and I almost trusted them, but long hard rowing was the only test that mattered. It would be difficult to make that repair out here if they did not hold up. There would be no boatshed, no warm bunks, no wise old man with hot coffee in a pre-war holdall, and there would be no carpenter to help. We pushed the oars through the rope strops and wiggled them into their most comfortable position so the rowlock post sat in the worn groove.

'Ready?' I said and we started to pull.

With the first strokes I prayed, but there was no need because the rowlocks squeaked and flexed and the repair held firm. *Kotick* slipped up and down and rolled from left to right over the waves. The oars popped and splashed and Shaggy dug his strokes deep into the ocean.

'Shallow, Shags, slow recovery,' I said. We were fresh and rested and I thought that we could work on the rowing again.

'Man!' I exclaimed as my oar popped out and the other one jammed.

'So Pete, on the other side of the island …?' Shaggy had a question, or maybe he was just trying to change the subject. My silence was tight and then my anger came.

'On the other side of the island …' he said again. My cheeks tightened.

'Don't worry about that, for chri'sake. Worry about the north coast, and getting to the next depot, and where to camp tonight. And ROWING THE FUCKING BOAT.'

Immediately I felt small because of my anger. We rowed in silence, rolling about but not quite so much. A black-backed gull flew over and circled before flying on. The silence remained. The gull was far, far off before either of us spoke. Someone had to speak.

'Black-backed gull,' I said.

'Another tick,' he said, and we returned to silence.

The swell seethed and broke on the seaweed of the last of the Kapp Mitra rocks and we turned to follow the pebble beach northwards. A breeze breathed over the beach embankment and the water close to the breaking foam was flat. The oar strokes came more easily because of the flat water and because we were now accustomed to rowing with two different rhythms. The kilometres began to come and the journey seemed worthwhile again.

We were closing on the edge of the map as it was folded in the map case so I rested for several strokes while Shaggy kept on. I pulled it out and unfolded and refolded it, so I could see the coast ahead through the plastic window of the map case. Refolding the map like that was always good, and now I could see that there were just eight kilometres between us and a hut marked Laxebu. If we could reach it then our day's run would be forty kilometres. That would be a good result for one day.

Shaggy kept time with me as I cut my blades out of the water. Small peninsulas of gravel marked the distance so we could judge the kilometres, and I counted the minutes as we built each one. Rowing in flat water for the first time was exhilarating, and our hands and muscles were tough after the hard row up and across Forlandsundet several days before. It was even a joy to go like this. At each catch the wooden shafts bent and swept the water, I tugged the oars towards my belly and popped them up at the finish, out of the whirlpools remaining. Then while I recovered I enjoyed the glide and Shaggy followed my time.

I was glad that he spoke as he thought, as if he were almost thinking out loud, because his worries were out in the open. Much better than mine, which I kept bottled in, until finally they exploded. I could only think logically in steps, like this, after the explosion had passed.

The boat was narrow and fast and the three of us, *Kotick*, Shaggy and I, ate the kilometres and completed them one after the next in twelve to fourteen minutes. That's five kilometres an hour, and the water boiled in the puddles from the blades and turned in the wake. Despite the pain in the crooks of our elbows we did not stop until the low rectangle we had been watching for an hour, became a hut. When we were close a thin man with green clothes and a goatee stepped out. We beached. The man was familiar.

'What are you studying?' I asked him as the rounded shingle crunched under my feet. I remembered his face.

'Fish,' he said.

His face fell into a slot in my memory: at the airport, a zoologist, the previous year. I tried to pull out his name but he gave it to me before I could. Slavomir. I went up the beach to meet his field party, not at all sure what to say because this was their camp after all. I had to say something.

'Here is my passport, I'd like to check in,' I said fumbling inside my jacket. The young Norwegian with big shoulders and wide blue eyes smiled.

'Velkommen,' he said, 'But actually, we have to go.'

'Is the weather always this good?' I asked him.

'No, it has blown a gale for two weeks. That is why we have to go.'

The two broad-shouldered Norwegians and the thin Pole spoke together, then the Norwegians pushed their ugly craft, in the form of a zodiac but made from air-filled steel cylinders, down the shingle.

'They have to track the fish, I will cook you supper,' said Slavomir. 'Do you like meatballs?'

'Yeah, man!' called Shaggy from the boat, where he was coiling line.

While the Norwegians pulled the starter cord on their huge outboard engine, again and again because they could not get it started, Slavomir lit the stove in Laxebu hut and filled it with the smell of simmering meatballs. He explained that he was here to research the migration of the only freshwater fish in Svalbard, the arctic char,[16] also known as the Spitsbergen salmon.

The fish spawn in the rivers and then swim out to sea. Where to? Nobody knows, he said, but they always return to spawn again. Their migration makes them easy to net at the river mouth.

Slavomir explained that the arctic char grow slowly, like most life in the polar regions. They only reproduce once they have reached the advanced age of nine to fourteen years, by which time they are around a foot long. Any caught smaller than that will have never reproduced and one heavy season of netting damages their numbers for decades.

'Such an impact is common in the Arctic,' he said.

The two Norwegians started the outboard and it growled

---

[16] The red-bellied arctic char is found in Arctic waters as well as some landlocked lakes, including the deeper waters of Windermere in England.

and spat for a few minutes before they cut it again and drifted.

'They cannot track the fish with the engine running.'

'You need a rowboat.' I said proudly and gestured towards *Kotick*. Less smoke too, I thought, watching a puff of blue exhaust rush from the cowling as the engines shuddered to life again. Then I stopped talking about *Kotick* because I realised that I did not want to make the offer. They would need help to handle her and we needed to sleep and move on.

Just before we slept, a scraggy polar fox-cub with a brown back and a yellow belly arrived. He licked the plates without a noise and was jumpy with curiosity not fear and more interested in the cutlery than anything we might do. It would have been easy to get him with a fox trap.

'He comes every evening, just before midnight. I think it's his first season,' said Slavomir. 'He's my friend.'

It was time to sleep.

* * *

When I woke up my muscles were stiff. The air in the hut was cold, and I pulled the drawstring tighter around my face. Slavomir was pumping his primus stove and then there was steam from his kettle. Vapour fogged the window and the air grew warm. There was the smell of hot oats, milk and raisins, then coffee. I pulled back my sleeping bag, leaned over to dig for my spoon and reached into my bag to retrieve my warm socks. It was time to get up.

The seven glaciers of the northeast coast were once called the Seven Icebergs by whalers, and each tumbles down from the ice cap of Albert I Land like a torrent of petrified water. Cathedral-sized icebergs calve into the sea, and as they fall into the water they send out waves similar to that which had drowned Gino Watkins. We would need a long day to pass them all and reach the safety of the inlets near Danish Island, which the Norwegians call Danskøya, and which is where a sad story ended many years before.

The story is called 'If We Are Found', and it started in 1922 at a geophysical station a few kilometres north of Ny

Ålesund.[17] Two young men, Møkleby and Simonsen, set off with the first of the springtime to visit a trapper in Krossfjord. They carried food and post for him after the long dark winter. The journey across King's Fjord started badly because, although it was free of drift ice, the water was heavy with the mushy ice crystals that are called grease ice. The rowing was difficult, then a wind came up and they were blown out to sea.

Drift ice caught them and they were carried by the wind and the tide for weeks. They did come close to the mainland but the ice cliffs of the seven glaciers prevented them from making a landfall until they came close enough to Danskøya to escape the ice and make a camp. They had long since run out of food but they did have a small rifle and they killed two birds for eating. The snow cave they built sheltered them from the wind but without more food they grew weaker. They saw a frigate searching for them, and waved and shouted but were not strong enough to attract attention.

Long after, they were found. They were cold and stiff and curled around the diary that told the story of their final days. The last words Møkleby wrote were these: 'If we are found please do not bury us with white flowers. Because all we have seen these last five months has been white.' He was buried in his hometown of Sandnessjøen and with respect for his dying wish the flowers were colourful. The wild pansies were red and the forget-me-nots were blue.[18]

The white ramparts of the seven glaciers were kinder to us, and inspired us to awe instead of crashing down. The first and third glaciers melted far back from the beach but the others tumbled down between their mountain ridges and calved into the sea. There was ice in the water. As we proceeded a little wind pulled the sails and because we were

---

[17] Kvadehuken.

[18] The trapper they sought was never seen again. A skeleton, thought to be his, was found forty years later with the skull caved in by the jaws of a bear. Nearby there was a bolt-action rifle with a round jammed at an angle in the breach.

winning confidence one of us would row while the other steered and trimmed the sail, which tugged us along.

North of the seventh glacier, the pointed summit of Hoelfjellet guarded the mouth of Magdalena Fjord, where our nautical guidebook, the *Arctic Pilot*, told us there was an 'excellent anchorage for smaller vessels' that was used as a base during the whaling period by hunters. There was fresh water and the whalers buried their dead 'after sea fights' on Gravsneset.

I wanted to go and see the plaque which the Norwegian state set up as a memorial for those who died with the inscription 'Svalbard Travellers 1600–1750', but the wind was fair and more than visit tourist spots I wanted to build kilometres towards the full circumnavigation. I did want these interesting extras. What kind of sea fights left so many whalers dead, for instance? But I was not confident of the whole circumnavigation. And without the full round trip there would be no story. That is how I was thinking, and Shaggy wanted to go on and on while the weather was with us. So we ignored the cliff of screeching auks and the intrigue of Magdalena Fjord and continued around the headland to Danskøya.

These mountains were colder and darker, more savage, or maybe the ice in the water made me fearful. Purple-grey cloud hung over us and to the north. Along the northwestern horizon the clouds were brighter than they should have been. It could have been light reflecting up from drift ice, an effect called 'ice blink', if drift ice had been this far south – but that could not be. It must have been an effect of the sun. To the south the clouds were broken, and out to sea there was a berg with the sun inside. A sea-coloured chunk of ice thumped the bow. This lurker was dimpled like a jellyfish and there was the sound of splintering as it bumped along the waterline.

'Careful Shags, we've got to watch for those.'

We both peered over the side and then aft as it disappeared in our wake. There was time and we could think.

'No more jokes about the *Titanic*,' he said.

Shaggy refolded the map and turned it, comparing the new sheet to the headlands around us. We turned inside

Danskøya and followed the beach towards Bear Cove.[19]

'Hey, it's a seal!'

Shaggy was the first to spot a huge rock on the beach.

'No it's not, it's a rock,' I corrected him.

'No it's seal, it must be.'

Then the rock twitched.

'Hey, it's a walrus,' I said.

The smell was terrible, like old sweat, rotten food and elephant dung at a provincial circus. It was sleeping like a drunk, leathery hide tightly wrinkled over hundreds of kilos of blubber. A sparse moustache of wiry whiskers trembled on his top lip at invisible irritations. He itched and wheezed and sneezed and snored and when we came close he arched his neck, opened one eye or two, and then sagged forward to snooze until another of our footfalls landed in the pebbles and woke him again. We went close, but not too close on account of the length of his tusks.

The hut in Bear Cove was drab and damp but we were tired so we pulled *Kotick* up the beach and unpacked. It was easier now that we'd practised what to do. Shaggy started the cooking stove. I went to check the beach and hillside for bears, and I returned to find Shaggy writing to Anna.

While we made tea he continued composing it.

'Go on, read it,' I said. Shaggy looked up and chose a place to start.

'Peter's either getting more disorganised or I'm improving; he does enjoy making piles but there's always something missing.'

'That's not true,' I interjected.

'We're getting on well … it's hard work for both of us … complaining is a waste of effort. I've just heard a growl. I'd better shut the door as Peter's gone for a walk with the gun.' He paused. 'Maybe it's time for some poetry?'

Before bed we put the new ticks in the *Birds and Mammals* book and measured the distance we'd come with a piece of string on the map. I was always happy for Shaggy to do this because he added a little extra for the zigzags and a little bit

---

[19] Bjørnhamna.

more to boost moral. According to today's official piece of string we had come fifty-six kilometres to add to the forty kilometres of the day before. Not bad for a rowboat.

Shaggy made the unselfish gesture of sleeping on the table. He was at pains to point out that it was six inches too short, but he would make the sacrifice of putting up with that discomfort. I should have been more careful before thanking him, because I found that the floor had been used as a lavatory by a previous expedition. But it didn't matter because that had been many years ago. Besides, I was happy.

I was thinking: we can do this, it wasn't beginners' luck; we have two hundred and forty kilometres out of the at-least-a-thousand. It is possible for us. The repairs are strong and we're in the real journey. It might not change my life but it'll be worth it somehow. I'm here and the real adventure is about to begin.

I fell asleep and dreamed of many things and the walrus.

7

Blubbertown

There was sleep in my eyes when I rattled the door handle and pushed the grey planks. My finger tips touched lichen filling the cracks and the door swung open. Light fell into our sleeping place and my eyes had to adjust before I could see a new boat on the beach with sixty-horsepower engines. The walrus had gone.

A white-haired lady in yellow waterproofs was bent over a kitbag and her man was walking up towards the hut. He was walking with a hand keeping the light from his eyes, looking into the light, towards me. His hiking trousers were tight and a magnum swung from his belt, banging on his thigh. He had a Hemingway beard.

'Ice everywhere,' said Hemingway. 'The whole sound is full of it.'

'That right?' I replied. I didn't like his confidence.

'None of the ships can get through,' he said without a tremor of doubt. He was happy about this, which struck me as strange. Why would he enjoy giving bad news?

'Uh-huh,' I said and blinked more than necessary.

'We're going south.' He extended a hand and I shook it.

'Good luck,' I said and he walked away. I didn't like the news of the ice and was happier when Hemingway had packed up and gone. Shaggy was still on the table under his red hat with earflaps. His sleeping bag was tied up around his face and he was looking at me and the light falling into the hut.

'Who's that?' he said, and, 'What time is it?'

'Some Dane with a big gun,' I said. 'He says there's ice everywhere.'

'That should be fun,' said Shaggy with a dead voice. Then he rolled and split open his sleeping bag by unzipping it. He wiggled his angular shoulders and struggled out. The *Birds and Mammals* book fell onto the table.

'Have you ever seen a Ross's gull?' he asked. 'It says they live in inaccessible places.'

'No I haven't, I've only heard of people talk about *not* seeing them,' I said.

'So, small bird, big tick, I hope that we see one.' he replied.

* * *

An hour later we were breathless from the short walk uphill and we found a comfortable patch of moss and purple saxifrage. Breakfast was hot inside our down jackets and I unzipped mine to release the warm air. Shaggy unwound the neck strap of his binoculars and I unfolded the map. Then we ignored both the map and the binoculars for quite some time. We were looking at the ice.

'Wow.'

'Amazing.'

'That's really something.'

Two small islands, Danskøya and Amsterdamøya, lay in the black water below us and the water was studded white. The Sound of Fairhaven and Smeerenburg Fjord reached to the right of the islands – that's where we wanted to go – and this inner channel was chock-a-block with white and blue chunks. On the far side of the fjord the wall of an ice cliff was strung along the water.

The tide flowed quickly in the deep channels and the stream pulled the large bergs with aquatic magnetism so they moved in line, overtaking the others. There was brash ice in the stream that roughened the surface of the water. Each of these moving icebergs, in the form of cracked and sculpted fairground castles, was many times larger than *Kotick*. In the shallows uncertain Henry Moore pillars of ice and canted blue mushrooms stood grounded.

The most beautiful bergs were the ones that broke from the glaciers, because both glacier and berg glowed with the same unearthly blue. Miles across the fjord a puff of frost smoke rose from the ice cliff and the face of it disappeared down into powder. Tonnes and thousands of tonnes of ice crashed into the fjord, sending out a mini-tsunami, but at this distance it happened in silence. The foam and splinters fell back into the water and long seconds later the crackle of the low thunder of its breaking arrived. My throat tightened and a noise rose in it.

There was a strip of cloud lying on the northern horizon, or a mantle of snow. It reached from east to west and out towards Greenland, but there it dipped into the sea in a confusing way. How could it fall below the horizon? I felt a rush in my chest as I realised that it wasn't a cloud or a mantle of snow. It was the great polar ice cap that floats on the Arctic Ocean over the spin axis of the earth, from Siberia, to Canada, to Greenland and Baffin, ice pans metres thick, the size of small islands, where the ice bears hunt. It was there.

'Look Shags, on the horizon, the white line. That's ice.'

I lifted the binoculars towards the east, and the hot rush in my blood died and turned cold because there, where we wanted to go, the barrier of ice, the polar ice cap, was joined to the coast of Spitsbergen.

'Man.'

'What?'

'We can't get through that.'

'We can't get through?' he asked.

'Seems like it, but we can't just turn back,' I replied.

'Well if it's one of those bad years then we'll have to.'

'Or wait, it may drift off north.'

'Wait? What for? For how long?'

'As long as we have food, and I'm sure we can get more.'

'Naah, I don't want to wait here all summer, I'd rather be climbing.'

Alone with the saxifrage and the ice, and a breath of cold wind, it was silent.

'Besides, Anna's boyfriend's coming back … I've got to get there first.'

'You never told me that,' I said. There was a pause, and I filled it. 'What d'you mean?'

'He comes back, in August, arrives at Waterloo.'

'So?'

'I've got to get back before then.'

'You never said.'

The chill in my chest cooled further.

'You could find somebody else, couldn't you?' he offered. 'Rich is free, or you said maybe Tim.'

'Nahh, for chri'sake, that's impossible. Imagine how difficult that would be.' Besides, it had taken a year to find somebody as good as Shaggy and I couldn't face teaching somebody else to row. He had to stay.

'Well,' I paused.

I wasn't going to stop. I'd come too far, put too much in. The journey was becoming me, and in that moment the journey was as important as I was myself. But I could not do it alone. I needed Shaggy too, especially if the ice was bad. Maybe it was best for him to go home to Anna. It was not best for me. So somehow, anyhow, I had to make forwards, around the island, the shortest way home for him. We had to keep moving. I picked up the map and looked up. I pointed.

'Smeerenburg, the ice is clear as far as Smeerenburg, we should find the depot there. Let's go see what it looks like from there. We should make that, at least.'

* * *

In the popular stories eighteen thousand people once lived at Smeerenburg, or Blubbertown,[20] a settlement founded by Dutch whalers in 1617. They worked through the summer to flense and reduce the blubber that the ships brought in. Smoke and steam from the fires and boiling fat curled up from vast coppers into the morning air and there are stories of shops, a bakery, a church and a brothel.

A recent excavation of the site by the University of

---

[20] *Smeer* is Dutch for blubber.

Groningen revealed two periods of activity divided by a layer of yellow ballast sand.[21] In the second period, judged to be from 1624 to the middle of that century, there were tents and buildings for all of the different whaling syndicates: Rotterdam, Middelburg, Veere, Flushing, Enkhuizen, Delft and Hoorn. The records show that the syndicate from Amsterdam was biggest so it had an extra tent. At the peak of the activity in the 1630s there were eight try-works and sixteen buildings. At that time around one thousand whalers, not the eighteen thousand of popular myth, lived in this lonely outpost. The archaeologists found no evidence of a brothel.

When a whale was sighted the crews launched skiffs much like *Kotick* called 'shallops', and rowed as fast as they could in pursuit towards it. This is a summary of the 'Method of Fishery' originally described by Robert Fotherby, the captain of the whaler *Matthew*, in 1613:

> When the whale enters the sound the whalers sally forth and row fast towards him with resolution and as soon as they are within a stroke of the whale the harpooner stands and with both hands darts his harpoon-iron at him. The whale, once stricken, dives to the bottom of the water and the men in the shallop give out 40, 50 or 60 fathoms of rope, sometimes 100 or more depending on the depth required, and this line is attached to the socket of the harpoon-iron and lies coiled in the stern of the boat ready to give. When the whale rises they haul it in again to draw the whale closer and because being shorter it will be stronger. Because when he comes up the whale swims away with uncontrolled force and swiftness, and drags the shallop with the bow pulled down towards the water so that it seems the shallop will be dragged under. Within a mile or more – which is done in a very short time – the whale comes spouting water. The men row up to him and strike him with long lances, trying to strike him as near to

---

21 The shells in the sand tell us that it originated from the coast of Holland.

the swimming fin and as low under the water as convenient to pierce his entrails. One man sticks the lance in but sometimes two are required to pluck it out. Now the whale does forcibly 'frisk and strike' with his tail sometimes breaking up the shallop and sometimes maiming or killing some of the men. For this reason there are always other shallops nearby. Once mortally wounded the whale casts forth blood where before he was spouting water and before he dies he will sometime draw the shallops three or four miles from the place he was first struck with the harpoon-iron. When he dies he most commonly turns belly up, and then the men fasten a rope or small hawser to him and tow him away to be cut up.[22]

Then the crew attached the whale to the stern of a ship, where they cut the blubber off 'as if the fat of a pig were cut piece by piece from the lean … into square-like pieces three or four feet long with a great cutting knife'. These blocks of fat were towed to the beach, where they were craned ashore and cut into smaller pieces by boys on chopping boards made of the whale's fin or tail. The small cubes were then fried, and the oil was drained off, cooled and poured into barrels. The whale fins were taken to the beach at high tide and when the tide receded the valuable whale bone was cut out with hatchets and scraped clean on trestle tables. The fins were tied into bundles ready for shipping.

There was clearly a lot of work involved in processing each whale, and the crews set up shore bases such as the station at Smeerenburg to prepare the oil to ship home, where it would keep the bright lights of Europe burning. Not surprisingly, soon after the whalers arrived in great numbers in Svalbard the whales moved offshore and the hunt and flensing followed them into the ice or out to sea, so the oil boom at Smeerenburg was over almost as soon as it had begun.

---

[22] *The Voyages of William Baffin*, printed by the Hakluyt Society in 1881.

Try works with cooper

* * *

Shaggy put the binoculars to his eyebrows. From the map Smeerenburg should be on the end of the spit. He looked down at the map and then up again. A breeze stirred the grass heads sticking up from the moss.

'Yeah, alright, let's see what the ice looks like from there.'

I was on my feet and tripping down the hillside towards *Kotick*.

'Come on Shags,' I called back to him, 'while the weather's good.'

I pulled on my wellington boots and we lifted *Kotick* into the water. I packed the equipment in as Shaggy carried it down the beach. My feet were in the shallows and I packed our kit into the right places, tying it down where I could. Shaggy clambered in and as I pushed off the water lapped over the top of my boots. The wooden keel ground free of the shingle and a shooting cold cut down my calf but I ignored it because of a presentiment of something great.

The sun broke. It lit the inside of the bergs and turned the water dark blue. There were flecks of gold. A breeze ruffled the sound and we gave it the yellow and green balloon jib. The small sail unfurled and cold air filled it into a perfect curve. It tugged at the wooden mast, the forestay and the sheets and cold foam creamed out from the cutwater. *Kotick* rolled gently with the following wind and the ice lay flat on the horizon.

Then one massive timpani drum boomed across the fjord and the echo rolled around the inside of it. I ducked and turned to look at Shaggy. His head was down as well and his eyes were looking sideways. I was confused. There was a rush of spray that was nothing to do with a drum. There was a blowhole and a cavernous lung and wet air rushed up in a V. A wide black back crested low in the water and a dorsal fin cut the waves up into the sunlight.

'Minke,' I said, 'it's a minke whale.'

The air hole sealed tight and sank, leaving foam and swirling water.

'Minke, are they common?'

'Used to be, used to be so many the whalers got them from the beach.'

'Look, Pete, look!'

'No ...'

The great black back crested again and this time it was heading for us. Its bow wave broke, driven by astonishing weight. It broke towards us and it broke fast. I felt a cold grip on my heart and I stood. I reached for an oar but there was no time to use it. The boom of the lung echoed and the fountain rose in a V. The blowhole sealed shut. The whale came, and came, then it dived and the dorsal fin breaking water sank into the fjord towards us.

I stood on the pine planks as this great dark beast passed beneath, a warm green breathing submarine flashing in the sunlight that fell around *Kotick* into the black water. The back was smooth and close, the blowhole was small and tight, the fins had white tips. I lost them under the gunwale. Suddenly I was small; very suddenly, very small; holding a matchstick oar, standing on a matchwood row boat. Its wide tail followed, gliding close beneath, and we all moved to the other side of the boat. We watched and we held our breath together. My fingers were tight around that oar. The minke surfaced and blew spray one more time. We, too, breathed and were smaller than before. The black back and dorsal fin trailed bubbles into the water.

The minke was gone.

We were not swimming in the water simply because the whale had not wanted it. We sat in a taught silence, half expecting it to return, not wanting the same excitement again. Shaggy was the first to speak.

'It would have been a hell of a swim.'

'We wouldn't have made it,' I replied.

'Did it make you wish for a life raft?'

'Maybe, no, perhaps, it was probably just friendly.'

With an effort I banished other more gloomy thoughts, and thanked our luck for quite some time as we reached on towards Smeerenburg. It was not so far but it would have been an eternal swim. There was time enough to think about being in the water and the boat being broken. *Kotick* sailed it well.

We found the depot on the beach, under the beacon, just where it should have been. There were breakers and small white bergs, rounded by the salt, washing up and down the shingle. *Kotick* was uneasy on that beach. We could not and did not stay long.

* * *

It was about ten kilometres across Smeerenburg Fjord to the Norskøyane, a small group of islands that we had seen were embedded in the pack ice from our hillside that morning. The drift ice that was piled up against them broke the waves that had gathered in the fjord.

A tour ship steamed up to the ice front and made a wide circuit before returning south close to us. It was one I recognised as an ex-whaling ship by the gangway that led high over the foredeck from the bridge down to the foc'sle.

That is where the harpoon gun would have been. We decided to practise with the radio. Shaggy picked up the VHF handset and switched it on.

'Hello *Globe, Globe, Globe,* this is *Kotick, Kotick, Kotick,* over.'

A thick and husky Norwegian voice crackled through the static.

'Hello-hssszss-station calling *Globe,* this is hssszsss-hzz *Globe,* over.'

'*Globe,* this is *Kotick, Kotick, Kotick.* Small rowing boat, near the ice. Let's go to channel six, over.'

'Channel six, hssszss, click.' Through the static I was sure I could hear laughter. Shaggy felt as if he'd done the formal part and now he broke into a more conversational tone.

'Yeah hello *Globe,* this is just a radio check and I'm ummmmha, telling ships where we are. We are a small rowing boat trying to row around the island. You'll see us near the drift ice. And yeah, my name is Shaggy. Over.'

'Ahhh.' At this point there was lots of laughter on the bridge. 'You are Shaggy! We came from Ny Ålesund. They told us about you.'

'It's a good party place,' replied Shaggy. 'How far are you going?'

'We have people stuck in Raudfjorden, but we can't make it. The ice is bad, we can't go in. They will have to wait at least one week. Maybe see you in Ny Ålesund,' said the husky voice. He wished us luck and called off. The *Globe* steamed south, out of sight.

Sensing the end, we paddled up to the edge of the ice. It was tight together and the wind was piling in from behind. To go in there would be suicide because the floes were jostling and grinding each other with the wind and the tide. With reluctance we turned and paddled back into Fairhaven. My shoulders and cheeks were heavy. We did not speak. There was a beach to the south. It was free of ice.

There were three kayaks among the boulders. From afar we could see a green one, a blue and a red. There were two orange tents and figures sitting, watching. As we came close one of them stood. We beached and they wanted to talk. They told us they were from Oslo, a plumber, a philosopher and a film director. We all shook hands. They thought we must have been shipwrecked. They were trying to paddle around the island and had been watching the ice for most of a week.

'There's no way through,' said the film director.

We unpacked the food depot that we'd packed in Shaggy's basement flat months ago and picked up off the beach at Smeerenburg. There were twenty man days of rations, matches, five litres of cooking fuel, loo paper and a bag of goodies from Granny with chocolate and a hacky-sack. Despite high security some of the chocolate had gone. There was a note: 'It's 2 a.m. You're not in and we're starving. Hope you don't mind if I borrow the Mars Bars, will pay you back later. Love, Andy.'

We looked at each other. Shaggy seemed to find that funny.

'Just great,' I said.

We pulled the equipment high up the beach among prehistoric boulders and pitched the tent on a platform of fine gravel. There would be bears with this drift ice so we needed a set of trip flares. I sat down and spliced loops onto the triggers of two mini-flare firing mechanisms, so that a safety pin would hold them back ready to fire. Then I cut lengths of string and tied them between stakes of bamboo driftwood. I secured the bent-open safety pins to the string and threaded them into the loops of the firing mechanism. A bear should trip on the string and release a flare that would scare him. It should also wake us up, and we would have the rifle if the bear was persistent.

Then we unrolled our sleeping bags and cooked supper. Shaggy added an instalment to his letter for Anna and he read it aloud.

'The pack ice goes on and on,
All the way to the pole
Not good for the soul,
And I'm lying in a hole.'

As was his habit, after each instalment he put the letter in a stamped addressed envelope in case we met a ship heading for a post box. Then he climbed into his sleeping bag and pulled out the *Birds and Mammals* book. He opened it at page 108, minke whale, and there he made one big tick.

8

Nelson and the North Pole

The prehistoric boulders were round like dinosaur eggs and our little brown tent nestled among them with the two orange tents of the kayak team. They sheltered us from the west wind and the wind rippled the water among the bergs in Fairhaven. Bright light played on the tent sheet as the sun turned around the sky, never dipping below the horizon. We slept far into the next day. There was no rush, because of the ice.

These last days of travel our urgency and focus had made the world smaller, there was the boat, the rowing, the sailing and the waiting, judging the weather and changing sails, cooking, eating and staying warm. There was nothing beyond that. We'd decided to follow the wind for as long as it blew, or row in a calm whenever we could, and since making that decision the weather had driven us hard. We had always been tired. That's to say that since leaving the Radio Station the weather had been good.

Our daily cycle was stretched beyond the usual hours: making breakfast, striking camp, preparing the boat, rowing and sailing, hauling ourselves and *Kotick* above the high tide mark, pitching the tent, setting the bear flares, then sleeping until we could sleep no longer. This all took time, more than the twenty-four hours of one spin of the earth, and in the eight calendar days since we'd left the Radio Station we'd slept six times.

The extra hours in the days that we lived meant that we'd lost two full ones, but we'd traded them for good progress. I'd

106

been squaring up to this challenge. And we both loved the scale of this adventure. Who could help that? It was an extraordinary wilderness. The whale had scared and thrilled us, and now that we were safe we felt good about that risk. But the next step was different. The pack ice blocked our way around the island, and while I wanted to wait, Shaggy had no time for patience. He would rather fly south to other mountains and to Anna. For this difference we did not rush to acknowledge that the ice was impenetrable.

We woke and we drifted in daydreams, thinking of useful things to do. I wanted to whip the frayed ends of the halyards and Shaggy wanted to clean the rifle but first we lay in our bags, with heads and elbows in the afternoon sun at the bell-end of the tent, and made tea and boil-in-the-foil bacon and baked beans. The breakfast orange glowed chemical pink until we mixed it with water, then we stewed porridge and coffee. By the time we had finished it was almost time for chocolate.

I boiled water for washing and we both found rocks to hide behind. My shave was jerky on account of the fresh breeze and cold stones but I made the effort because I loved the hot water on my face and the clean feeling afterwards. The scarcity of hot water in my mess tin made me take care over what to wash first, and then, and next, and what to wash last. I don't recall the order I chose but I do remember that I followed it quickly. With clean underwear next to my skin and plenty of warm clothes over the top, I stretched out on my kip mat outside the tent next to Shaggy, who was reading. He'd been quicker because he'd skipped the shave, having decided to let his stubble grow.

He had more coffee steaming in the cooking pot. I poured a cup and opened my expedition book. The hobbit was making friends with Tom Bombadil. Shaggy hacked some driftwood with his penknife. He looked up to the mountains.

'So d'you reckon we could pack everything up and walk inside?' he asked.

He was trying to make a fox trap.

'What, over the ice? Or around the coast?' I continued, 'The coast is way too rocky, and the ice would need to be joined up.' I was inventing this. I didn't know anything about crossing sea ice. Except for the stories of painful hours pulling sledges through sastrugi[23] and making long detours around leads between the ice floes.

'I don't want to get caught in ice,' he said.

'That's what your ice screw is for.' My idea, formed long ago, was that an alpine ice screw would anchor a pulley block and be strong enough to haul a fully laden rowboat out of the water in case the ice came crashing in from all directions.

'I'm not sure that'll work,' he said. 'Maybe best just walk up this glacier and down the next one.'

'Nahhh, no way, too dangerous,' I was afraid of crevasses, 'And way too much work. And anyway, we've got to make the full circumnavigation, around the whole island. Let's see how far we get in the boat.'

Shaggy was bored of the fox trap and started leafing through the *Arctic Pilot*. There was a photograph of the Norskøyane islands and the channels were completely free of ice. He showed me.

'If only it were like that.'

The ice floes rocked and grumbled in Fairhaven and the flood tide crept up the beach. One by one the bergs floated and a shore lead developed. I realised that with the flood tide the surface area of the water was growing. Of course it was, how obvious. I went down to the prehistoric boulders by the water to see how the swelling of the tide had opened the ice.

'It does that every day,' explained the Norwegian plumber, who was sitting on a rock. I called up to Shaggy.

'Look Shags, near high tide, leads all over the sound.'

'Yes, but they'll close up again,' said the plumber. 'There's no way through.'

'Shall we give it a go?'

Shaggy and I looked at each other and we both dipped our heads just enough to say 'yes'.

* * *

---

[23] Sastrugi are sharp, irregular ridges formed on a snow surface by wind erosion and deposition.

There was a lot to do and not much time.

We pulled the tent down and wrapped our various belongings into bundles that fitted into the barrels and waterproof bags. The trip flares went in the dry barrel and we strapped the rifle and map case onto the thwart amidships. The shore lead was still opening and the water lapped more seaweed on the beach. It kept rising towards the high-tide driftwood. When we drove *Kotick* down the beach to meet the rising level there was clear water out in Fairhaven. It was scuffed by a light west wind.

We paddled out, and inside the hour we set the mainsail and pattered along in the open water, then towards the edge of the pack a kilometre beyond. It was rafting far out to sea but I thought there was a gap. We found more water and shook out the jib. Then the ice closed around us.

'The sail's too much,' I said. 'Need to row.'

We smothered the sail and paddled downwind. I was standing up and steered for an eight-foot gap between two large floes. We entered the quiet water of a lead and the ice foot of each floe came close on either side. It closed us in. We rowed some more. The lead was blocked. The two floes rested hard on each other and we could not turn back into the open water because the channel was too narrow. Ice was drifting in behind us now. We had to go on.

I leapt onto one ice floe with an oar. There was a step where the two bergs pressed onto each other and I kicked my boots into the soft spring snow so the balls and heels of my feet were firm on the sea ice, then I jabbed the blade into a hollow in the other floe and I gripped the handle. I leaned into the shaft of the oar and the muscles of my arms bunched up under my cotton windproof. The sight of me trying to push apart two islands of ice made Shaggy stand up and laugh.

'Give up, Pete, they'll never move.' He reached for his camera. 'But hang on a sec. I want a photo.'

As I hung there on my oar, crying for salvation, with Shaggy fumbling in his bag for a camera, a hot rage ignited inside me. There was no time for photos because there was more ice drifting in behind. This boat would smash into matchwood. If that happened because of taking holiday photographs then that would make us imbeciles, quite probably cold, wet, dead imbeciles, and having just escaped a similar fate with the whale, unbelievable. I drove my rage down the oar and the heat of it blocked out the danger of the ice arriving from behind. It seemed the heat of my anger would melt the ice itself.

They'll never move

I was pushing one lump of ice, standing on another. Shaggy was standing up in the boat with his camera laughing at me. I wanted to throw the oar down and jump into the boat and swing at him and knock him down, then pick him up and point his nose at the icebergs that were about to break *Kotick*.

'Look behind you!' I yelled.

Then Shaggy was jousting with the new piece of ice and for long seconds our tiny world hung in a balance between the wind and water and the ice, and all we had was the light wooden hull and the oars in our hands. Then the long seconds were over because a narrow lead of clear, quiet water opened at my feet: two inches then four, six inches then one foot. I blessed it and drove the oar harder because the ice was moving. The one foot gap became two, then three, then four and still growing. That was almost enough.

'Come on, Shags,' I shouted and he, still standing, paddled

Kotick towards me and through the now six-foot gap. The ice bumped on the pinewood. As they glided past I jumped for the stern seat and landed with a thump. The oar banged on the gunwale.

'No trouble,' I said, meaning that it had been as much as I could stand. 'Let's get back to open water. This is crazy.'

Back in the open water of Fairhaven I realised that it was only crazy because of the wind and despite the wind I'd separated two icebergs with an oar. It was quite something to learn what we could do, it was extraordinary.

* * *

In 1773, one hundred and fifty years after the Dutch drove the whales away from Smeerenburg, two British bomb-vessels, the *Carcass* and the *Racehorse*, were caught in the drift ice, just like us, here in Fairhaven. Horatio Nelson, then fourteen years old, was on board and they were making an early attempt for the North Pole when they were trapped and driven towards shoal ground. The sailors prepared to abandon ship. This is Nelson's version of the story:

> When the boats were fitting out to quit the two ships blocked up in the ice, I exerted myself to have command of a four-oared cutter raised upon, which was given to me with twelve men; and I prided myself in fancying that I could navigate her better than any other boat in the ship.[24]

Before they abandoned ship the wind changed and the ice opened up so they did not find out if Nelson's conviction was justified. Well over two hundred years later we were discovering that Nelson had a good point, even though further progress (for us, right now) was impossible.

There was wind in the open water and we sailed around the tight pack towards the outermost island. I grabbed a radio and went up onto the ice. I was surprised at how secure I felt

---

[24] Captain A T Mahan, *The Life of Nelson*. Sampson Low, London, 1897.

up there. I considered jumping from floe to floe as far as the island but that would not help get *Kotick* any closer. So I turned back. Shaggy was paddling into the wind to stay still in the open water, dodging the drifting icebergs. I called him on the radio.

'Shaggy, Shaggy, this is Peter. Doesn't look good.'

'Peter, Shags, oh well, are you coming back then?'

'Yep, see you on the edge, back where you dropped me.'

Then a new voice broke out of the radio set in my hand.

'Shaggy, Shaggy, Shaggy, this is *Waterproef, Waterproef, Waterproef*, over.'

I recognised the voice, it was totally familiar, but who was it? Where could it come from? Who else was at this end of the earth crackling in the radio set? I looked at the loudspeaker under its plastic holes. Rudolph? Was it Heleen's boyfriend? I called Shaggy on low power and the familiar voice broke in again. What was the *Waterproef* doing here? They should be on the other side of the island. And why would Rudolph call Shaggy using his name as a call sign? The call came again.

'Shaggy, Shaggy, this is *Waterproef, Waterproef, Waterproef*, over.'

'Waterproef, this is *Kotick, Kotick, Kotick*, over.'

'*Kotick*, this is *Waterproef*. Is that Peter? This is Rudolph.'

It was. He had recognised my voice and called me, thinking the boat was called *Shaggy*. I asked for his position, and he sent numbers back that did not mean anything, and his course and speed.

'To the northwest, we are making half a cable an hour, over.'

I didn't know what a cable was and I didn't want to ask over the air.[25]

'Did you put in the depot?'

'No we couldn't make it, nobody can make it.'

'How's the ice?' I asked, not wanting the answer.

'Nine tenths,' he said, 'too heavy, we've damaged the ship's screw.'

---

[25] A cable is approximately 185 metres, or one tenth of a sea mile. A sea mile is one sixtieth of a degree of latitude, or about 1.1 statute miles.

'How about for a rowboat?'

'It's very heavy, too heavy even for a rowboat. We have damaged the screw and need to return for repairs. We can't put the food. It's a bad year. I'm sorry about that.'

And there it was, the end of the summer, just like that. If there was no food on the far side of the island there would be barely enough to make it round, even if there had been no ice obstructing the way ahead, and the ice was bad, and Shaggy wanted to go home. And we'd been properly scared twice in two days. And, and, if I wanted a reason, an excuse to give up with honour, then this was surely it.

We turned south and rowed back to the beach in Fairhaven, where the Norwegians were not surprised to see us.

'That's what we expected,' said the philosopher.

'You can't get through,' said the plumber.

But I was thinking of Shackleton, and thinking to hell with the food depot, we can do it without. And I was hoping that Shaggy was up for it too.

9

'You can't get through'

Shaggy and I spent the time watching the ice. For now we were united against it, but if we had to resort to waiting then we would want to go in different directions. I wanted to wait for as long as it took, and possibly wait out the summer, but he wanted to get back to the warm sun, to alpine rock and to Anna.

The pack ice breathed with the tide, relaxing and opening as the water surface swelled with the flood, crashing back together with the ebb. The sun turned around us. If we reached halfway around the island then Shaggy's anxiety to go home would work in my favour. But thus far we had made less than a quarter. From my point of view it would be better to be stuck *in* the ice, further around, than to be waiting here with a clear run back south.

The Norwegians were bored. They talked about home. It was still July, less than a month after the summer solstice, but already the sun was dipping lower in the north and the air cooled around the hours of midnight. In four more short weeks there would be six-hour sunsets heralding the end of the summer before the sun finally dipped under the horizon in the second half of August.[26]

Every twelve hours the pack ice relaxed and then crashed back together. I whipped the halyards and Shaggy unpacked the rifle. Doing these small things gave us the feeling of

---

[26] For reference, in Longyearbyen the sun first sets on 23 August.

progress and helped us avoid the argument about what to do if we could not go on.

The rifle was rusty again, which surprised us because it had been in a waterproof bag all of this time. Shaggy withdrew the bolt and dismantled the firing mechanism, then laid all the pieces on his kip mat. He scrubbed them clean with scotch-bright and gun oil and reassembled them so that each part glided.

He worked the mechanism and held a round up in his hand.

'There's no way that would stop a bear.'

'Kind of agree,' I said.

He laid the shell in the breach, worked the mechanism and took aim at an iceberg. The rifle crashed and kicked up in his cheek and a piece of the ice splintered into powder. If a bear splintered like that then we might be alright. He held out the rifle and I worked the mechanism. I laid my cheek on the stock and held the butt in my shoulder. It crashed and the wood of the stock kicked up into the bone on my cheek and more splinters of ice flew off the berg. The wood of the stock was hard and the rifle worked fine. It was fun. But it did not convince me it would stop a charging polar bear.

Shaggy went back to his letter to Anna and I went back to my book. The hobbit met Strider. Shaggy looked up again.

'So how long do you want to wait?' he asked.

'Not sure,' I said.

'The Norwegians say we can't get through.'

'You know, if there's no wind at all, I reckon we might.'

'So we're waiting for a flat calm? There's nothing wrong with you.'

* * *

That evening the wind died and it was flat like glass, even out in the open water. The sky was grey and the air was still. The tide was creeping up through the boulders and the pressure between the ice floes was coming off a little. Two hours before high water we leaned forward into the stroke, dipped the oars and started to paddle. It was just before midnight.

The air was close and I took off my shirt despite the cold.

In this flat calm with the high tide opening leads and no jostling in the ice from the wind, we could cut through small gaps and creep along the shore leads. Once among the ice I stroked alone while Shaggy stood up on his seat and picked a good line. He was happy up there choosing and I could concentrate on the oars, keeping my own rhythm. As I stroked the boat my muscles were hard and my shoulders were strong. The rough grain sat easily in my palms. The water rushed out from under the bow, and behind us the bubbles stretched in one long taught line.

Fugleøya, or Bird Island, was sheer-sided and the rock shelved steep into the fjord much like the body of an iceberg. There was no beach, no shallow water with grounded bergs, just deep water breathing with the twelve-hour cycle of the tide. We skirted the island, close to the rocks, and just as the ebb came, and the first grinding and crashing started in the floes, we stopped in a tiny cove between two rocks. It was barely large enough for *Kotick* but we could run lines out and there were convenient boulders. Then we climbed onto the island and stretched.

The five kilometres between us and the Norwegian camp was white with pack ice. There were groans from out there.

'You can't get through,' they'd said. But we had and I felt euphoric for that.

I was concerned as well as elated, because despite wanting to make Shaggy commit to the whole journey I was wary of getting into a place with no escape.

We had made it through five kilometres of ice. Now we had to be safe, eat, maybe sleep a little and then make another five kilometres, and another five, until we discovered open water or realised that there was, truly and without doubt, no way through. Once we knew more about the ice we could calculate how fast, how far, and on how much food, we would have to travel.

It was too big, this whole adventure, so again I focused on the next short step. What, I wondered, did the next kilometre hold?

* * *

We sat on the mountainside looking down on the island that fell steep into the water. Thousands of tonnes of ice moved out to sea no faster than the driftwood, but jamming against the rock that protected *Kotick* the ice rotated and crushed itself. The bergs growled and cracked and ridges blew into the air wherever two ice islands were forced together. The sound was awful and it made my belly feel cold and empty.

Every acre of water that we could see was filled like this. There were pans the size of tennis courts with plenty of space to camp on, one football pitch, and in between there were chunks of clear blue and snow-white debris. There was no way through. Except – except for one thin blue thread six kilometres away. The innermost channel leading around the coast was free. It was shallow, so the icebergs had grounded before it, keeping the smaller ice out, and *Kotick* would be fine in the shallow water. If we could cross the deep channel of thundering, groaning, splintering ice then we could continue around the island. We might even make it to the point where the quickest way home would be around the island and not back.

'You can't get through,' the Norwegians had said.

'It's too heavy even for a rowboat,' the Dutch had said.

If we could just reach that thin blue thread six kilometres away then the journey might still be possible. We glanced at each other and smiled.

'Let's go for it,' we agreed, but first we had to wait.

'What's for supper, Shags?' I asked as we tripped down the hill.

Shaggy declared that there were no pears in 'Pears in Chocolate Sauce' but that we were going to try eating them nonetheless. They were brown and runny, and halfway through the packet he declared that he had never tasted diarrhoea but if he had, he would not have been surprised if it tasted like Pears in Chocolate Sauce.

When hot it tasted like fruity hot chocolate, but Shaggy's strong point of view put me off and I couldn't help thinking that maybe he knew something that I did not. So after we'd eaten just one packet and a half between us we decided to consign all Pears in Chocolate Sauce to a black bin liner and save them as emergency rations. If we were going to make this bid around the island we had to save all we could, because the next depot would not be there. And it was a very long way to the depot after that. As well as being good emergency rations, Pears in Chocolate Sauce were ideal as sea-boot hot-water bottles for our ever frozen feet. I pulled out my harmonica and watched the ice.

When the sea had exhaled a six-hour sigh with the ebb and drawn nearly six hours of water with the flood, we set out among the bergs that were becoming loose from one another again. But they were still moving, and despite the quiet water the ice was groaning.

As before, when the leads were blocked I climbed onto the ice, kicked my feet into the snow, leant on an oar and strained my arms, back and legs, trying to prise the ice apart. Often I didn't think I could do it, but there was never an option except to believe that it was possible. Sometimes it took five, ten, twenty minutes. Sometimes I couldn't move the ice at all, but most of the time the ice opened just enough to allow us through to open water on the far side.

The heaving of the water and the swing of the ice was unpredictable. We could never guess what would happen next, and one time a huge pancake twenty-five metres in diameter and at least two metres thick swung across the bow. We saved *Kotick* with hard back-paddling, and the two bergs met and crumbled with a long, deep groan. In that groan there was an echo of the Norwegians.

'You can't get through,' it said.

But we did cross those six kilometres where the *Waterproef* had broken its propeller, and we made it to the thin ribbon of water where the bergs had grounded. The glacier ice glowed with ethereal blues even though the sky was grey. We both settled at the oars to pull hard together, shooting over the shallow ground with the power of two. Those kilometres were today's victory.

The blue sculptures of ice glowed in the grey seascape, the large pans crumbled on each other and perfectly calm leads let us slip on towards the black mountains beyond. I was thinking this is it. It can't get better than this. We are further than all the rest. We took the big risk carefully. It worked and we are good enough. I don't want this to stop.

At sleep time we made a camp at Flathuken and argued about how to leave our kit on the beach. I wanted to stack it and weigh it down with rocks for fear of sudden strong winds and curious bears. Shaggy was happy to leave it all over the place.

'What's the point of leaving it tidy?' he said.

'If the wind gets it we're done,' I replied.

'But it's a flat calm, Pete,' was his answer.

I couldn't convince him, so I stacked the kit on my own and walked around the hill to look out over the eight kilometres of open water to the other side of Raudfjorden.

The *Globe*, whose crew had recognised Shaggy's name on the radio, had a field party stuck in there. He came and sat beside me, and we looked together. There was broken ice across it and two bands of thick, white, solid pack across the mouth. There was no route through. We decided, almost at once, to confirm that there was no route through, ourselves, in person, in the middle of the fjord. But that would have to wait until tomorrow. Now it was time to sleep.

* * *

I awoke ten hours later on a ledge of moss, with the screams of schoolchildren echoing in my dream. Above me hundreds of guillemots chattered to and from the crevices and ledges of the cliff above. Below was a steep scarp slope and my sleeping bag was on the edge, not far from falling. We were up there for fear of the bears.

There was still no wind and a low grey sky. We had a breakfast of corned beef hash and several pints of hot chocolate. Then we packed it all away and loaded *Kotick* in the shallows. I stroked and Shaggy followed my time. We came to the ice and invented ways for working through it, and made names for the different methods to make our discussions easier.

In open water or if there were just a few bergs we rowed in 'four-wheel drive' which meant that we both rowed. The one in the bow would keep looking over his shoulder to check that there was no ice nearby and if there was just a little of it he would call out instructions.

'Right oar, just a little, there' – and we would both choose a point on the horizon and use it to maintain a new course. If there was more ice Shaggy would stop rowing and face forwards as the ice-pilot. We called this 'two-wheel drive'. Shaggy liked this because by now he found the view of the back of my neck very boring indeed. And, I suspected, he liked it when I did all of the hard work.

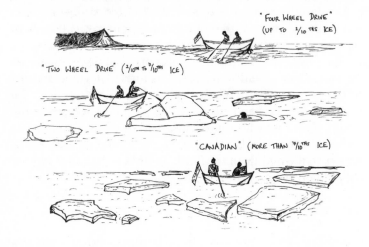

Manoeuvres in sea ice

Shaggy had to be careful calling instructions. Sometimes when he wanted me to go left I might misunderstand and pull on the wrong oar, so he would say, 'No, left. Right oar, right oar.'

Of course I would be looking in the opposite direction so he'd mix up my left and right and I would pull the right oar, which would make us go right not left. Then I would call out with a strong and loud obscenity because we were about to hit a berg. Then Shaggy would go into the bow with an oar to push away from the iceberg.

'No. That way, that way,' he would be shouting.

And of course that was a useless thing to say because I was

looking away from him. Then I would throw down my oars, turn around and work out precisely what he was trying to say. It would be so simple I couldn't see what the trouble was all about. Then I would pick up one single oar and paddle in the stern, pushing off from icebergs whenever necessary and giving Shaggy tips on how to paddle through the ice.

We called this 'going Canadian'.

By now we knew that if we found ourselves far up a narrow lead then one could get out and push the ice apart. Sometimes this meant that the lead closed behind us. If you draw a diagram of the forces involved you will soon see why this is, although it did catch us by surprise the first few times it happened. That was fine so long as the current and the wind were calm. But when the wind breathed, just slightly, the ice started to heave and the forces were terrible, like a steel press.

'Did you ever hear about the *Southern Quest*?'

Shaggy had not, so as we paddled into the thickest ice in Raudfjorden I told what I could remember.

'Rob Swan's boat in Antarctica, he was trying to get to the Pole, got trapped. Should have been OK, the ship was Ice Class Three.'

I tried to remember the account and, with a little editing, this is how it goes:

> With growing concern they struggled for hours. The floe on the starboard side was slowly rotating, and the pivot on which it turned was the ship. The pressure on the hull increased as the teams exhausted themselves without effect. They were caught in a trap and the outcome looked inevitable. Slowly the ship was being crushed.
>
> The hatch to No. 3 hold on the port side burst open as the foredeck buckled. Inside, the bulkhead could be seen slowly altering shape, the plates at the waterline bulging inwards until the steel ruptured. In the engine room two frames suddenly split down their length and water gushed in. Nothing would stop that.
>
> 'Well, I ain't welding that,' cried the second engineer as he scrambled up the ladder from the

engine room. It was time to abandon ship.

The pontoon was unleashed and the life-rafts and the two inflatables were removed to the ice. They unloaded tents, sledges, skis and radios from the hold. They threw cheese, chocolates, biscuits, cake, fruit and drinks on to the growing pile of debris on the floe.

Aghast, the crew stood and watched as the Mate and then the Skipper leapt down on to the ice. Then the ship went down – slowly at first, the stern dipping under the water, then more quickly the funnel, then the bridge, and the deck at 45 degrees and the railings and the barrel at the masthead. Last of all went the great red prow pointing to the sky, with the words Southern Quest in big white letters disappearing one by one in a consuming rush.

She was gone.

Where there had been heavy, hard, red-painted steel, now there was emptiness, distance, a flat white sea of pack-ice beneath a flat white sky. It began to snow.[27]

The lead ahead of us was blocked and as I drove to make a gap, the ice pivoted and closed behind. More ice came and floes closed in on all sides. The pool of water in which we floated shrank and the pressure point between two of the floes rose with a splitting noise into a ridge. The pool of water was still shrinking, *Kotick* would be broken into splinters. Pushing with an oar was as useless as whistling in the wind.

The ice came on and on. I stepped up and out and with one foot either side of the gap looked down into one hundred and twenty metres of dark water. It was four kilometres to the nearest beach.

I tied a rope to the bow and up through Shaggy's ice screw. We pushed the boat to the far side of our shrinking pond, then jerked and pulled *Kotick* and with a heave lifted the bow out of the water and onto the ice step. The ice was sharp and it would scratch the paint but I didn't care at all.

---

[27] R Mear and R Swan, *In the Footsteps of Scott*. Cape, London, 1987.

There was no time to unload her but with the ice screw as an anchor we could pull her, fully loaded, away from the pressure ridge building in the ice.

The ice was too heavy 'even for a rowboat', just as the Dutch had said. But we were fit, dry and hot from exertion. We had all of our equipment with us. I watched the steep screes on both headlands with my compass and it became clear that we were drifting. I made a calculation. We were drifting north at one sea mile per hour. At this speed we would reach the Pole in twenty-four days' time. I told Shaggy about my discovery and then the loneliness of it struck me.

That drove us to set off across the ice towards the far headland, and straight away we broke the keel by turning the fully laden hull towards the direction that we wanted to travel. The break was along the line of the keel and to fix it required re-working twelve broad-faced wood screws. Lying there on the mush of water and ice, I took the multi-tool and turned the first screw. The multi-tool buckled and trapped my finger. I swore and tried the second screw, and the third. Each time I pushed to twist the multi-tool, it collapsed. Then Shaggy tried, with the same result, then I tried again. I swore. It was cold and wet, we were floating to the North Pole, and it was not clear what we should do next. I was angry again.

'We could really, really do with a broad-faced screwdriver.'

Both he and I recalled the discussion when he'd persuaded me to leave it behind, and then Nick had offered one and we had, or I had, refused. Neither of us referred to these conversations but they were very close to us as we worked on what to do next. We stood back and puzzled. Then we emptied the boat, lifted the hull, and with that better position managed to re-work four of the twelve screws so that we could at least push *Kotick* when empty. Once that was done we carried the barrels and bags, the oars and spars, the food, the equipment, and finally the hull, towards a large floe that lay between us and the far headland.

Then Shaggy fell through the ice. If you want to know how he managed to do it without getting his feet wet you will have to ask him. I heard a crack and a shout and turned to see him landing without ceremony, on his bum. A block of ice and the dry barrel with all of the dry clothes were floating off into a lead.

I ran over with an oar and hooked the barrel with the blade. Just in time. It wouldn't do to lose all of the spare clothes. Especially as we're floating off to the North Pole on an ice floe. With the barrel bobbing back towards us, I turned and picked Shaggy up.

'Good, my theory worked,' he said.

'What do you mean?' I didn't know what he was talking about.

'My theory. When I felt the ice breaking I gave it a really hard push down and forwards with my feet. It sank the block of ice, and in line with the laws of physics I went up and backwards. I got back to the good ice. That was my plan. I'm glad it worked.'

'Quick, get the barrel.'

And we both leant down over the ice foot and gripped the rim of the barrel. It was not easy to hold and pull at the same time, but we did it. Then we collected all of our kit and the boat into one pile. I took a bearing on the headlands. We were outside the mouth of the fjord and still drifting north. Then a lead appeared. Another led to the far headland, the ice was opening up, and – without stopping to think why this was happening – we launched *Kotick*.

Suddenly back doing what we understood, we worked fast. The gap was closing so we piled our four hundred pounds of kit into *Kotick*, Shaggy knelt in the bow with an oar, I gave a running push and we glided out of the miniature harbour into the narrow lead heading east. We each held one oar and we 'went Canadian'.

'The lads in the Corps would love this,' Shaggy said, 'lost in the cold with no food, moving obstacles, heavy weights, not much time. Can't wait till I tell them about this.'

He loved this episode so much he designed a game called 'Help Pete and Shaggy get to the food barrel before they starve'. The board was made up of ragged squares much like snakes and ladders. There were moving bergs, immovable bergs, bergs which broke and bergs which crashed into each other. There was a walrus, squadrons of suicidal arctic terns and a hidden polar bear with big teeth. There were just three pieces to move, and they were the two of us, our kit, and the boat.

He sketched a version of it in his next letter to Anna.

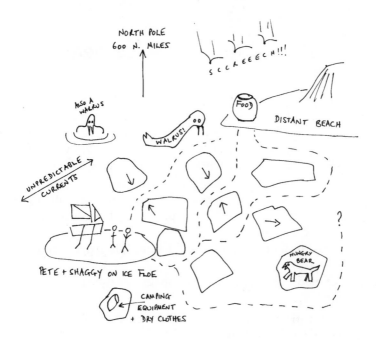

Help Pete and Shaggy get to the food

10

Kingdom of the ice bear

There was less ice on the far side, and when we reached the shallows the water was open again. There was a hut marked on the map and we rowed for that mark. I wanted to hide from the wind and the light, and warm my feet. But when we reached the headland with the mark there was nothing but six vertical sticks on the raised ground with a pile of planks and rocks. It was possible, this journey, but goodness it was hard.

'Probably flattened by bears,' I said. 'They get hungry in the winter.'

'I'm glad I didn't fall in,' said Shaggy, 'I'd be hypothermic by now.'

He'd been saved from mountain hypothermia by huts before, and if he'd been cold and wet he might have needed this one. But the view we found from where the hut should have been was far better than the shelter I wanted, because across a bay and as far as the northeast horizon the sea was almost free of ice. We could row through wide flat water like that at five kilometres per hour. And at that speed we might do what we had been hoping was possible, make it to the next depot, not the one the ship had failed to put in, but the one after that, far, far around the island at Kapp Lee. We had not measured the distance. It might be four hundred kilometres.

'Cool, look at that.'

'Does that mean we still can?'

It was true; we could. So we went on towards a fast-approaching point of no return. We rowed and rowed, and our hands grew stiff, driven by the need to make distance. The sun sank lower in the northern sky and the day-coloured night arrived so when we stopped rowing the cold gripped our hands and leaked up our arms. It was time to sleep but we continued, denying that we might have limits, pulling an extra hour and a half along the low shingle bank before we finally beached and lifted *Kotick* out of the surf.

When the boat and kit were up the beach, we turned *Kotick* bottom-up and I gripped the multi-tool in a comfortable way, and with time and in comfort I re-worked those twelve screws that we'd damaged on the ice floe. Shaggy set up the cooker and worked on supper. Then we turned to our rituals.

I handed the map to him and he measured how far we'd come with his lucky piece of string. This evening he announced, 'Right, I reckon we did forty kilometres, as the string flies.' And he wrote that down and counted up from his notes.

'Three hundred and fifty K so far, not bad for seven days rowing.' He was referring to our days on the water, defined as one waking and sleeping cycle, and not the days of the calendar.

Then we ticked off new animals and birds.

'That was a long-tailed skua at Flathuken,' I said, and he looked it up.

'It says they follow ships,' he chuckled. 'There aren't any of those, so I guess that's why he followed us. *Kotick* is now officially a ship.'

Then when supper was finished we put any leftover food into the black bin liner with the packs of Pears in Chocolate Sauce that were already there. Shaggy had saved a Mars Bar and so I had to put something equally valuable from my twenty-four-hour ration pack. I had a rich assortment of sugar sachets, chewing gum and tea bags but none of these was as valuable as a Mars Bar. Maybe a packet of squashed-fly Garibaldi biscuits and a tin of cheese spread was as good as one Mars Bar, or a packet of oatmeal and raisin mix. I reluctantly threw my biscuits and spread into the bag, all too aware that I would wake up with hunger in the morning.

Then, our rituals complete, we counted the kilometres to the depot at Kapp Lee and worked out that, if we didn't count our escape rations or saved rations, we had to average fifty kilometres per twenty-four-hour ration pack. That was a very long way to make every day, without fail, whatever the weather. So we decided to improve our chances by extending each rowing day, and by eating less. We could not afford another three-day blizzard. My hunger was worse because I was thinking of that.

The weather was calm and for efficiency we did not pitch the tent. Without it we were more exposed to polar bears. This was fine when we were awake, because we had a good view up and down the beach, but when we had the drawstrings of our bivvy bags tied above our heads we must have looked like big brown worms or dried-out seals. We zipped up and hoped that the trip flares would work and scare the bear away, should one arrive.

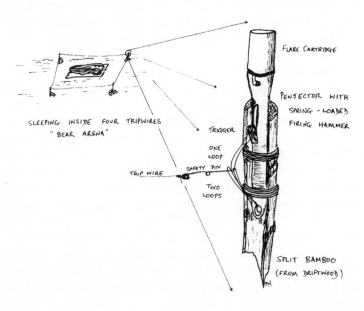

FLARE CARTRIDGE

PENJECTOR WITH
SPRING-LOADED
FIRING HAMMER

TRIGGER

ONE
LOOP

TRIP WIRE SAFETY PIN

TWO
LOOPS

SLEEPING INSIDE FOUR TRIPWIRES
"BEAR ARENA"

SPLIT BAMBOO
(FROM DRIFTWOOD)

Sleeping arrangements

The last one to bed always pulled the rifle into his sleeping bag. When the gun metal had warmed up I worked the action and put a round in the breech. I clicked the safety catch on and off, and on, and I fell asleep with the loaded weapon beside me.

* * *

When I woke up I uncurled my hand from around the rifle. The safety catch was still on, that was good. My sleeping bag was warm, that was very good. We had hundreds of kilometres and ice behind us, which was good, and there were unthinkable kilometres ahead. They were too many to imagine. If we turned back now we could make it to Ny Ålesund, but very soon there would be the point of no return, when we would no longer have enough rations to get us home. So far we had been feeling our way, pushing the limit, seeing how far we could go, always with the option of retreat. In the next day or so our escape route back would close. On my own that morning, with my feet finally warm after a dry night at the far end of my sleeping bag, the threat of that complete commitment made me restless. The sky was settled and low waves washed the beach. I wanted to go on.

Shaggy stood up and exclaimed, 'I feel like a new animal today!'

And off he went looking for driftwood. He brought logs, planks, twigs and dried seaweed and piled them into a pyramid. He struck a match and with the help of a solid fuel tablet and some chocolate wrappers the flames licked up around the kindling into the dry wood which caught quickly. Once his bonfire was properly alight the wall of heat was a welcome relief and he constructed a frame over the flames and hung our still-damp boots from it. While they steamed into the fire we ate our rolled oats and hot milk out of their foil bags and licked our spoons clean.

Pushing *Kotick* out, we shot through a narrow tidal stream which was carrying a procession of ice against and across our path around the next headland. We had to be careful to avoid the chunks of broken ice because they were moving fast, but that was easier than it sounds because once in the fast tidal stream we moved at the same speed as the bergs. I was rowing in the stern and Shaggy was in the bow taking the odd extra stroke with a single paddle that he held in both hands. He called my strokes and from time to time I looked over my shoulder.

'Right one, then pull hard, now.'

His voice changed, his calling was faster.

'Two quick strokes, Pete, quick and hard.'

I looked up and a grounded berg towered above me; there was a deep cave melted by the saltwater and an overhang reaching towards me. Shaggy was trying to cut it too fine and it was not at all clear that we would make it around the up-current side of this iceberg. It was dark in the ice cave.

I pulled harder, once, then twice.

'Hey,' I said.

'Pull,' he said.

The current swept us underneath and I dug another hard stroke before my oar was obstructed by the berg and I could not take another. The roof of the overhang was four feet above the surface of the water, I turned and saw that Shaggy had his head and shoulders low next to the gunwale, the smooth corrugated ice brushed my scalp and I leaned down and sideways. With the mast down the tip of the flag pole was the highest point on the boat and the red ensign, which we had spent so many hours lining up on points on the horizon, scraped and juddered on the corrugated surface.

Don't snap, I thought, don't snap, I like the flag. I don't want to lose it.

I imagined *Kotick* trapped and dragged under. How could we fight a weight of water if it was this cold? There would be no help, they may never find us. Maybe some flotsam would make it to the beach. We still had plenty of speed through the water, but we hardly moved towards the upstream side of the berg. I pushed on the ice roof and my palm caught then slipped without friction. There was nothing more I could do but hope the momentum would carry us. The momentum had to carry us. There was no other way. And it did, just. I straightened my neck, and my shoulders relaxed. I took two more strokes.

'Don't *do* this to me, Shags,' I said. I was not questioning his judgement, which I should have done. It was his style that alarmed me.

The wind came again and after a hard row to the next point, Velkomspynten, the wind increased more and thick tendrils of mist reached out from the far side of the fjord. The spray and the bucking of the boat were exciting, and the beach disappeared in the fog. I wanted to call out but instead breathed freedom and shouted silently to myself. The tour ships and kayaks were far behind. If anybody tried to find us they would not look for us here. Raudfjorden and the Norskøyane islands were impassable, after all. The commitment was in me now. I sensed the threat of no return, breathing freedom in the mist.

The island goal, the full circumnavigation, was nothing to this – shouting with the wild, pushing the limit, with the spray flying in the sun and the fog. We were going for the depot. The dream, the success, whatever story might come, was all secondary to this, to being here, cutting a wake, out at sea.

Then the mist wrapped *Kotick* like a shroud and the wind died. Our world shrank to a small silver disc of sea and the damp, heaving boards of *Kotick*. The mist was spinning around so I fixed the compass to the stern thwart and we took the sails off and rowed on a bearing until we reached more ice.

The combination of pack ice and fog filled me with dread. Neither Shaggy nor I wanted another scrape like Raudfjorden, nor did we want more damage to the boat, and it would be so much worse if we were disorientated and blinded by fog as well. So we turned by the compass needle for a beach which should be behind us and paddled that way until there was the relief of waves breaking, not on ice but on a shingle beach. Grey pebbles came out of the mist. The bow crunched and we beached.

Shaggy laid out his kip mat and sat cross-legged. He put a flame to the jet line of his petrol cooker. Then he heated water and made tea, we drank it and he made more for the thermos flask. Caught between two fjords blocked by ice, we discussed what to do if our food ran out. It seemed quite possible that we would be caught here; unable to continue or return.

Shaggy claimed 'pangs of vegetarianism' whenever we talked about shooting wildlife. I suspect he didn't like the idea of fishy blood and blubber on his down jacket. But his alternative suggestion of shooting a duck seemed unreasonable. After a seven-six-two high-velocity rifle bullet smashed through a duck there would nothing left but eider-down and tail feathers. He pulled out a pocket catapult.

'Maybe we could use this,' he said, and took pot shots that missed several times. The duck didn't even notice. Then he hit a boulder and the duck flew away. Hunting might not be as easy as it seemed, so we made a plan that if our progress fell much behind the target of fifty kilometres per twenty-four hour ration pack then we would hunt opportunistically before the food ran out. Reindeer, we decided without much conviction, would be the best option.[28]

Our conversation, and the pot shots that Shaggy was taking at the ducks, came to a sudden end when the fog lifted and a light breeze started blowing off the beach.

'Hey look at that!'

'Best we go, let's go, let's go then.'

The fjord was clear of ice except for one small raft of it in the middle, which we'd run into. And with clear water ahead, after so much rowing, we wanted to catch this following wind.

It took longer than I expected to leave and after we'd spread the sails out on either side in a goose-wing they soon sagged and flipped as the wind died. When the breeze seemed utterly dead Shaggy untied the shrouds and we put the mast down and started to row with stiff hands. Then a southerly wind picked up. It was a good one so we put the

---

[28] Reindeer were officially protected in 1925 (I later discovered) and with the exception of trappers, who have a meat quota of five reindeer a year, and some limited and carefully controlled hunting in the autumn, the shooting of reindeer in Svalbard is prohibited. We should have chosen seal.

mast up, but it was short-lived and the southerly died. So we put the mast down again. Should we have been quicker putting it up? Or should we have not bothered putting the mast up at all? We laid the oars inside the rowlock loops and started to pull again. Idleness was a luxury we could not afford with so many kilometres to the next food depot.

As we pulled our toes went cold, then numb, and then our ankles froze. With the hours a deep chill nestled in the bones of our heels and toes and climbed through the ankle joint to the two shin bones in each calf. The circulation shut down and it seemed a pool of liquid nitrogen settled in place of the fluid in the joints. Stiffness collected, making a dull pain. Whenever we re-warmed the pain intensified as the joints moved, so it was more comfortable to leave them cold.

By this stage we'd tried many different combinations of socks, sea boots, mountain boots, toe wriggling, re-warming with jumpers and armpits. It was all to no avail. Today, like every day, our feet froze, and the best we could do was joke and ignore the pain. If we did not acknowledge the sensation the agony was easier to take.

'No, not cold at all,' he maintained.

'A little chilly at the tips,' is what I gave.

We pulled on the oars and the wind breezed, so we stopped to debate putting the mast up again. We put it up and the wind died and we cursed the wind. With all of the erecting and dismantling of the mast, sailing to the wind and running around the drift ice, it took an age to cross the mouth of Woodfjorden – but eventually the low cloud and mist that had been swirling with the fickle breeze cleared into a hazy blue sky and a handsome scarp ridge rose out of the screes above the rocky foreshore. The beach at Gråhuken was easy and came with relief.

My limbs were heavy and my back ached and it was all I could do to lift my share of *Kotick* up the beach to where we laid her above the high-tide seaweed. Feeling the weight in my arms and legs I could only look at the ground at my feet. I was determined to sleep in the tent. If I did not sleep in the tent I would wake cold and hungry the following day. And if I did that I did not have faith in myself to pull through the next day if it was as hard as this one. I opened the dry barrel and dragged out the tent.

'I'm happy to sleep on the beach,' said Shaggy, 'it's almost the same.'

'Not tonight, we need the tent,' I said and shook it onto the ground. Then I pitched it very slowly so as to give Shaggy time to do everything else: digging out the food and choosing what to cook, refuelling the cooker and getting fresh water for the food, bringing our bags and kip mats up from the beach. I ate the food he cooked, threw the remainder of my ration into the bin liner and, the second my head hit the rolled-up towel and clothing I was using as a pillow, my eyes closed and sleep hit me.

Shaggy wrote in his diary, 'Pete snores but only quietly, he's very run down; to keep ourselves going it's almost a game pretending not to be tired. We've made rationing into a game: who can discard the most into the black bag. At the moment we're neck and neck.'

I woke up many, many hours later with a weight in my head. This was a wonderful, long, adventurous trip, but so what? I crawled outside and my shoulders were heavy. It was hard and special but it would never save me. The very best I could see was that we'd make it to the food and then back to the world of men. It was a beautiful, aching empty wildness of ice and rock and cold, cold water but utterly devoid of human warmth.

I loved the space and freedom but with this fatigue I could not take it. My body was small and I needed something, some human warmth, to take me on. Shaggy was alive. He was rowing for Anna and he seemed just as strong every day. Should I be doing the same? Did I need an Anna? Not many of those around here. I saw for a second time that this big goal of mine, this circumnavigation, might not be all I wanted it to be. I needed something else. So in the long hours at the oar that followed I turned more and more to the people and the warmth I'd left behind.

I rolled up the tent. Shaggy was looking at the *Birds and Mammals* book. He called out the pages we had not ticked and made a list of the birds we had not seen: red-throated diver, king eider, pomarine skua, Ross's gull and the Svalbard ptarmigan.

While he did that I turned my thoughts to the challenge of crossing Wijdefjorden, the last and greatest fjord of the north coast. It was carved out of the earth's crust by prehistoric glaciers cutting northwards along a cataclysmic fault line.[29] With all the water that filled it now there was also plenty of ice. We needed an idea of how much there was, and where it lay. And for that we needed a vantage point.

The nearest mountain top was three kilometres inland over pebbles and beach ridges, so on that fine morning we walked towards it for a better view of the ice and the water between us and the land on the far side of Wijdefjorden, forty kilometres distant.

'Hey, it's a ptarmigan!' Shaggy was squinting. But this ptarmigan took off and flew a circuit around us with a whirr of guillemot wings. It croaked like a guillemot. It was a guillemot.

A little later there was a growling 'arrgh' from behind a ridge.

'Now that's a ptarmigan,' I said, and we ran up the next ridge of scree.

'Arrgh,' it called again, but we could not see it.

'D'you reckon we can tick it, even if we didn't see it?' said Shaggy.

'Don't see why not,' I said, 'it's definitely a ptarmigan.'

'I hope we see a bear,' said Shaggy, 'but not too close.'

The fjord stretched away in blues and whites, and the far shore seemed far closer than the forty kilometres the map told us it was. There were two thick bands of ice lying between us and the other side. Standing here we would never know if we could make it through that ice, but we did know that this calm day, this blue sky and the liquid mirror that stretched over the water ahead, were the best possible conditions for trying to do so. And we knew for sure: out there was the point of no return.

---

[29] Locally called the Billefjorden Fault Zone.

On any ordinary day in my life what we set out to do would have seemed a tremendous challenge, but today this impossible feat was just one more routine day of our rarefied existence. It was no more to us to set out into forty kilometres of open water broken with ice, than to boil the breakfast rations that gave us nothing to chew, to eat the oat biscuits and fill the thermos flask with tea, to row with stiff hands and ignore our cold feet, or feel hunger for the sake of the black bag.

I sat on the thwart, threaded the oars, reached forwards for the first catch of the day, and as I pulled the water into whirlpools with the tips of my blades I thought, where is this taking me? Beyond the point of no return.

Droplets of spray bounced off the water from the splashing of our blades and we enjoyed a blue day of crystalline clarity. Sure of ourselves and our ability, we used all the rowing-in-ice lessons we had learned. We travelled four-wheel-drive, two-wheel-drive, and when the ice was close together we went Canadian. We pushed our limits, like we did every day, and seeking warmth I turned my thoughts to a girl in Norway and another in England, because I needed that to get me home.

11

Great wanderer

The girl in Norway had a copper bob and wide eyes that creased at the edge when she smiled. She'd squeezed my hand when we kissed goodbye in a haze of perfume at a nightclub door. The one back home had cut her long hair into a bob and moved away the year before. I liked that bob and the smell of her hair. As I pulled my blades through the liquid mirror of the fjord I pulled for their warmth and measured the very great distance between me and them, and the world of men.

Verlegenhuken, Hinlopen Strait and Sørkapp all lay ahead, they were aspirations and obstacles, places on the map, coloured ink tempered with advice and hearsay. I tried to imagine: the northernmost tip of the island, its beacon and the relief of turning south, the infamous Hinlopen Strait, known for fog so cold it cracks the skin and the katabatic blasts of wind that crash off the glaciers, and Sørkapp, the local Cape Horn. There were bears and icebergs and the risk of capsize, likely disappointment and possible death. All this lay between me and the warmth of the world that I was rowing for now. I was not at all sure that my desire to reach the world was strong enough. This was such a wide cold coast, there were hundreds of kilometres of it, and my desire for warmth was no more than a pinprick.

Forty kilometres is a lot of fjord, and I tried to imagine the scale of the force that made it from the fault plane of prehistoric earthquakes, millions of years, gallons of water, tonnes of ice – and all the quantities of each were beyond comprehension. This great Wijdefjord ran north–south following the fault line that divided the ancient basement rock on the far side of the fjord, around a billion years old, from the more recent but still timeworn, four-hundred-million-year Devonian sediments that were tumbling down the screes behind us. It's a lot to understand a billion years.

If the entire life of planet earth[30] were twelve hours, from six in the morning to six in the evening, then the ancient basement on the far side did not appear until mid-afternoon and those sedimentary deposits behind us didn't appear until around five p.m. Each million years would have been eleven seconds, civilisation just the last fifty milliseconds. My life in all of that was shorter than the electric snap of a synapse; less than a fraction of a millisecond.

I'm a really small thing in all of this.

The textbooks describe the far shore as 'gneiss with bands of deeply cooked mudstone and marble', and there is evidence of glaciation. This suggests that, as Svalbard was at the equator at the time, the whole globe was covered in ice. Imagine that; mid-afternoon in the twelve-hour planet-lifetime, the whole globe was one snowball. Life would never have started in such a place.

Then the super-continent began to break up and, coincidently or not, there was life. The tectonic upheaval which ensued buckled and cooked the ancient rocks and created a sedimentary basin where vertical kilometres of Devonian sediment (this side of the fjord) were deposited along with fish and trees and the first beds of Svalbard coal. How the world changed in that long hour in the late afternoon of the twelve-hour planet-lifetime.

As the super-continent continued to fragment the continental shields of Greenland and north Europe were compressed and sheered. Much as some of the icebergs around us were shattered as the wind and the currents heaved them around headlands or across each other, the continental crust broke along deep planes miles below the earth's surface. And the two bodies of rock, the ancient

---

[30] Usually estimated at four and a half billion years.

basement and the Devonian sediments, were displaced hundreds of miles along a sinistral fault plane until they lay next to each other. The same fault movement tore Scotland apart along the Caledonian Canal, and all of this time Svalbard was drifting northwards. By the time the faulting had finished it had reached the latitude of latter-day England.

Then as the rain and snow fell in the last half hour of the twelve-hour planet-lifetime, it naturally chose these fault lines when running back to the sea. It scoured channels, and when the climate cooled again the glaciers chose the same river channels and scoured it into a U-shaped valley. And all this time Svalbard was drifting northwards into the Arctic Circle.

The Atlantic opened up, first as a rift valley between Europe and America and then as a volcanic ridge on the deep ocean floor. Greenland moved away from the coast of Norway and the most recent rocks were deposited: alternate desert sand and shallow sea deposits with an abundance of mollusc and squid shells. Dinosaurs left footprints on the east coast of the island and then in the last ten minutes of the day there were volcanic eruptions when lava flowed into the forests and petrified the trees. Other forests and swamps turned to coal.

In the last few minutes of the twelve hours the continental shield was heaved and compressed by more tectonic activity between Europe and America, and this deformation threw up the current mountain chains which were cut by new rivers and glaciers. One vast glacier, forty kilometres wide, cut the Wijdeford valley into the size it is now and then melted, allowing the sea to flood in, and other glaciers cut the western mountains into the needle peaks discovered by Barents in 1596.

I pulled on my oars and the screes of the Devonian sediments at Gråhuken seemed no further away. I pulled and that hour seemed to last for ever. The sun dazzled on the ice floes and drops from my blades bounced on the surface of the liquid mirror. A billion years takes a lot of understanding, and forty kilometres is a lot of fjord. I was just a pinprick of warmth. And the sun was burning my skin.

The next hour stretched ahead of me and seemed, if that were possible, even longer than the last. The red ensign was draped on its pole and it stirred with the breaths of wind that came with our motion towards the heavy ice. This fjord was wider than all of them but we were strong in our own small way. The sun was hot and I felt good. From time to time Shaggy stood on his seat to pick the best line through the ice. He took his time up there because that's when I was rowing alone and I gave him kilometres for free.

I pulled for the Norwegian girl and the one back home. In the long stretches of clear water I could hear Shaggy counting behind me. He reached five hundred, then six hundred, then went back to one again. There was some ice and I was counting the strokes per minute, but we were so far from shore I couldn't tell the distance of the minutes and the hours. The fjord was forty kilometres. Shaggy reached one thousand. At twenty-four strokes a minute that's forty minutes of counting. Each of those strokes had taken him closer to Anna. I settled into the rhythm as Shaggy fought for his Anna. I suspected the goal would defeat him. Then he shifted in the boat behind me.

'Let's try this.' He had his hands in his rummage bag. He pulled out some speakers and some waterproof ziplock plastic bags, and then the walkman which he'd pulled out of the dry barrel the night before.

'What were those tapes you brought?' he said.

'Just three, at random,' I said. 'Umm, let's see, one classical, one Scottish rock and ummm, *Grease*. I took them at random, I didn't think.'

One had been a favourite on my trip the year before.

'The Proclaimers, that's cool.' He plugged in the speakers and arranged the wires in the plastic ziplock bags so the walkman would not be splashed. He pressed the play button and looked to see that the cassette was moving. The speakers hissed. The beat hummed in the thwart as their steel strings and bass struck through the intro. The lyrics came in and so did Shaggy. He knew them word for word.

'When I wake up, yeah
I know I'm gonna be
I'm gonna be the man who wakes up next to you, g'dang, g'dang,

And when I go out, yeah
I know I'm gonna be ...'

We pulled, and the rush of music from Scotland was suddenly in the boat there with us, so we did not feel so far away. A ring seal bobbed up nearby and it looked at us for longer than usual. We pulled with a new rhythm and even Shaggy's deep strokes did not bother me. The water was calm and it didn't matter if he lugged the blades out of the water. We drove on to the next song. I knew the chorus from the mapping project last year, and we both wailed with the cassette –

'While the Chief, puts sunshine on Leith,
I'll thank him for his work
And your birth and my birth.'

That gave us something to think about, but the tape was over in an instant. He turned it over, it played, and then we played the A-side again. I was trying to work out how to find the copper-haired girl in Oslo. Maybe she would go to that bar again. It was ridiculous for me to be thinking like this but I needed something to help me through. The music gave me hope.

What would John Cooper have done? What about Gino Watkins? Did they feel weak before they died? Did they imagine the warm people waiting for them? Their striving and fighting wasn't enough in the face of bad luck, the long fall and the sudden capsize. What were they thinking? Were they here now? Would I join them in their cold eternity? Would I be young forever? I wanted to live. Maybe fear will help me through; fear of failure, fear of the bears, fear of death. I pulled harder.

The music was helping.

As we skimmed across the placid mirror of Wijdeford among the wide floes of the polar ice cap I could not help thinking that all of these friendly seals would bring bears. Nothing can move quite so fast in drift ice as a polar bear. Their agility and strength to leap and swim is legend, and to hunt in sea ice is their reason to be. I calmed myself with the thought that in summer the bears are seldom hungry thanks to the quantity of seal.

They eat whale and walrus and the occasional expeditioner but they prefer seal, and seal blubber in particular. Eskimos often find the bones, muscle and hide of a ring seal untouched, but the hide has been stripped from the carcass with cuts around the flippers and head, and then turned inside out and stripped of its blubber. The Eskimos envy the seal-hunting skill of the bear. Their stories describe bears stalking behind a block of ice that they push to camouflage their black nose, or more comically by hiding it under a paw.

Whatever the truth of those stories, because of the seal that bobbed and watched us, I kept looking for bears. That fear helped me pull on my oars. Then I rested on them and I took the rifle from its bag. It was rusty again so I checked the action, put a round in the breech and clicked the safety catch. It was simple and powerful, a good rifle for hunting, though not quite strong enough to inspire faith that it would stop the charge of a bear.

One hunter who nearly found out what it takes to stop a bear was the fourteen-year-old midshipman Horatio Nelson, out on the ice near Fairhaven shortly before his crew were nearly compelled to abandon ship. While the ships were caught in the pack he ventured out in search of a bear, wanting a skin to take for his father. According to Captain Mahan's account of that voyage:

> Nelson in high spirits led the way over the frightful chasms in the ice, armed with a rusty musket … Between three and four in the morning the mist somewhat dispersed, and the hunters were discovered at some distance, attacking a large bear.
>
> The signal was instantly made for their return; but it was in vain that Nelson's companion urged him to obey it. He was at the time divided by a chasm in the ice from his shaggy antagonist, which probably saved his life; for his musket flashed in the pan, and the ammunition was expended.
>
> 'Never mind,' exclaimed Horatio, 'do but let me get a blow at this devil with the butt end of my musket, and we shall have him.'[31]

---

31 A T Mahan, *The Life of Nelson*. Sampson Low, London, 1897.

At this point his Captain saw the young Nelson's danger and fired one of the ship's guns so that the bear ran off. If nothing else, this story suggests that turning a blind eye was a habit Nelson developed long before he lost one of his own, and that he would probably have done the same at the Battle of Copenhagen[32] if both his eyes had still been intact.

I took a break from the oars and searched the broken pack with both eyes and there were no bears. The sun was hot and I didn't want to sweat because later it would freeze, so before I resumed with the oars I took off my trousers and kept the rifle within easy reach. Shaggy said that he'd rather face a bear with dignity and he kept his trousers despite the sweat. He turned the tape over.

'Change it, Shags, try *Grease*,' I said, because I'd had enough of the Proclaimers and bizarre and banal as it may seem, we pulled our way through that frozen kingdom to the funky, funky beat of Summer Nights, Hopelessly Devoted, Greased Lightnin' and Blue Moon. Shaggy had never seen the film, so I had to explain.

'High-school kids, they met on holiday, then end up at the same school. He's got a gang; she's a daddy's girl. He's too cool, they break up, there's a beauty school drop out ...'

As we turned the cassette over and over I explained how each song fitted into the story (several times) until 'lunch time', when we tied up to the largest ice floe we could find. The puddles on it were fresh and slightly salty. I scooped some water into a tin. Shaggy fired up his cooker and I walked a long circuit to check the ice beyond the pressure ridges was free of hostile wildlife. There was a family of ring seals.

The water from the surface of the ice floe was perfect for soup.

* * *

Despite all of the pulling and counting, and turning my thoughts to the girl in Norway and the one back home, and

---

32 When he famously exclaimed, putting the glass to his blind eye, 'I really do not see the signal' (to retreat).

thinking about bears, eventually my mind stopped revolving. Hours later my head was empty and I imagined my brain in a jar of aspic. My thoughts were still as the oars creaked in their rowlocks.

It was my way, to enter a calm place with few thoughts and not hold out for a goal as Shaggy did. I had to strike level with the oars as if I could strike like this forever, row within myself as if I would row forever. I found the level feeling. I found the groove and held it through the rest of that day while the sun beat down.

My left wrist hurt. It ached and I was afraid for it, how could it be bad? Did the boat always pull to the right? To be weak from injury was dangerous. I wrapped my neckerchief around the wrist and pulled more carefully. My life depended on strong hands, my strong back and the desire to live and fight for home. The wind started against us and I pulled hard but smoothly, thinking of my wrist but not too much, all the way to the hut on the east side of Wijdefjord, just twenty-five kilometres south of Verlegenhuken, the northern tip of the island, where we would turn to head south.

We saw Rekvik Hut from a distance. It was made of tree trunks pulled from the driftwood and I was happy that the bears had not flattened it in the winter. There was a hole in the roof but the hole was small: there would still be shelter from the wind and the light.

'How've we managed to come so far?'

'Oh, I think we've been pretty naive,' said Shaggy.

Supper was over and we were eating some of Granny's Toblerone, saved for eighty degrees north. My cheeks and ears and neck were burning with the sun and now they were wet with cream. It had been a big day for the walkman and we were listening to the third cassette, a Mendelssohn violin concerto played by Jascha Heifetz. Shaggy pulled a hip flask.

'I think it's time for this,' he said. 'Whisky?' He poured twice and I tipped mine. The alcohol diffused in warmth through my arms and neck and up to my temples.

'Yes, maybe we've been stupid. But we planned it. And we coped with everything, and the weather's been good apart from the ice. But we learned how to get through it. We never took no for an answer. That's why we came so far. Just didn't take no for an answer. It's amazing what you can do when you only try.' I was speaking to myself. 'And don't listen to the advice that says no. Maybe we're naive, but that's not the only reason we've come so far.'

Shaggy was reading the *Birds and Mammals* book again.

'Go on, read it out aloud. This is bear country.'

'Snow white in winter and yellow-white in summer. The neck is long, the head and ears small. The claws are stronger, the canine teeth longer and the cheek teeth sharper than in other bears, a sign of its purely carnivorous way of life. The soles of the feet are covered with fur except for the footpads. Males have powerful shoulders and limbs, an arched nose ridge, and their ears are lower and further back. They have facial scars.'

The whisky was warm and when the tape ran out I started blowing my Lark harmonica. These lips were getting into shape and I went through all the simple tunes I could remember. I put one more whisky in the bottom of my mug and zipped up my sleeping bag.

Shaggy was in his sleeping bag, writing to Anna.

'I'd love to fall asleep in your lap but a loaded mini-flare gun will have to do. It's more ethical to scare a polar bear than to kill it. And an injured bear is problematic because it starts eating delicious young children and things. Pete's started on the Christmas carols with his harmonica; it's time to sleep. I'm going to try and dream about you. I do all day, I hope I do tonight.'

I felt better. The hours of sleep at Gråhuken and the day in the sunshine had made me stronger, and I was happy to be rowing for something other than the dream. Even if it was just for girls who didn't know I was rowing for them.

I lay awake.

The Eskimos tell stories about bears because of the centuries they've lived and hunted with them out on the ice. In the stories the bears have human characteristics and they are known as Great Wanderers.

One Great Wanderer fell in love with a beautiful Eskimo

girl, young and lovely, and she, though recently married, fell in love with him. The polar bear made the girl promise never to tell her husband of their love because the bear knew that then the man would try to kill him. The girl and the bear lived and loved happily for years. Then after a long hard winter when the man had been unlucky in the hunting of bears the young girl told her husband where to find her lover.

The bear was far away but with his preternatural ears he heard the girl whispering to her husband. Leaving his sleeping place long before the dawn he went to their igloo, where he found them lying together. He raised his paws to smash them both but realised that he loved the girl despite her betrayal. He put his paws down again and set off on a long solitary journey. The girl never saw her Great Wanderer again.

My cup dropped and I did not hear it strike the floor.

* * *

I was thick and comfortable with sleep. Through the warmth I heard a great scratching, like pebbles rubbing rough on each other.

'Shut up Shags, let me sleep.' The scratching continued.

'Shut up Shags, shut up.' And I dreamed that I was in a bed that was too comfortable to be awake in. Then the washing of pebbles came through again. It was disturbing my sleep and I needed to sleep to be strong, good and strong so I could row hard when the new day came. Why can't he shut up, it's still time to sleep. I slept again.

'Shut up Pete, can't you?' Then something thumped the bottom of my mattress. It was Shaggy. He was in the bottom bunk, I was on the top bunk and my legs were lying along one of the window sills. He was calling me. Why?

'Shut up Pete, shut it.' And there was another thump on my mattress. I opened my eyes and there was the passing of a shadow. Then he spoke faster and his voice was tight.

'Pete, Pete, quick, get up, there's a bear at the window.'

'Balls, Shags, let me sleep.'

'There is, there is.' I peered down over the edge of my bunk. He was frozen in his sleeping bag. I was blinking awake. It must be a trick, although he'd never tried it before. He just wants me to make the coffee. He called out again.

'There's a bear at the window, I swear there is.' I was not quite sure why he was still in his bunk. Why did he want me to get up and not him? Convinced I would be the joke I climbed off the top bunk. The boards were cold on my bare feet. I pulled a fleece over my Norwegian army shirt and padded over to window.

The long and empty beach stretched far in both directions.

'There's nothing,' I said.

Shaggy was still frozen in his bunk. Then I saw the shadow again. This time I could see the shape of a neck and snub nose craning up to the roof of the hut. It was the shape of an enormous snake, just by the wall, at the head end of Shaggy's bunk.

A profanity filled my mind but I held my voice steady.

'It's a bear,' I said.

Shaggy ignored my new information, and that surprised me.

I stepped twice and lifted the rifle. There were five rounds in the magazine, and I worked the action. I pushed and turned the bolt down. There was a round in the breech. It was ready to fire. I took the first pressure on the trigger and the stock was comfortable in the meat of my thumb. With my left eye I took up the iron sight.

The bear stopped digging and came to the window. His nose was on the sill, smelling us. He was curious. I took the first pressure on the trigger, looked across to the gap in the roof and put the bead of the fore-sight on his forehead. All I had to do was take the second pressure and the stock would kick in my cheek while a supersonic round whipped from the muzzle. The window would crystallise, there would be splinters of wood and the bullet would sting his face. With luck it would break his forehead. If not the first round, then the second round would. But I didn't want to break his face, or smash the hut. He was just looking at me and I was looking at him. We were both alive in this empty place and we shared that. He looked like a young one, an outsized puppy even.

Shaggy was standing beside me now. His presence made me braver and I stepped towards the window. Then I clicked the safely catch and put the rifle down, I picked up my camera and went close, the window framed his muzzle and ears: an enormous white dog with questioning eyes. Shaggy got braver and put his hand to the window. He held it out towards the bear.

'Just want to touch the window, touch the bear through the window,' he said but some invisible force repelled his hand and he could not touch the window. Then the bear moved back and put his paw on the window and my cheeks burned and the blood rushed in my chest. My hands were throbbing on the camera as the bear scraped at the window, then the bear tapped and the Perspex made cracking noises. He tapped again.

The tapping of the bear made the driftwood trunks vibrate and I stepped back to where the rifle was standing with a round in the breech. Shaggy stepped back too. The bear went down from the window and then up on his hind legs. The fluff on his belly filled the window and his paws were on the roof. His weight came down, the hut was strong but I did not trust it. And there was that hole.

I went for the mini-flares. I pulled the mechanism and screwed one in and pulled it from the case. I put my thumb on the trigger and took it back, then I put my hand with the flare through the roof. I didn't like having my hand out there. I tried to point the flare down to the beach, that would be best, and I fired quickly because of the bear being out there. He jumped back and looked at us and sniffed one more time. Then he turned and ambled away up the beach with all the poise and confidence of an Olympian. The sight of him moving fixed us to the floor of that hut.

I was nervous when the bear smelt the boat because they are known for smashing kayaks, but he did nothing more than sniff. I was glad that everything was packed in waterproof barrels or here with us in the hut. There were no interesting smells so he walked north, supple and powerful, up the beach. We watched him out of sight.

Sniffing the food barrel

'So, not top of the food chain any more,' said Shaggy.

'I think he was a young one,' I said.

Our bladders were full of tea and whisky but we tightened our legs for nearly an hour before venturing out as gingerly as you can imagine. I held the loaded rifle in my shoulder, forefinger along the trigger guard. And I answered that call of nature with it cradled in my arms. Much later, after coffee, breakfast and reading, and when the coast was entirely clear, we packed the equipment, looking up and down the beach many times.

We rowed north along the beach, following the bear (as it happened) and much further from the shingle than usual. There was mist again, and out of the mist came two zodiacs full of European tourists zipped up in fluorescent waterproofs and lifejackets. Imagine our surprise – well, imagine theirs. I was looking bookish, wearing spectacles, and Shaggy hadn't shaved for weeks. Their presence told us that Hinlopen Strait was clear of ice, which was the best news yet, and I don't want to speculate what our presence indicated to them.

They said they'd been following a bear and were lost. They could not find their ship with its warm cabins, fresh food and hot showers. I imagined a comfortable table for writing postcards and freshly ground coffee. But they were not sure which way to go. Shaggy and I, however, knew exactly where we were going, north, and the compass told us where that was. While we were there, hanging on to the zodiacs that were lost in the mist, I tore a page from my diary and scrawled a note. I reached over.

'Can you send this, or call by radio to Nick Cox in Ny Ålesund, Nick Cox.' I pointed to his name.

The coxswain looked at the paper, read it, smiled and nodded. Then he stuffed the page into a zip pocket. After we'd said our good-byes and good lucks and gone our separate ways in the fog, they found their ship – because the message reached Nick: 'Hi, we are OK. A bear woke us up this morning at Rekvik hytte. Love and hugs to everybody – Peter and Shaggy. 80° N.'

12

Most desolate place

Despite the many thousand oar strokes and running with the sail, the beaches and the pack ice, the whale, the walrus and this morning's polar bear, we were little more than a quarter of the way around the island. The bear had shaken us both and we moved more carefully now, any bravado was gone. We were very aware, very alive. There were more colours in the mist.

My grip on the rough wood of the oars was warm, my blisters were hard and the sinews in my fingers curled around the handles in an easy way.

The long sleep had done my wrist good, and we pulled carefully through the fog following the compass needle. The two zodiacs had disappeared into the mist, searching for their mother ship. There would be light below decks, polished brass and clean lino, the smell of floor polish, and fresh coffee in the galley. Despite this I was happy without a mother ship, on our way around, with a long way to go and no way back. Hinlopen Strait was free of ice. That was great news, and we had to make it through while we could.

The waves rocked us as we left the shelter of the drifting pack.

'That bear, how close do you think I was?'

'About a foot, it was amazing, you couldn't get closer.'

'Something invisible pushed me back,' he smiled.

'You just lost your nerve,' I said.

He dug deep and the boat lurched into a roll, one of my oars popped up and the other one stuck deep as I tried to pull a finish. The tendons in that elbow shot with pain.

'Not so deep,' I said.

I'd given up trying to teach Shaggy how to row distance with minimum energy, but when it hurt I had to tell him, 'Smooth and shallow,' I said. 'Try to make it smooth and shallow.'

The mist cleared for a moment. Over our shoulders the beach curved away and the rocks of the northern peninsula were starting. I couldn't see the beacon. It was difficult to navigate in the fog. It could not be far away.

'They'll be post at Kapp Lee, right?' said Shaggy.

'Small chance,' I said. The depot at Kapp Lee was three hundred and something kilometres distant and we were looking forward to it. He wanted that letter from Anna. He'd been trying to tell her something important, or maybe he'd already done that, and he didn't know if she'd understood. Or if she had understood he wanted her reply. Which way would his life go, along with Anna or apart from her? He was anxious to know.

'Just got to bring things to a head,' he said. 'It's worth rowing for.'

'They'll pick up mail in Longyear. If Anna sends it, and it doesn't get lost in Cairo, it'll be there.'

'They've got to fix that prop.'

'And if there's ice at Sørkapp, the *Waterproef* wouldn't get through. Then we end up walking out overland after all.'

'The depot'll be there, and the post,' he said. 'It has to be.'

'The depot has to be there.' I replied and pulled my neck back into the handkerchief tied inside my collar. My cheeks and neck and ears were sensitive with sunburn. That was one reason to be happy for the fog.

The beacon emerged from the mist. It stood alone, a dry timber pyramid among the rocks in swirling fog on Verlegenhuken. The cold water broke on the rocks off the point and we could navigate among them easily. We slipped into a bay beneath a rocky stack where the wind was quiet and opened the thermos flask. Steam tumbled from the mouth of it, and the tea scalded and put heat in my chest. I stood up and shook my arms and the blood rushed in my ribs and shoulders while Shaggy paddled forward and back to keep us steady in the bay.

'What a fuck-off lonely beacon,' said Shaggy.

'Eighty degrees and zero-four minutes north.' I was looking at the chart and measuring its position against the graduated scale of latitude.

'Off the end of most world maps,' he said, and I concurred.

'On the way home now.'

* * *

Something had moved inside me. Perhaps it was the bear that morning, the tourists in the mist, perhaps the forty kilometres of fjord, or our manoeuvres in sea ice – there was something different and now I wanted to go home. I wanted to go the long way, around the island, but more important was that I wanted to go home.

Through that long row up to the beacon I had been anticipating the relief of turning and hoisting the sails. After the rowing, sailing was always a gift because the kilometres came for free. But now each time we paddled around the next rocky stack the wind veered to the east and did not fill our sails.

We rowed north again, off the end of Spitsbergen, trying to make it to windward so we could hoist our sails and have kilometres for free. We rowed and rowed and then hoisted the sails.

The wind barely filled them and we ghosted across the gravel banks as the coast turned away southwards. A spit ran out into the sea. We clawed into the wind to clear it and ran aground. The sails pushed us onto the bank and the light swell knocked us up and down on the stones. I swore, let the mainsheet fly and grabbed an oar. Shaggy leapt overboard. The water was shallow and it should not have come over his boots, but he landed in a bank of quick sand and sank up to his thigh. I winced for him. My feet were as cold as they could be. Jumping into the water like that was stupid or brave, and if he pushed us off again then I was happy to call it brave.

With the sails flapping and me punting and Shaggy

pushing we inched around that headland, bumping on the sand and gravel, floating free then bumping again. The beach shelved away and *Kotick* came free, and Shaggy leaned forwards into the boat. Water dripped into the sea and then into the boat as he tumbled in. I doused the sails, packed them in bags and picked up my oars. The wind was no good.

'Downhill all the way!' he said, trying to bury the pain of his cold feet in a joke. I didn't think that I could have done the same. His trousers were drenched and he pulled off his boots. I paddled along the beach with the fluky breeze on our beam and Shaggy dried his feet and trousers. My feet were too cold and I couldn't imagine his. I imagined all the things I might give for a pair of warm dry mukluks: not *Kotick*, not the food, not the rifle, but almost anything else. I'd give double the money we'd decided that we didn't have when we saw the boots for sale in Longyearbyen.

'How are your feet?' I asked, breaking our pact of silence on them.

'Almost SNAFU,' he said, meaning situation normal, absolutely frozen up. I rowed some more. His must be really bad.

'These feet stay cold like nothing on earth,' he said, angry. 'When I get home I'm going to use them for keeping my beer cold.'

He picked up his oars and joined my rhythm.

'The fifth law of thermodynamics,' Shaggy said, taking a stroke. 'On the same day in the same conditions in the same clothes,' he took another stroke, 'it is always five degrees colder in a boat than on the beach.'

'Amen,' I said.

The sun came out of the mist, no more than a silver disc, and its warmth was lost in the fog. Blue sky tantalised us and I could not be sure it was there. More ice came into view, two hundred metres out. Was the mist lifting? It was difficult to tell. Which way was south? I sensed this light grey blanket cleared just above us, but it may as well have gone up forever for the distance we could see. An ice floe with two walrus grew into sight. They were quiet and still, disconsolate sunbathers on the drift ice piled up against the beach. We could not land because of it. What if our way was blocked by as much ice as before? The prospect of fog and closed pack turned my belly to ice, just like before. What if there was a bear just beyond? He would smell us long before we could see him. There was drift ice between us and the beach.

It was long past lunchtime and the thermos flask was empty. By now we would usually stop and walk around, fire up the cooker and drink hot soup, then refill the thermos ready for another long row. But we couldn't reach the beach thanks to the drift ice piled up on it. A breeze had settled into the northeast and so we ghosted along. It was silent and grey. Was that a ghost ship, the *Flying Dutchman*? No, it was an iceberg in the mist. I was hungry and Shaggy was cold.

'Right, d'you fancy a hot drink?' exclaimed Shaggy.

'Would love one,' I said, 'but we can't beach.'

'If I'm careful, I can make one here. I've got a chain so I can hang the cooker from an oar.'

'Uh-huh? Don't spill any. Fuel, I mean, seriously Shags, if we burn the boat it's over.'

'That makes the challenge more interesting. D'you want tea or soup?'

'Soup, just don't burn the boat,' I said.

'It'll be OK, it'll be fun to try,' he said and I watched him over my shoulder with tight lips as he hung the stove, heated the fuel line and pumped for pressure to vaporise the white naphtha. He was right, it was fun. The cooker made heat and the soup warmed me from the inside.

Shaggy filled the thermos with tea, and as the wind was quiet he took the oars again. It was satisfying to be self-sufficient at sea.

'All we need to do is learn how to use the bucket and we'll have ocean-going capacity,' I said, relishing the freedom to travel in open water. The shallow water near to land with its rocks and people made for complications. In open water life was simple and you could be alone with whichever God you believed in.

* * *

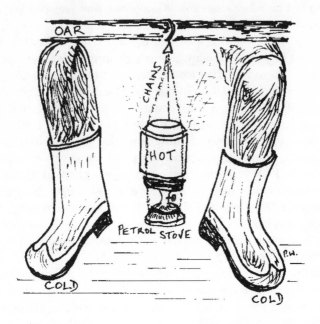

Cooking at sea

After many hours the heat from my rowing muscles reached my face and we pulled on towards the depot at Kapp Lee, pulling for food, for post, for human warmth, and pulling for distant home. The map told me that we were near the mouth of the next fjord and five kilometres of open water.

'Guess we better stop then,' said Shaggy, disappointed and frightened by the fog. If we could cross Sorgfjorden then there would be a feeling of progress, despite the frustrating day with poor visibility and fluky wind. But it would not be easy.

'We could try if you want. I can go by the compass,' I said, 'but you've gotta follow me.'

Shaggy looked all around, and watched as we drifted gently along the pebble beach littered with slabs of ice. He looked out into the mist.

'Five kilometres? Yeah, let's try,' he said.

I took the compass and set it on the line that the map told me I needed to follow. We paddled out into the grey space ahead and beyond the warm wood and dampness on the ropes and barrels in *Kotick* there was only the grey water and the grey mist. As the hard grey stones of the island faded away we were swept south by the tide and I had to aim off to hold the line. I checked the bearing that compensated exactly for the tide. If we kept this speed all the way across, then we should be OK. The beach disappeared and I leaned forward to twist the compass dial to account for the tide.

My world shrank to the plastic dial with the red and black needle swinging to and fro.

'Left oar, there, one more, not so much,' I called. I watched the minute hand creep around my watch face. We should see the far side in fifty minutes. I told myself to hold this course for sixty. Nothing was more important than my faith in that compass needle, the offset for the tide, and that we should follow it together, for the full sixty minutes. And that we not doubt ourselves or waver before that.

'Gives me the creeps, are you sure this is right?' The fog was spinning around us, it seemed we were turning and turning but the needle was steady, rocking with *Kotick*, in line with the marker lines on the compass face.

'Left one, hold it Shaggy, you've gotta trust me.'

The fog grew in towards us. I hated the claustrophobia and the feeling of being lost. If we disappeared nobody would know. It would not have surprised me if we were the ghost ship I'd just seen. The one that was following just out of sight. Gino Watkins would have managed this, and John Cooper, they were out there in the mist. Be good, be calm, there was a voice out there, be good and you'll be OK. I wanted to be good, I wanted to be OK. I wanted to get home again. I wanted to play John's music from Belfast on my amber violin. The compass needle rocked in its alcohol.

Out there to the south, with those ghosts in the fog, was the safe anchorage of Hecla Cove.[33] Twenty years before, Tilman in his pilot cutter met Brian Harland in *Salterella* and another cabin cruiser. And years before that Parry anchored HMS *Hecla*, in preparation for his 1827 expedition to the Pole.

---

[33] Heclahamna.

He shot seventy reindeer and three bears, which would have been plenty of food for the Pole team of twenty-two. But his bid was defeated by miles of open and broken sea ice, and a strong southerly drift. When he realised their goal was untenable they turned back to travel with the drift, leaving a furthest north record that would stand for forty-eight years.[34]

A grey form fluttered in the mist, long neck thrust forward and arching downwards, wings beating the wet air, grey head and darker brown behind, on its breast a flash of russet, or blood red? My heart was thumping and I could see the flash of red-brown there in the mist despite the distance. It veered towards us then away. The croak, croak of it reached us as if from another world and another time. It made me sad to see it cackle on its way.

'Red-throated diver,' I said. 'Not many people see that.'

'Cool,' said Shaggy. 'There's life out there after all.'

Then a beach came out of the mist, quite close.

'Well done Pete, I didn't think you'd do that,' he said.

I smiled and felt tingling. I thanked the compass. The ghosts had gone.

We rounded the headland and the tide started to run with us, then a headwind started, fresh off the Nordaustland ice cap. It was just a breeze with enough to resist our blades but it cut and cracked my neck with astonishing cold.

I turned my head against it. Why was I here? To be different, to be special, to make my name, what rubbish. The whiplash of that glacial breeze cracked across *Kotick*, shooting us through with an electric jolt. I can't go on. I want nothing more than to be safe.

The beach on this side was free of ice, and the bow crunched in the stones. I was unsteady on my feet. Shaggy wobbled as he carried the bags and barrels up the beach. I wobbled too and tried to hide it. We lifted *Kotick* and pitched the tent then dived inside and fired the cooker and the warmth came back to my face. Shaggy measured the distance.

'Only thirty-five K today,' he said. That was not good enough.

---

[34] 82° 45′ N, 700 kilometres short of the Pole.

'That's about the same as crossing the channel,' he said. That made it feel better.

'Not bad for a seventeen-foot rowboat,' I said.

'We've got to do that, every day from now, to make the depot.'

We both knew.

While I set the bear flares Shaggy checked the rifle. Our close encounter at Rekvik had made us vigilant and we practised with the rifle again. There was plenty to shoot at: buoys, bottles, rope, wooden crates and shoes. Looking at this beach in the middle of nowhere on top of the world one could only conclude that sailors spend their whole lives throwing rubbish overboard. I snapped the bolt down with a round in the breech. I closed my right eye and the rifle cracked and kicked in my cheek. A buoy far down the beach jumped and rolled to a new place.

Shaggy tried to cheer the tent up by putting on the walkman but it was so cold all the batteries ran slow. He tried swapping them and warming them but it was no use, John Travolta sounded terrible. He gave up. Even beef stew and dumplings did nothing to warm us.

He ticked off the new animals, the bear and the diver, then I tried to write my diary but it was too cold. I wrote one sentence then fell asleep hoping that my feet would warm up. My diary remained open at the same page.

'This is the wildest most desolate place I have ever been to.'

13

Hinlopen Strait

Hinlopen Strait is exposed to strong winds of gale
force which largely blow northwards or southwards
through the sound and bring mist. Pack ice can be
troublesome. The sound has been navigated by
whaling and exploration ships but there has been no
systematic surveying and the greatest possible care
must be taken when navigating these waters.

Norwegian Polar Institute *Arctic Pilot*

The deep cold was there in my feet when I woke up. Most
nights they recovered some warmth with the hours in
dry socks and tent boots. But not this time. The invasive
cold that cut with the wind and seeped up from the stones
chilled the end of my sleeping bag. It was like a deep freeze
down there. Should I take my feet outside and pound up
and down the beach, crashing the blood back into them?
No, I tried to sleep again.

The progress was good – the forty-kilometre fjord, the
ice bear, crossing Sorgfjorden in the fog. Next it was
Hinlopen, with its many stories and warnings. It was still
the best part of three hundred kilometres to Kapp Lee. That
was a quantity of kilometres in water that I did not know,
and it would be further if my feet stayed cold like this. Of
course they should be cold, whoever heard of warm feet in a
small boat at eighty degrees north? How good that we are

going south again, it's quite something that we are going south again. I wonder if all of this will turn my life.

Sleep had left me, so I pulled out my expedition book. I'd hardly touched it since the idle hours in Fairhaven. What next for the fellowship of the ring? When Shaggy stirred he cracked open the next chart. I closed my book and we followed the western coast of Hinlopen with our eyes.

There were kilometres of cliff, both ice and rock. It was difficult to know how far from the cliffs we should go. Their cold and their size fascinated me and I wanted to be close, but if they fell, if an iceberg calved, then even if we survived the tumbling ice a mini-tsunami would swamp the boat. I didn't want to die like Gino Watkins. I didn't want to leave the unpacking of my rucksack to my mother in England. After porridge we stomped around with blocks of ice for feet and loaded the boat. Then we paddled south into the wind.

It was a difficult wind to row into and nearly as cold as the night before. I looked to the Norwegian girl with the copper bob and then the girl back home. This was so much journey, so much adventure, goodness it was hard. I didn't think we'd make it without some extra luck. Then a wonderful thing happened. The wind died and within hours the water became glass.

The ice cliffs of the Valhalla snowfield[35] towered above us and lay a second time, upside down, on the water. They were alive with the noise of falling rocks, and waterfalls tumbled from the cracks. Layers of moraine made the white giant dirty and the cold brushed our faces in glacial puffs. We paddled too close and then further away, afraid of waking this sleeping giant, wanting to see an iceberg fall but not from close. We tiptoed past and the ice did not fall. It was ten kilometres to the next beach of grit and moraine.

After two hours we stopped and drifted among the broken bergs from the Ny Friesland ice cap. The sun was hot now and our shirts were off. We put on sun-cream but our faces were

---

[35] The Norwegian name is Valhallfonna, after the dwelling place of the gods in Norse mythology.

cracked with sunburn. It seemed that we were too small to talk and our feet were cold like before. I rolled two cigarettes and Shaggy poured out tea, I opened a pack of Garibaldis and we called it elevenses. Then we rowed two hours more.

At lunch we drifted far out in Hinlopen. There were no ships, just birds and the high clouds reflected in the water. We drifted in circles and ate 'biscuits brown' with meat spread, drank bottles of water, and finished the meal with Rolos.

'How long d'you think this'll last?' We could not believe it.

'Don't know, but we've got to go make the most of it,' I said.

We set to the oars again. There were more cliffs. Acres and acres of sheer rock streaked with guano, and many thousands of guillemots wheeled and screeched along the pink ledges where they were nesting. The air was alive with the sound and the smell of bad fish. The reflections in the water were just as beautiful as the rock cliff and the ice cliff but there were no beaches.

Valhalla ice cliffs and Kotick

With the hours, rowing became as natural as walking and we were becoming accustomed to each other's different stride. We kept ourselves going in different ways. Shaggy went for goals, for numbers, for landmarks and for Anna. If I went for these many different goals then I rushed and tired too fast. The goal was always further away than my optimism expected it. So instead I focused on a level of exertion I could maintain, and I rowed within it, pushing that level but never breaking it, whatever the short-term goal. I treated each hour like the first lap of a middle-distance track race, pushing hard but within myself for fear of losing my strength too early.

While Shaggy drove for his goals I settled into daydreams, of the girl in Norway and the one back home, of my fiddle in England and the ghosts of John and Gino. Shaggy was groaning and counting. I told him to settle but he had no ears for that and he started counting again. He wanted another thousand. There was a fulmar skimming the water with sickle wings that were reflected in the water. Together with the reflection the wings made a perfect circle.

Chocolate was a friend that helped us cover the distance because we both agreed that looking forward to chocolate is a Good Thing.

'Right, bar of chocolate in an hour's time.'

'Sounds good to me. Which one?'

'Marathon, hmmm, no, that Dairy Milk, with nuts and raisins,' he'd say.

So we settled into our strokes, the water swirling where we flicked the blades from the surface, and the whirlpools of the puddles turning in the wake. We were good at holding a straight line, we'd pick a spot on the horizon in front of us, I swung the bow through the line and Shaggy would call –

'There!'

I'd blink and take a snapshot of the flag pole and the clouds behind and then Shaggy would look too and we'd keep that line, all the time thinking of Dairy Milk. That was his goal for the hour, and the thought of chocolate made my daydreams sweeter. I put the chocolate in the sun so the ice in it melted. As chocolate time grew closer my anticipation grew sweeter. Shortly before the hour was up one of us would say –

'I reckon I could do another fifteen minutes.'

'Nahh, twenty-five, easy.'

'Twenty?'

'Twenty.'

Then when the hour and twenty was almost up, we'd push the time out some more, extending the joy of anticipation further still. The game had no logic and it was a little annoying, but each chocolate bar took us further than an hour. And it gave us conversation and the talking helped. When we finally cracked the lumps of Diary Milk and felt the cocoa fat between our teeth and cheeks it was bliss. Then the sugar would reach my blood and my muscles would buzz.

Twelve hours out and there was still no beach.

'How long will it hold?'

'Let's keep going.'

I paddled slower and Shaggy dug out his cooker and flashed it into flame. He brewed soup then tea for the thermos and in the hot water he put two foil bags of chicken and mushroom pasta. While I drank my soup and spiced the pasta with garlic salt he paddled on alone. In this way we continued slowly southwards, eating supper in relays. Then I rolled two cigarettes and stitched a glove. The sun was in the north and it was cooler than before.

Shaggy pulled out his sleeping bag and curled up in the bow while I paddled like before until the wind came. The wind came with us and so I moved him to put up the mast and set a course for an island far out in the middle of the sound. He slept and when he woke we were in the lee of the island. I climbed into his sleeping bag and the wind pushed us south. The wind gave us kilometres for free and my feet warmed up in his down bag. The last time they'd been warm was the night before the polar bear.

Twenty-nine hours from the Most Desolate Beach the sailing wind died and tongues of drift ice reached across the horizon. There were many small islands and the mainland of Spitsbergen was far away on the starboard side. The islands were no more than igneous lumps and the snowdrifts clung to them all the way to the waterline. We came to a snow ramp and I stepped up onto it. It was a lift to take everything onto the rocks, and then we lifted *Kotick* out too. Ever since the storm damage in Ny Ålesund we had always lifted her high out onto safe ground. I tied the painter around a boulder that would never move.

We were tired, cold again, isolated and absolutely completely alone. If the weather trapped us here then nobody would find us inside the short time our food would last. And there would be little hope of hunting animals on such a small outcrop. There was nothing, it was inaccessible, except maybe a Ross's gull? But we didn't see one. After supper I was nearly as hungry as I had been before, I tried to think of something to say.

'In a funny way this is the happiest I've ever been,' I said and realised my lie. I'd been happier one week earlier, fighting through drift ice, when the journey was still impossible. Now that I could see a way through the magic had come out of this dream.

* * *

After a long sleep we made coffee and surveyed the horizon ahead of us with binoculars. The mountains above Kapp Payer wore their glaciers like shawls, and the white of the ice cap stretched into the white of the sea which reached across the horizon ahead of us. There couldn't be bad ice here as well, but there was. It reached across the horizon. How could we possibly cut through that quantity of ice? I tried to imagine how we might get our equipment onto the glacier. My chest settled as I breathed, and I pushed my lips forwards.

'But look, on the horizon,' said Shaggy. He had the binoculars pressed to his eyebrows. 'It's free!' he said, and I took them.

Far beyond the white of the pack ice a thin filament of aquamarine lay on the horizon below the grey-blue sky. I tracked left and it joined the open water between us and Siberia. The deep water was free. It was fifteen kilometres to reach it, but the deep water was open and it was free. We celebrated with hot chocolate and prepared to leave.

The ice foot below *Kotick*, the one we had landed on twelve hours before, had broken and gone. This shocked me and I thanked God that we'd hauled her high among the rocks. It would have been easy to leave her lying on that ice foot. To the near horizon there was no ice in the water. The ice foot had floated far out of sight. Shaggy and I lowered her into the water and packed with great care. We hardly spoke, thinking, what would have happened if *Kotick* had broken away with the ice.

A shine of six-sided crystals lay on the black water because the air was freezing it. The new ice flexed and we broke it easily. It crackled as we broke it and it held us back, but hardly at all. It made the smallest resistance. We sped over the flat water in silence, already many hours out, and Shaggy was asleep again. My oars creaked in the rowlock posts and the crystals of fresh ice crackled under the bow.

A harp seal bobbed to the surface, he was right in our line. We were far out in open water and he was looking away. My stroke was a strong one and I watched him as we glided; he didn't look round. Behind you! I thought but did not say it. Then he saw, and before he dived beneath the gliding cutwater I saw quite clearly the comical panic in his eye.

At this time we were one or two kilometres from the coast and there, far away, the shore line drew back into what looked like a bay. From the map it was the channel between Spitsbergen and Barents Island, a short cut to Storfjorden called Heleysundet but I didn't want to go there because of its other name, 'Hell Sound', and because of the *Arctic Pilot*'s warning: 'In the narrowest part the tidal stream runs at nine knots. It has happened now and then that whalers have been crushed in the ice. There are no slack periods at the change of stream.' We lay those few kilometres off and I looked into the narrow sound. It was tempting to try, and it would be great if that strong tide was with us. But I didn't know the tide times, and even a favourable current might break us. So we continued south.

Far away on the beach there was a bear patrolling southwards too.

It was my turn to sleep. I woke Shaggy and showed him the bear. Then I slept.

* * *

'Pete, Pete, there's a bear!' Shaggy was shouting at me. 'Look, look, it's close, it's close!'

The water was swirling around his blades and I pushed my sleeping bag down. We were far out to sea. He was backing the oars and then pulling one and pushing the other. The bear was behind us now and he took one oar stroke.

The bear was swimming away.

'Quick, the camera, grab the camera!' Shaggy was urgent.

I pushed down the sleeping bag and pulled on my boots. I didn't want to do anything without my boots. Then the camera was in my hands and the bear was far away. Shaggy pushed and pulled opposite oars to spin the boat again and then pulled them together. Now he was paddling after the bear. I was in the bow with my camera. The walkman speakers were out and a song was playing.

'You're the one that I want, ooh, ooh, ooh,' sang John Travolta.

'Give me the rifle,' I said. I clicked the shutter. Shaggy pulled, and I was surprised that he wanted to row so fast after the bear.

'You're the one that I want, ooh, ooh, ooh,

The one I need, oh yes indeed ...'

The bear was fast and Shaggy pulled hard. Slowly we gained. The speed of his swimming surprised me. The bear filled my zoom lens and I clicked the shutter. The exposure was way too long.

'A bit closer,' I said. I clicked the shutter and suddenly we were very close, what happened if he turned and came? It would take too long to spin the boat. I didn't like being so close.

'OK Shags, that's enough, easy now.'

Shaggy stopped stroking. He touched the blades on the water and the surface broke up like a sunlit dish smashing into glass pieces. The song finished and the bear swam off, keeping its extraordinary speed, off and out to sea. Where was he going? There was no drift ice on the horizon. The next land was Siberia. It was one powerful bear.

* * *

By now we knew the sea and it spoke to us. When a fast swell came in smooth water we knew there was a distant storm. If there was a short chop on a headland then we knew the tide was tumbling over shallow ground. If there was a cross-swell it told us the wind was about to change. Each wave rocked *Kotick* in a different way and the sea talking reassured me.

We were drifting at rest and Shaggy was dangling his petrol cooker from an oar, heating stew in two foil bags.

'Hey, look at the water,' I said, 'something's different.'

A cross-ripple rocked the boat and slapped the small icebergs in the water nearby. I tried to tell what would happen. *Kotick* pitched in a different way and I could think of no explanation for the waves coming in many directions.

Then a smooth ivory back broke the water, arched and disappeared, and another smooth and wet, and then while the cooking pot was steaming, a school of white whales surrounded us: ten, twenty, thirty belugas arching, blowing spray into the air. We were all going south together and three white backs came up close to us. They arched and sank, arched and sank. One came up higher than the others, then it arched and sank.

'Are we looking at them, or are they looking at us?'

* * *

We turned into Freemansundet, and the mountains of Barents Island and Edge Island climbed away from either shore. We stayed close to the north side. There was a ship in the distance. She came and she came and it was the *Lance*, the Norwegian Polar Institute supply ship with the bridge as big as a boatshed, the one that Nick had taken me onto in Ny Ålesund.

I picked up the VHF handset and clicked to sixteen.

'Hello *Lance, Lance, Lance,* this is *Kotick, Kotick, Kotick,* over.'

My call was long, slow and measured because they would not be expecting us. There was silence, then my set crackled to life.

'Hzzz, click, hsszzzz, station calling *Lance,* this is *Lance,* over.'

'*Lance, Lance, Lance* this is *Kotick, Kotick,* over.'

'Station calling *Lance, Lance,* did not copy, come again, over.'

'*Lance* this is *Kotick.* That's Kilo, Oscar, Tango, India, Charlie, Kilo, *Kotick.* Very small boat on your port beam, over.'

'Hey, you didn't have to say Very Small Boat like that!' Shaggy cut in.

I imagined Norwegian binoculars in the bridge the size of a boatshed, turning towards us, to above us and then down and down, we were really very close. They saw us.

'Ahh, hello *Kopeck,* I see you now, I see you now.'

'It's *Kotick.* Please tell Nick Cox in Ny Ålesund …'

They promised they would. They were laughing when they signed off and the bow butted into the low chop sweeping in from Siberia, out towards Hinlopen.

'Nearly there,' said Shaggy. He'd aimed for Kapp Lee.

The hut was further.

'Bit further,' I said.

'Are you sure?' The map had deceived him. He'd already given everything. 'It can't be. How can they get that wrong? Bloody idiots can't make a map.' He was angry, and that surprised me.

I turned to the pulling again and listened to the silence behind me. It was black and sullen with an occasional sigh. I was happy for the last hour. It had been thirty-four hours since we'd camped on the inaccessible island in Hinlopen Strait and the progress had been good.

Unfortunately as we pulled into the open water of Storfjorden[36] a chop came up. Each wave tugged the blades in an uncomfortable way. Shaggy dug deep with his blades but

---

[36] The Great Fjord.

his heart was not there. He wanted the end, he'd counted on it, and this was too far. For him the last hour was a bleak one.

* * *

The hut was locked so we put up the bear fence and unrolled our bags. We fired both cookers and ate beef stew and dumplings followed by chicken and mushroom pasta loaded with paprika. We drank the whisky and took chocolate from the black bag. The food barrel was not here but it should arrive any day now. I could not remember the date the *Waterproef* was due, and anyway we were unsure of today's date. They could not be more than a few days away. We would work the details out tomorrow.

Meanwhile Shaggy took out the charts and the magic string. He measured our two days' run from the most desolate beach: one hundred and thirty-three kilometres in twenty-nine hours to the island in Hinlopen, and one hundred and thirty-eight kilometres in the thirty-five hours just gone. The numbers were nothing but the distances were vast, for a rowboat. We'd made it to the barrel. Hinlopen was behind us. We were more than halfway around the island and I started thinking about full success again. What would it look like? It really seemed that we might find out.

Our campsite was out of the wind and we slept with smiles. When the *Waterproef* arrived there would be food, whisky for sale and, Shaggy's hope against hope, post.

14

MS *Waterproef* and the post bag

The hills behind the Dutch hut at Kapp Lee on Edge Island caught the afternoon sun and sheltered us from the wind. The warm light fell on our bags and for twelve hours we slept. My feet came warm. It was a relief that the sensation was returning after so long.

'So, when does the *Waterproef* get here?' Shaggy was awake. He was making coffee. I rolled over and I sorted through the charts and papers that had been tucked inside the dry barrel, looking for the *Waterproef*'s long-cast.

'Not sure, what date did we say it was?' I replied.

It was three o'clock and the sun was in the south, but I still didn't know the day. I tried calling the *Waterproef* on VHF channel sixteen. There was no reply. That's what I expected.

'I reckon there'll be post,' I said.

The Dutch hut was a couple of hundred metres away, and the door swung open. A man came out. He looked up, then sat on a crate and looked down at a box in his hands. He stayed there looking down with the box in his lap and his hands working in it.

'They're back,' I said. 'Let's say hello.'

'Let's have breakfast first.' Shaggy had planned what we would have.

'They might give us breakfast.' I was indifferent, and sick of soft food.

'No, let's have breakfast and then go. It's nearly ready.'

The flames of the cooker were growling and the steam was

blowing out from under the lid of the cooking pot. It was bumping with the boiling of the water. The man on the crate stood up and went back inside.

We took the foil bags of corned beef hash from the cooking pot and tore them open .

'Best that ship comes in, we've only got two of these left.' I said.

* * *

A Swedish geologist and his local field guide Heinrich were spending the summer season in the Dutch hut at Kapp Lee. Our arrival had surprised them. It was not every morning that two seal-shaped forms appeared on the beach. We knocked on their door.

'Hi, I'm Peter and this is Shaggy, we're rowing around the island.'

'Where from?' said Heinrich. He had disturbingly blue eyes.

'From Isfjord Radio, by the north,' I told him.

'We left Ny Ålesund two weeks ago.'

'In that?' said the Swedish geologist.

'How did you make the journey so quickly?' Heinrich was curious.

'The weather was good, we didn't have enough food. We had to rush.' I said, not expecting him to understand.

They invited us to supper and then Heinrich surprised us by offering polar bear. He explained it had climbed on the tent of a nearby field party. The geologist inside shouted, trying to scare the bear off, and when the bear did not move off he aimed his revolver between the two paws weighing on the canvas. He fired through the tent wall and caught the bear in a soft gap between his ribs. There was blood and a struggle and the bear died a short distance away. The geologist washed and repaired his tent.

They called the Governor because bears are protected: you can only shoot in self-defence. The environmental police came in a helicopter and checked the shooting was legitimate, and they checked the sex of the bear. They took the skin and left the carcass. The field party wanted the meat, and discussed the merits of bolognaise sauce versus chilli with beans. Heinrich chose the Mexican option and when we arrived for supper he was stirring his cooking pot.

'Would you like ein hot toddy?' said the Swedish geologist, and he told us he'd seen mast heads to the south, quite possibly the *Waterproef.*

Heinrich was cooking with care because polar bear is difficult. It's at the top of the food chain so the muscles are peppered with the muscle-wasting *Trichinella* larvae. It's also famously rich in vitamin A: a crew of whalers stranded on Spitsbergen in 1631 suffered an overdose when they ate the liver. According to the account 'they were all attacked with a kind of eruptive fever and their skin peeled off'. I was keen to avoid that.

Heinrich knew all of these things. He'd already cut away the liver and simmered the meat for nearly an hour.

'Chilli con Ice Bear!' he said when he put it on the table. The meat was sweet and tender like veal and a little strong like game. The beans and rice were good. It had been a long time since we'd had food we could chew properly, and to chew and cut with our teeth for the first time in weeks was a relief. All the garlic pepper in the world was no substitute for fresh food that you could chew. They had red wine.

It was not the first time that Heinrich had used his cooking pot to sort out a polar bear, and over supper he told us about the time the front page of the Svalbard newspaper had proclaimed, 'Schoolboy Knocks out Ice Bear with Frying Pan'.

'I was up at Texas Bar Hut, on the north of the island, early in the year.'

'How old were you?' I wanted to know.

'Fifteen, the hut was full of snow, I was with a friend. We dug it out and went to sleep. When I woke up the window was open, there was a bear and cub right there by me. They were sniffing the window sill. I grabbed the first thing that came, a cooking pot. I tapped it on the windowsill, tap, tap, tap and the two bears ran away.'

'Yes, so why the newspaper story?' The geologist asked. He was laughing. He'd heard the story before.

'On my way home I stopped by Harald, he's the trapper at Kapp Vik, I told him the story. He gave me food, he was drinking Cognac, by the time I left he was singing. When I left he called Longyear to tell them I was coming. When I arrived they were all waiting. The newspaper had my story with the headline – Schoolboy Knocks out Bear with Frying Pan. I couldn't believe it.

'I told them the bears were outside not inside, I told them it was just my camping pot. But they preferred Harald's version, that I fought the bear with a huge copper frying pan and knocked it down.

'There's a stuffed bear in the museum. They gave me a frying pan, sat me on it, I held the frying pan up. That was the picture that went with the story. But everybody knew the real story, that Harald was drunk. Would you like some Cognac?'

'Yes, please.'

It was warm in there and so was the Cognac. The stories continued for hours and we provided some of our own.

* * *

When I woke up there was a paper sign taped onto our polar bear trip wire. It said 'Please Feed the Animals'. There was a figure in the Dutch hut watching us with binoculars. He waved – it was Heinrich – and down on the beach there was a huddle of people in colourful anoraks herded by a guide with a rifle. They came towards us and some of the tourists bent forward to read the sign. One tourist tapped his jacket and pulled out some mints, he offered me one and they all smiled. The MS *Waterproef* lay at anchor a short way off the beach. I smiled and took the mint.

The tour guide came. I recognised him from before.

'Here, this is for you.' He was holding out a bundle of envelopes. There was a blue one postmarked Cairo and a brown, padded one from England.

174

'Rudolph says, would you like to come to the ship? We can take you in about an hour.'

'Yes, definitely, would love to,' I said.

'You can have a shower if you want, and bring your laundry.'

'Thanks, that would be great.'

On the beach at Kapp Lee

The land party moved off and we opened our post. The brown envelope had spare parts for my cooker. The blue envelope was from Anna. There were some others, and we withdrew into our own worlds, the ones that we would be returning to, and we re-read the best parts.

There was still a long way, back to where the letters were coming from, but from here it would be different. I knew we could make the distance, and work in ice, there would be plenty of food, and the quickest way home was around the island, so Shaggy would be with me. All of these things would take us onwards. I was looking forward to that. But what would I be telling them, the letter writers? That this journey was big news? It did not feel that way. That we were making history? It was small history at best. That we had come through impossible ice, rowed unthinkable kilometres and been close to a young ice bear? That might be interesting.

Shaggy finished reading.

'Well?' I was looking at him.

'It's OK,' he said. 'She feels it.'

'What do you mean?' I said.

'Let's just say it's good news.' He was smiling and didn't talk more.

Shortly before we left Shaggy asked if he could borrow the seats out of *Kotick*. He'd been eyeing the power of the zodiac's outboard engines.

'Could you take me for a water-ski?' he asked the Dutch boatman.

'If that's what you want.' The boatman was surprised.

Shaggy lashed his trainers to the two wooden seats. He pulled on a dry suit and tied a good-sized rope to the zodiac. I loaded all of our wash gear and dirty clothes into the zodiac and climbed on board.

'OK,' he waved from the water. When the boatman eased the throttle forwards Shaggy came up in a curtain of spray. Imagine the surprise of the tourists. The coxswain made one circuit of the ship and then went alongside. Shaggy swam to the ladder and we picked up his skis.

On the *Waterproef* it was warm, there was the smell of polish and the brass was shiny, the water was hot and there was cake in the galley. For the first time in weeks the blood ran as normal in our feet and they burned white-hot like coal. It was real pain.

'It's the lactic acid,' said the doctor. It seemed unjust.

Rudolph was there and we sat and talked. It had been a good summer except for the ice on the north coast; Heleen had gone home early; the ship's propeller was not as badly damaged as they had feared, and a diver had checked the shaft bearings in Longyearbyen.

Rudolph was the first officer now because the last one quit and he was building his log book so he could move up to larger ships. They'd seen dolphins near Aberdeen.

'When you see dolphins, whatever else happens, it's been a good day,' said Rudolph. We didn't see dolphins that day, but it was a good one for us.

'Sleep if you want,' he said, and that's what we did. There was dry linen on the bunks and the pillows were soft.

Then, with clean clothes, a full food barrel, a new bottle of whisky, and with our post stamped for abroad, we put on warm clothes and returned to the beach. The Dutch boatmen helped lift *Kotick* and watched us pack our equipment. Shaggy put the seats back in.

The wind was blowing gently offshore, straight for the main island that lay low on the horizon, sixty kilometres distant. The weather was good for travelling so we were bound to go. My feet were still burning with fresh circulation and I waited for the cold with anticipation, looking forward to the relief that must come.

It was time.

15

Distance run

If you can fill the unforgiving minute
With sixty seconds' worth of distance run –

From 'If', by Rudyard Kipling

Shaggy climbed into *Kotick* and sat with two oars to steady her in the shallow water. Rudolph, Heinrich and the Dutch boatmen were standing by with their cameras. I stepped into the waves to push her off and welcomed the metallic cold of the glacial water pressing on the outside of my waterproof boots because it calmed the deep burning of the acid in my feet. With relief I pushed a little further.

Kotick stuck on a gravel ridge. I pushed, paused, caught the breath in my lungs and pushed again. The water was at the lip of my boots. It needed one more but the water rushed. The cold burn of it inside my boot made me suck and pull my lips tight. I'd welcomed the cold while it was dry but to have water and absolute cold inside my boots now shocked me.

The boat eased out deeper as the water spilled over my boots. On the beach they were talking, taking photographs. I scrambled into the boat. Cold dry feet were one thing, subzero wet feet were quite another. My thickest warm socks were soaked in freezing brine. I wanted to empty my lungs with anger but instead I turned and waved, then took the rudder bar and set a course for the mainland.

The straight-line trip back to Spitsbergen was sixty

kilometres from Kapp Lee on Edge Island. We could have followed beaches and ice cliffs to the north, Shaggy would have preferred that, but it would have added another hundred kilometres and there would have been the other more complicated dangers of tides across shoal ground, more ice in the water and dangerous wildlife. So I'd chosen the open water. Rudolph had questioned this, but I'd told him *Kotick* was good enough, that we were good enough. The water washed in my boots; that did not feel good enough.

As I smiled and waved, their cameras clicked and they waved back. Inside I was bitter and angry. Wet feet at the start of a voyage like this, how could I be so stupid? Shaggy had a towel and spare socks. He gave me some coffee, then a shot of whisky. I took it in silence. Damn this dream.

'Thank goodness those socks are warm when wet,' Shaggy said. I was wringing them out. 'Warm when wet' was their advertising strap-line. It wasn't funny now. He opened a bar of rum-and-raisin chocolate that Granny had put in the top of the depot we'd received at Kapp Lee. He broke a piece off and put on a faux-Caribbean accent.

'Have some Jamaay-can rum and raisin, with that totally tropical taste.'

Finally I smiled.

* * *

The southwest wind kept *Kotick*'s small sails brimming with the breeze and her hull swung in the sea as the sun turned around the sky. Waves broke under the bow and bubbles turned in the wake. It was warm again and so were my feet. I pulled out my book. The hobbit and his friends were deep in the mines of Moria. Then I slept.

Accustomed as we were to making distance, it was easy for us to while away the time. One of us held the line straight, steering for the mountains of Spitsbergen, while the other would sleep or read. Every two hours we changed places.

After six hours the wind died. It died slowly and we sailed quietly for as long as we could, listening to the timeless roar of the ocean swell breaking on two vast tabular bergs grounded on a shallow bank. I loved that crashing, it was the oldest in the world, as old as the sea itself. Then with the drifting and waiting and listening it was clear that the wind had really died so we packed the mast away and started rowing for the coastline, still fifteen kilometres distant.

We rowed, and the swell roared on the icebergs, and I grew hot from the rowing. We'd been exposed for many hours now and it was time that we arrived at the far beach. A cool breeze turned around my neck and cat's-paws turned the smooth shoulders of the swell opaque. The air resisted my blades and the hull dragged in the water.

'Too good to last,' I said.

Kotick pitched. The climbing of each wave slowed her down and made the next stroke stiff. She rolled so our blades caught the water while we recovered to the next catch. An hour more, and freezing spray flashed in the sun and the water under the bow crashed more often. Water broke in the air and spattered my hair. It happened again, but in my ear, and it trickled under my collar. The waves came with white caps.

A good headwind came and *Kotick* pitched some more. Behind me Shaggy swore. We pulled hard. The main island of Spitsbergen was trying to shrug us into the sea. The wind kept increasing and the waves came with breaking white caps.

A headwind came

'Bastard,' said Shaggy.

'Must be twenty-five knots in the gusts,' I said. 'Pull, Shags, pull.'

'I am pulling,' he said.

It gusted twenty knots and more and *Kotick* pitched on a wave. The oars were deep in it. I heaved mine through the water, my muscles were burning. Another hour and I was tired and needed to rest.

'How about a smoko?' I said, 'I'll get the thermos.'

When I started again, when Shaggy was drinking tea and dragging on the cigarette that I'd rolled for him, then I discovered how hard he'd been pulling. The water felt like concrete on the end of my oar, and it was all I could do to force *Kotick* up the waves as they came with the wind stronger than ever. I was wet with sweat and spray and hollow with anxiety. There was a growing doubt: we might not make it; something, something has to change.

'It's no good Shags, we're not gonna make it, we've got to run.'

'Where and how? Back to Edge Island? No way ...'

'No, with the sails, we can reach into Agardhbukta.'

The bay of Agardhbukta reached out from the coast to the north of us, and it was the only shelter we could make, other than returning to Edge Island. But we wanted to go south. And we couldn't reach the coast with this wind blowing offshore. It was a depressing thing to go twenty kilometres north when we wanted to go south. But it was better than going back fifty kilometres to Edge Island or, worse, being at sea forever. This might be the start of a stronger blow.

'If that's what you want. You sure we can sail?'

The pitching of the boat made rigging the shrouds to the mast a wet thing to do, but we pinned out the mainsail with the yard and I pushed up my sleeves and ran the rudder over the stern onto its steel post. My sleeves still came up wet through.

Shaggy pulled on his right oar and the wind cracked the mainsail and filled it, the sheet pulled tight against the pulley block and I tied it off. The foam moved along the gunwale again and the water tumbled in the wake.

'Look how she's sailing!' I called. My shout was higher pitched, optimistic.

Spray crashed across the green canvas that covered the equipment tied into the bow. *Kotick* heeled to starboard and the downwind gunwale hissed with the foam. She was sailing like a keelboat, fast and into the wind. Pointing well to windward like she had never done before. She'd only managed seventy degrees in Ice Fjord, but now with twenty knots of wind she sailed like a racing keelboat. We pulled up our hoods for the spray and sat her up to windward.

'Let's put her round' I said.

'Yeah, put her round,' he called and I looked at the water to windward with the heavy gusts in mind.

'Ready about.'

I put the rudder bar down. The sails beat around us. Then they filled to bursting on the southbound tack and the waves crashed out from under the bow. It was cold. It was wet. It was frightening. But we were going south, around the island not back, in a boat that could sail to windward, with a crew that could handle her in anything. I could not ask for more.

* * *

We reached calm water in the wind shadow of the hills to the south of Inglefieldbreen. Their scree slopes tumbled down, red and brown and dirty. They were solid and earthy, enough to shelter us from the wind. We paddled to the shore but did not land because of the large boulders and because we wanted more distance. So while Shaggy continued pulling south, I unpacked my little stove and stood it on a mat on the floorboards.

I lit a fuel tablet and vaporised the paraffin. It spat and growled and I stood enough water for rolled oats and raisins upon it, then more for hot chocolate and coffee. We were twelve hours out so we started a night routine and rowed one at a time, while the other slept. Boulders were tumbling down the screes.

The bay below the hut at Kvalvågen was full of rocks. I didn't want to suffer wet feet as at Edge Island so I put on the waders and walked most of the equipment ashore while Shaggy stood off at the oars. We landed *Kotick* and it was easy to lift her out of the swell that crashed on the beach. We stood and breathed. Our feet were back on the mainland of Spitsbergen for the first time since the Most Desolate Beach all those kilometres behind.

A plaque said that the hut was built for the Dog Club by the coalminers at Svea. It was locked so we slept on the roof to be out of the way of bears. It was a flat roof with roofing felt, warm to lie on and with a good view. But it would have been easy for the bears to reach up, so we set the trip flares just the same. Then we surrendered to fatigue and slept for many hours.

* * *

The greatest of the journey was behind us. We'd come at least two-thirds of the way, we just had to keep going, keep doing what we were good at: rowing and sailing, keeping our heads, filling each unforgiving hour with sixty minutes of distance run. Then the circumnavigation would be ours.

'Downhill all the way.' Shaggy said cheerfully.

'There's still Sørkapp,' I said, sensing that we were relaxing. Sørkapp was the South Cape, the southernmost peninsula, and I was apprehensive about it. Nick had warned me about the fog and gales, the unpredictable set of the tide.

'Just pretend the coast goes straight on,' Shaggy said. I did not think that was very helpful.

After a windy start and plenty of progress southwards, the shadow of the hills killed the wind, so we took the mast down. Once we'd tied the mast down the wind started again. We waited to be sure that it would hold. We discussed what we should do and put the mast up. The wind died.

We argued, then took the mast down, and the wind came back. We decided that before erecting or dismantling the mast we would wait five minutes. I timed five minutes on my watch, the wind held, and we put the mast up again. Then the wind died.

'Unbelievable,' I said.

We left the sails hanging, we were still moving, just. Neither of us wanted to argue any more. I timed the bubbles in the water: a metre every five seconds. That was too slow. So we laid the mast down and determined to row, and only row. Of course the wind came back.

Then we set the mainsail and while one of us sat on the stern barrel like a Buddha and steered with the rudder bar, the other sat on the thwart and rowed in the lulls. Sometimes the oars beat the sail, and sometimes the sail pulled away and the oars made little help. We didn't go so fast motor-sailing like this, but we saved the time previously spent erecting and dismantling the mast and rigging. And without the debates there was more goodwill between us.

We passed a procession of glaciers calving into the sea and realised how the wind came rushing down off them. The wind was strong on their snouts and fluky-calm under the mountains between. At the end of that day's run we reached across Markhambreen, the wind driving us through the broken ice. Chips of it tapped and chocked against the hull and I stood in the bow keeping an eye for lurkers and growlers. If we'd hit one at speed it would have splintered the planks. I rocked up and down on my toes trying to make them come warm. The cold and fatigue made me wary and the ice passed us by in the water.

The wind swung around to the west and knocked up small waves that broke on the beach, and Hamberg's Bay[37] opened on the starboard side.

'That's the headland.' I pointed.

'Nahh, it's this one.' Shaggy was at the helm.

'Further,' I said, 'it's further on.'

'Look,' he pointed down at the map without looking at it, 'it's there.' He paused. 'I'm usually right.'

God how arrogant, I thought. Which one is it?

It was a mistake to think that we could beach with the sail up and the wind blowing us on. We hit the gravel and took the yard arm out of the mainsail to take the wind out of it so it

[37] The Norwegian name is Hambergbukta, after Hamberg's glacier, Nathorst (1900).

could billow like a flag. A wave lifted and dumped *Kotick*. I winced, and then a wave broke across her back.

'Quick Shags,' I shouted. Another wave broke, she was filling with water.

He pulled the canvas cover off and started piling the equipment out onto the beach. I fumbled at untying the shrouds and threw the mast down too. I grabbed the bucket and bailed the water and another breaker washed into the stern. What a shambles.

We lifted *Kotick* out of the surf, then carried her up the beach and prepared to camp for the night. I went for a walk and found the location of the hut. There was a cairn of three black rocks, the nest of two long-tailed skuas and no hut in sight. We'd both been wrong but he'd been more wrong than me. When I returned I told Shaggy what I'd found. He was dismissively cantankerous so I kept my lips tight.

We had come one hundred and seventy kilometres in the two days' run from Edge Island but that distance did not excite us. We'd done more in Hinlopen. Then we couldn't decide what to cook so we had oxtail soup and peanuts. I couldn't be bothered to write up my diary so I had whisky and a roll-up instead.

16

Here be katabatics

I opened my eyes and felt the cold on my cheeks. There was a gap in my belly. The peanuts and soup had not been enough. The clouds were quiet and grey and out at sea the long swell had died away. We'd been quarrelling the night before. It had been good up to now, but now we were bitter, uneasy with each other.

'Hey, who's gonna make breakfast?'

'Your turn.' Shaggy was awake in there. 'I made it yesterday,' I said.

'Yes, but I did lunch.' That was a fair point.

'That doesn't count,' I said, nonetheless.

'Let's spoof for it.'

'Alright then, spoof.'[38]

We both sat up in our bivvy bags and looked around for stones. I picked up three comfortable pebbles and looked at Shaggy. Taking care he couldn't see how many I held, I put one stone of my three in my fist and extended it towards him. He held out his fist against mine. He had between three and one stones in there, or he might have none.

'You call,' I said. It was better to call second. He shrugged.

'Five,' he said, trying to guess the total number of stones in both hands. He'd called high and so implied he held two or

---

[38] Spoof is a game we'd learned from the Royal Marines in Norway. It's a game of skill and chance, and more fun than spinning a coin.

three. So I should call three or four because I held just one stone, unless he was bluffing. He might be bluffing because he wanted second call in the next round. That was most likely.

'One,' I called and uncurled my fist. He did the same and my lips twitched. He held one stone, and with my one stone that was two in all. Yes, it had been a bluff, but I'd called one not two. That was unlucky. We put our hands behind our backs, shuffled the stones and then extended our fists again. We locked eyes. He smiled and I smiled too. My curled palm was empty.

'Four,' I called, playing back to him.

'One,' he said.

We opened our hands and there were none this time. He'd been right about the bluff but wrong about the number, touché. We shuffled the stones. I held three.

'Three,' he called.

'Four,' I said.

We uncurled our palms and there were just my three stones. He'd won. That was no good. How had he guessed that I'd go high? Had he read me? It had to have been luck. I swore. Anyway, what did it matter? We were smiling and had agreement on who would prepare breakfast. I unpacked my cooker and he snoozed for fifteen minutes more.

As the blue flame sputtered under the cooking pot I looked around. Here on the southeast coast the world seemed bigger, the beaches higher, the swell longer and the waves reached up the shingle beaches in long sighs despite the offshore wind. The bays were wider and the ice cliffs ran down from higher mountains far inland. Sørkapp was closer and the sea was darker blue. It was more ocean than before.

The last two days' run had been a full one hundred and seventy kilometres, so our distance was matching the scale of this place. We were up to it, and like this we would finish inside a fortnight. Then it would be over. I didn't want that yet. There was still Sørkapp. We could not relax.

'Hey, rolled oats, they're hot,' I said, kicking his bag harder than I needed to, 'and tea.'

The shape in Shaggy's bivvy bag sat up, a hand reached

out and I passed him his measuring jug full to the brim with tea.

'Ah-hah, oh yes, the King of Drinks,' said Shaggy, 'oh, yes please.'

* * *

There was a similar fluky wind but that did not frustrate us because we motor-sailed. Then the wind grew strong and steady so we shipped the oars and ran to the last spit of moraine before the eighteen kilometres of ice cliff that surrounded Isbukta, or Ice Bay. We decided to beach and wait and see what the wind would do before committing ourselves to all of that ice cliff.

Shaggy collected driftwood and I walked up onto the shingle bank to check out the snout of the glacier, which should have been a few hundred metres inland. I topped the bank of blocky and muddy moraine and looked out. I was looking into space. The glacier had gone. In its place there was a moonscape of bare boulders and dust down to the blue of the water, then there was a wide channel before there was another low beach, and the snout of the glacier was beyond it. We were not on the mainland at all.

One degree of warmth over the year might mean an early spring in East Anglia, or an inch of tide in the Thames estuary. But in Spitsbergen for whatever reason this majestic glacier had been cut back by two kilometres since the map had been made. That's a lot of melting and there was a moonscape of debris where it had been. I looked over the open water at the snout of the glacier. We were standing on a new island, an unknown island, maybe as yet unnamed.

'Hey Shags, come and look, we're on an island!'

He was stoking a bonfire of driftwood and had almost boiled the water for hot chocolate, so I went down to him and we drank it. An ivory gull came looking for scraps. Then we walked up and around the unknown island. Maybe Kotickøya would be a good name.

* * *

With the white sail set, *Kotick* reached across the glacial bay. Blue water piled up under the bow and spray smashed around the pine planks and caught in the sun. We'd often talked about the threat of immersion. Especially as the dry-suits had proved impractical for everyday use.

'So, how long do we have? If we go in ...'

'Five to ten minutes, that's if the shock of it doesn't kill you.'

'We're not very good at wearing the dry suits, are we?'

'They're a pain. We've just got to go carefully. And we've got the life raft.'

'As if that'll help.'

Once the sails were pulling, I rolled two cigarettes and lit them in my cupped hands. We were warm and dry and in control.

Unknown to us, far up the glaciated valleys above Isbukta, super-cold air was slipping down snow-covered mountainsides to collect in wide bowls. The colder air brimmed against the lip of valleys and when it started to spill the whole mass of it became unstable. It tumbled down into the bay where we sailed in the sun.

The noise of water and rock falling from the ice cliffs was lost as the wind stiffened and it shifted onto our nose so we tightened the sheets. Spray flew over the bow and I sat in the bottom of the boat sheltering from the wind. It was cold. I'd been cold for many hours now and my mind was working slowly. That was dangerous. Shaggy was holding the rudder bar with both hands. The wind was stronger again.

The tell-tales flying from the shroud showed the wind was behind us, but Shaggy was whooping like a cowboy with the sails pinned hard in. The water crashed out from under the bow.

'Look out Shags, you've got to free those sheets.'

'Yeeee-hah, whoooah,' he responded, deep in a fight with the weather helm. He could barely hold *Kotick* straight with both hands. I reached for the mainsheet but it was tight on the cleat.

'Look out, there's a gust!' he shouted.

An invisible hand pushed the mast firmly into the sea. The

mainsail flogged on the water and as the hull went over a shot of heat surged inside me. Suddenly I was a gymnast, scrambling on all fours over the topside that was coming up out of the water. My knees and boots were on the hull and my hands were pulling the gunwale back towards me. Water washed halfway into the cockpit and it rushed across the shrouds and semi-submerged hull as the bow swung into the wind, driven by what was left of the mainsail and jib, and hull above the waterline. *Kotick* was down, and the killing water was all around, very close. We had to stay dry.

The gunwale eased back towards us and then the mast popped up. I crashed forwards into the wash inside *Kotick*. The food, rifle, passports and map were all swilling around and the boat lay low in the water. In that instant the sea water froze my legs and feet and for some reason that annoyed me. The sail banged out a drum tattoo on my head and I chucked bucket-loads of water overboard. Shaggy's kip mat was flipping off in slow somersaults towards Siberia.

'Get the sails down,' I shouted, 'and bail, bail out!'

Shaggy wanted to row after his kip mat. He sat and pulled the boat around to chase it, but the mainsail drove us back into the wind.

'Get the ...' I said. And he freed off the mainsheet. We found a way for him to row while I bailed, and he paddled like a madman for his kip mat. We caught it, and then we both chucked water overboard, one with a bucket and one with the bilge pump. Nothing moves water like a scared man with a bucket. I was that scared man, and *Kotick* rose out of the water. My back was tight with the throwing of the water but she was higher now. I reached forward, took the jib off, and took down the mast. Shaggy was holding her into the wind with an oar. I made space to row and sat down on the thwart and threaded the blades through the rowlock strops. I took a stroke and *Kotick* responded to my oars in the water. Shaggy sat down and we stroked together.

We pulled for the wind shadow of the cliffs and the following wind buffeted the blades of the oars, driving the hull at top speed. And when the vortex spinning off the top of the cliff came the other way, and we were pulling into it, the wind pulled

Kotick's bow off the wind so both of us had to stroke with one oar to pull her back and back down with the blade on the other side.

A deep chill took me in the chest now, and it shook me. We could have died. What if these cliffs go on forever? What if we're stuck between ice cliff and rock cliff and there is nowhere to land? What if we die out here alone? They will say we were stupid. There was an alluvial fan under a heavy water fall. It was solid ground and we could have landed there, but it would have been pointless to try and recover in that cold shower.

The vertical rock cliff stretched out. There was a buttress and the wind was still spinning over the lip, turning to head us and follow us as the katabatic raced out to sea. I imagined an Arctic panther, chasing us and spitting foam.

Between gusts I shook the water from the map case. The chart was still dry. There should be a beach around this buttress. We stayed close to it. What if we hit a rock now? Our strength was gone and we could not withstand another accident. The buttress was just ten metres away and it disappeared into the sky above us. Please, we need dry and solid ground. The beach has to be there, around the corner.

It was.

* * *

We beached with relief and turned the boat upside down. We tied the kit together in a hollow and we made a camp while the wind was flying over us. I changed into dry clothes. The wind was still there but we lay on hard dry ground that did not move. We had dry clothes and this campsite could not turn upside down. The glacial water could not come rushing in. We were safe.

Shaggy counted the day's run and added all of the kilometres together.

'One thousand,' he said. That was a great time for good news, so we celebrated with whisky from the *Waterproof* and chocolate from Granny. I wanted to see her again, not send her my rucksack from a watery grave. Maybe I would not tell her about that last bit. That was too close.

The following morning the wind was still beating out of a blue sky and sweeping across the water, so I explored the pebble dunes behind the campsite. I walked further and longer than I intended, just to the next hummock, up and up, then along a summit ridge to a mountaintop.

The needle peaks of the nunataks stretched out inland and the high mountains in the centre of the island scratched the clear sky white. Out to sea the dark blue horizon curved ever so slightly downwards. My practised eye searched for drifting pack and there was none. The only white was in scuffs of troubled water, which fanned before katabatic blasts blowing down from the glaciers. Down there it was hell on water, Gino had died in such a place, but from here it was smooth and blue and amazing.

I sat on a stone in the sun. The blue barrels and brown tent where Shaggy slept nestled among the piles of shingle and the wind flew across the bay. What's it all about? I thought. This struggle for life and death, which only matters to ourselves and each other, what's it all for? Why do they argue about who made it? I'm warm, I've slept, and there's hot food in the tent. It's beautiful and I'm alive.

I ran down the screes and flicked back the tent sheet. Shaggy had hot tea in a mess tin and he'd saved half a pack of wine gums, my favourite.

I ate them and then I slept.

* * *

The tent sheet rippled in the wind and the light scattered on our sleeping bags. The high wind streaked the clouds into long tails and as the sun went through the north it was already reaching down towards the horizon. The white of it was dimmed into oranges and yellows by the dust in the polar air. That is to say, it was beginning to set and the high-latitude summer was drawing to a close. We could not wait for ever.

After two days of waiting, some kind of calm settled the water and we decided to try. So shortly before midnight under a sky of yellow fish scales we pushed out into the dark water one more time. My easy confidence to drift kilometres offshore had evaporated and I wanted to be near the beach, near to dry stones and shallow water where we could lay down our oars and build a small castle. And be free to walk up the mountains. The force of the katabatic was still fresh in my memory but there was no time for the luxury of getting over it. I was fearful.

For the first time since leaving the Radio Station we pulled on dry suits. But to wear them while we rowed was impractical because of the quantity of condensation and because they restricted our arms. The rubber neck seal was too tight, so we wore the trousers pulled up and the arms knotted around our waists.

'Near the beach Shaggy, let's stick close.'

'Nahh, straight to the headland,' he said.

The bay was glassy and I could see no harm in taking the direct line. But taking it made me uneasy. We agreed a line that brought us to below the next headland. The light surf on the beach stretched away and the distance to it grew. And it grew. There was a flat calm.

The glassy patch in the bay drifted out to sea and it was replaced by ruffled water. A breath stirred across *Kotick* and it settled into an offshore breeze. It might even fill the sail. We put up the mast and the jib but could not keep into the wind, which kept on rising. Now because the mast was up only one of us could row, and we tried motor-sailing but it did not work with the jib and the wind ahead.

Then a column of dark water rushed out towards us from the beach. It had to travel the full distance before it reached us. There were flecks of white in the rush of it and we heeled in the spray. The jib beat on the forestay and cracked the sheet. It caught and released and then cracked again. It cracked and the cleat flew out of the gunwale. I swore. We needed four oars just to pull back to the beach now that it was far away and directly upwind. I released the shrouds and shook the mast down. Yet again this was a race we could not lose. I swore again and tied the mast on the thwart and we both took our oars. Shaggy was in the stern and there was no time to change so he set the time.

His blades went deep and his recovery was fast: lug-chuck, lug-chuck, lug-chuck. The spray was flying in the icy sun, and the oars were smashing in the waves as the boat rolled from side to side. We couldn't make it into the wind. The rush of wind was too strong, and it caught our blades like before. Instead of making for the beach we turned away and crabbed sideways, hoping to catch the next headland. It was four kilometres to the south of us. If we missed that, the next landfall would be Siberia. That was eight hundred sea miles away.

We watched the relative proximity of the beach and the headland. It changed: the beach was further away and the headland was closer, or was it? Twenty minutes, then forty minutes, and the water crashed into the boat and our biceps and wrists were aching. The muscles bunched in my shoulders and the sweat ran freely down my temple and inside the collar of my shirt. The headland curved away. The closer we got the further it seemed to be.

'Are we any closer?'

'Pull, just pull. Just concentrate on pulling.'

I was rowing for my life. We both were, cut by the wind with freezing spray. And we both had guns at our heads, one at mine and one at Shaggy's. If we relaxed or missed a stroke, or did any of those things that people do to lose a race in England, then those guns would crack us away, out to Siberia, a bullet in the head, just like that polar bear. I didn't want that bullet. And while I was there I felt that there were two of me. One Peter was there in the boat with the pain and the heat and the exhaustion, forcing the power from every aching sinew down the flexing shafts, feeling the hot skin in my palms that ached from the pressure, heaving the oxygen into my lungs and battering the base of my spine.

The other Peter was watching the boat, watching the two men splashing in the sun and the strong wind, losing their balance and slopping with the chop that built in the short fetch from the beach. The detached Peter bore no pain, did not think this was the end. I tried to make a true description of being there. How to say all this? I surprised myself by that floating, and I saw quite clearly: Shaggy, myself and *Kotick* in that bay, with the sun and the strong wind. I looked for words that never came and never managed that true description, but that other Peter could stand the pain, and not for one moment did he think that I might die. That helped me keep my head.

'Follow me!' Shaggy was yelling.

'Be controlled,' I called. And he wrenched one of his blades out of a wave and rushed back to catch again, half a stroke ahead of his rhythm.

'We must be closer?'

'Just fucking pull.'

Then I could see a large crate and old rope. We continued to stroke the blades through the water. The surface was flat and *Kotick* did not roll as she had done before. Our rhythm came back and I was breathing more easily. The spray had gone. The wind rushed by and we had nearly made it, but oh what pain. Then I could see dry wood and plastic debris, the grey-green seaweed; there was a shoe and strands of kelp and the strokes came more easily. Are we nearly there yet? I was thinking.

Then the water was flat and the beach was there. I could smell the sand, the wood and the dried weed. Then, crunch, the bow rested in the gravel.

I filled my lungs with air.

'Thank Christ for that,' I said.

'That was one hell of a time.'

'Not doing that again,' I said.

'Good effort,' he said. 'Nothing like rowing for your life.'

After running along the beach to warm my feet up, we both had the same idea and decided to tie lines to the bow and stern of *Kotick*. We each held one and walked her along in the shallows. When there were rocks we held the gunwale. It was slow and painstaking but we were making progress. We probably could have paddled safely but we were reluctant to leave the security of the hard beach. Then a spit of rocks reached out. It was the headland we had been rowing for when our lives depended on it, and that was as far as we could go. There were two glaucous gulls sheltering under the beach embankment. Even the seagulls were walking.

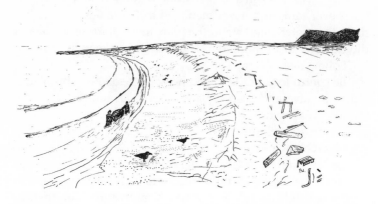

Even the seagulls were walking

We built a shelter with the mainsail stretched over an oar. The bow was just under the level of the beach embankment. The wind ripped and whistled over, carrying a fine spray of moisture. We slept alternately and when the sun was behind us rainbows danced in the sky downwind. I dreamed of going away with a Norwegian blonde girl to ski. Shaggy thought that was a great dream until I told him we'd gone to Antarctica and that yes, we really were skiing. After that he no longer wanted the details.

As we lay there, warm and dry, watching the rainbows, there was a suspicion eating me. Could it be that even here, now that we had come so far, our best might not be good enough? There was still Sørkapp. And the Arctic kept surprising us. Shaggy scratched another poem to Anna. He was counting down to the Radio Station and I wanted my old life back. We just had to keep going for a few more hundred kilometres. I didn't care where this journey took me, if anywhere, beyond that.

We sheltered there with the seagulls, drinking tea, watching the wind in the sunlight, hoping for calm, waiting until we could go home.

17

Sørkapp and Storm Bay

The colours of the rain danced in the sunshine as the wind swept it out to sea. My sleeping mat was comfortable in its hollow in the gravel with the mainsail stretched over us and my sleeping bag kept me warm. There was blood in my feet. I turned the pages of my expedition book, the wizard was killed in the mine and the hobbit continued to Mordor. Shaggy continued his letter to Anna. The seagulls were still walking.

There was a wide bay to the south of us and the flat-topped mountains beyond the bay fell away in cliffs and pinnacles. The sleep and the sun under the mainsail restored us and my fear of being on the water subsided. The tide filled the beach and ebbed, the wind relaxed and the white cuts of cloud in the high blue sky drifted offshore. The seagulls took to their wings.

The sea grew restful and air moved from the north, breezing along the coast with slow fat clouds. The tide ebbed and returned. We let it ebb and flood one more time, steeling ourselves for the wind and the cold, waiting for the moment to push off and the answer to the question: are they good enough?

I pulled on dry socks and a fresh shirt, brushed off my mountain boots, laced them and zipped up my yeti gaiters, put my arms in the down jacket sleeves and shook my shoulders so it sat with plenty of air. I knelt and pushed my sleeping bag into its compression sack and packed the food back into its watertight barrel. I took the rocks and pebbles off the mainsail and unfolded it from the mast – there was no damage – and I rolled it into the sail bag.

It was three-thirty in the morning of the fifth of August.

* * *

I worked the action of the rifle, dropped some oil into the mechanism, worked it again, then wrapped it in plastic and zipped it into its case. The water crept up the beach towards us and I read the *Arctic Pilot* while Shaggy was picking out soup and biscuits for the next leg.

'It's not as easy as you think,' I said, worried about his 'downhill all the way' attitude. 'This is what it says,' and I read from the *Arctic Pilot*:

> The coast around Sørkapp is among the most weather-exposed in Svalbard. The summer temperature is low because of frequent fog. Periodically there are strong easterly winds and mariners must be prepared for the pack ice to close in under cover of fog ... There may be undiscovered shoal ridges ... The tidal streams run violently to and fro at five to seven knots.

Kotick's top speed was four knots in calm water. 'Looks tough,' I said. 'We'll have to be careful with that current.'

'Just pretend the coast goes straight on,' said Shaggy again. His logic still did not convince me. I did not trust this wild island to make it easy. It wanted to shrug us into the water, and Siberia was far away.

When the tide arrived and it was time to leave I was as warm as I had ever been. We pushed *Kotick* down the beach, lifted her bow up off the gravel and took up the oars. I poled off in the shallows taking care for rocks because we were leaving the certainty of the beach. The fat white clouds drifted with the breeze from the north.

A black guillemot jinked up and down around *Kotick*, chased by a skua. Left, right, up and down, the skua wanted the guillemot's fish. After dancing across the sky the smaller bird skimmed low across the water. There was a wave toppling up on the beach and the guillemot smashed into it. The skua was confused, lost; it made one slow circuit and flew away.

'I hope that's our excitement for the day,' I said, my voice dead-pan.

Shaggy remained silent, then he grunted and we rowed south under mountains that rose like ramparts from the coastal plain. It was a surprise that the tide was running with us and the channels near Sørkapp were calm. There was no fog, no pack ice, no five to seven knots of current. But there were shoals and we hit one, gently. There was no need for drastic action, no need to jump overboard to push her off, an oar in the shingle bank was sufficient.

'I bet we're the First Ever to run aground on the northernmost tip and the southernmost tip of Spitsbergen,' said Shaggy.

'Better with dry feet,' I said, remembering how he'd jumped overboard at Verlegenhuken.

* * *

At Sørkappneset there was a beach and a hut and we found a ten-kilogram block of cheese and tins of ham. We ate some cheese and in the visitors' book there were names in biro grouped by the date, several parties of skiers who'd made the journey from Longyearbyen in spring time. Further back I found the carpenters who'd sold me *Kotick*. She'd already completed a full circumnavigation. Shaggy and I still had a way to go.

We couldn't stay long because the current was running with us and we didn't want to waste it or have it change on us. We licked the cheese off our fingers and signed in the book.

'Peter and Shaggy and *Kotick* around the island, from Isfjord Radio via Ny Ålesund, Hinlopen Strait, Edge Island and Isbukta. Lean and mean, going for home. P+S.' Then we drew a cartoon of *Kotick* with the sail up and us pulling on the oars. There was a speech bubble and it said, 'Just another 1000 km to go then'.

* * *

There was a long hard pull up towards the fog around the islands off Sørkapp. And the wind started against us, but it was a wet breeze and *Kotick* was comfortable in these longer waves. Fog arrived but we were not lost in it because of the compass and my watch. We pulled through, driven by excitement tempered by fear. Like this we knew how to use our strength. I pulled watching the clock face, fighting the temptation to think we'd arrived at the turning point. With patience and nerve we kept on and only then changed course, and when the fog lifted we were emerging onto the southwest coast, in the middle of the channel that I'd chosen.

Then longer waves and more damp air came. The mist cleared and the coast opened to the north of us. The long waves and the steady breeze and the tundra moss were familiar. I felt safe. There were no more corners to turn before the Radio Station.

The coast had turned and it had changed. The west coast was a better one. There were no katabatics here and the island protected us from Siberia. Many hundred metres back from the beach there was a wide streak of red snow that I remembered from two years ago. I'd been the youngest of four on the survey team. My curiosity had drawn me to the red stain and I'd discovered it was real and natural, like a frozen watermelon. The field guide said it was algae.[39] I hadn't expected that. As we rowed I remembered that first field season.

The *Isdronningen* or 'Ice Queen' rolled like a pig in the southwesterly gale and I had to break-dance in the shower to stay upright. Katie was comfortably comatose thanks to an overdose of seasickness tablets. With the exception of the captain there was no sign of the Viking sailors, least of all the cook. So I ate tomatoes and rye biscuits then with three violent spasms I threw them shamelessly into the loo. It splashed up and I felt better. Much later, when there was still no sign of the crew, I boiled some eggs in the kettle and

---

[39] The red stain is caused by the presence of *Chlamydomonas nivalis*, a species of green algae containing a secondary red carotenoid pigment in addition to chlorophyll. Unlike most freshwater algae it is cold-loving. The epithet *nivalis* is from Latin and refers to snow.

enjoyed the exhilaration of the sun in the gale on the black water. There was a night, then a calmer day and a run ashore on Bear Island. Then north some more and they left us here at Storm Bay, close to the red-stained snow.

Then on the ridge above the ice cap, with the nunataks stretching away, I had stood with the same field party, looking down on the light and swirling cloud. A halo of misty colours grew out of the whiteness and then giants were walking on the carpet below us, each with a halo from the colours of the rainbow, moving in time. The sun was behind us and we watched in wonder as the giants moved together and then moved away.

'Shags, have you ever seen a Brocken spectre?'[40]

'Yeah, in Scotland, with my dad, you?'

'Up there.' I nodded towards the needle peaks above Storm Bay. 'Two years ago. It was the first time I arrived,' I said. 'I missed the May Ball.' And, I thought, I was in love with that girl the whole summer.

The wind was calm now and while Shaggy paddled in the rolling waves that swung across Storm Bay I made hot soup. We had twelve good hours of turning water in our wake since our last campsite where the seagulls had been walking. The wind was calm but the swell breaking on the stones looked dangerous to beach in so we rowed on and on, until the fatigue was really in us. We approached the beach again and the breakers swept and sighed as we talked and we chose a stretch to land on. We chose a wide sweep and a shallow incline so the waves toppled gently. There was a path up through the low cliffs, and there were not too many rocks.

I sat on my thwart and pulled on the waders and Shaggy paddled as far as the place where the breakers toppled before they crashed, and I lent over with an oar and jabbed for the bottom. It came up just three feet wet. I could easily stand in that. So we untied the barrels and equipment and made everything loose and I jumped overboard. I held my hands

---

[40] An observer's shadow cast upon a cloud. This usually happens when the observer is on a mountain top or ridge and a low sun casts the shadow onto a fog or cloud in the valley below. It is named after the Brocken, a peak in the Harz Mountains in Germany where frequent fogs mean it is often observed.

high in the air and the water slopped up towards my chest but it stayed below the bib and armpits of the waders.

Shaggy passed me the food barrel and I carried it ashore through the surf and went back to where he was steady with gentle strokes of the oars. He passed me the escape bergan. I carried it ashore, then the bosun's bergan and the rifle together, then the dry barrel, then the life raft and the sails and spars. When there were just the 'fiddly bits' in the bottom of the boat – the sponge, the baler, a bilge pump, rummage bags, map, canvas spray cover and anchor – we could lift *Kotick* with all these smaller things onboard – Shaggy bailed the bilges dry and watched for a big wave.

He turned to the beach and just before it caught him he paddled deep and hard and rode the wave to the beach. He arrived on a froth of turning water and grounded far up the pebbles and sand and the turbulent wash left him there with his oars in the rope strops around the wooden rowlocks.

With two swings of his arms he shipped the oars and jumped over onto the running shingle. I was standing at the stern. He bent down over the bow, reaching for the cross-piece that only he could grip. He heaved and I heaved and the strain cut down my spine. *Kotick* came up and we walked sharply up the beach with the boat between us, and the next time the water broke on the beach we were above the high-tide seaweed.

'Cool. That worked,' I said as we laid *Kotick* down.

We packed our equipment between the rocks at the top of the beach and set apart the sleeping and cooking equipment. Then I walked up onto the coastal plain. It was soft with moss and there were stains of purple, and white saxifrage, and the yellow of the whitlow-wort. There were low hummocks stretching to the scarp slope of the needle peaks four kilometres to the east.

In low dips there were pools of water and hoof marks in the earth. Stalks of grass grew in the shelter of a boulder and on its rock face there was a splash of orange lichen. Three reindeer grazed on the tundra and the sun was beating down. I walked and drank the space and the smell of fertile tundra, and left my rucksack where we could sleep. A shadow cut the sun and a cry pierced the air.

'Ji-ahh, ji-ahh.'

The silhouette of a great skua circled above me, broad dark wings flashed with white, a stout hooked bill. I tipped my head back and the silhouette was following me. 'Ji-ahh, ji-ahh,' it was mewing. There were more silhouettes circling in the south. I remembered from Bear Island that a great skua at the bottom of a dive is a ferocious weight, two kilograms of stabbing beak and razor talons, that takes your hat off then cuts whatever lies beneath. It is a lot of skua.

I moved my rucksack and the skua circled away.

'Ji-ah, ji-ah,' it called at the reindeer.

Reindeer and great skua

We ate our boil-in-the-foil chicken and mushroom pasta and Shaggy opened the chart. We'd been over two folds and around Sørkapp so I knew we'd done well today. He pulled the magic string out of his pocket and started to measure.

'That was a good run with the tide,' he said.

'Yes it was strange,' I said. 'With a falling tide I'd have expected the current to be against us.'

'Whatever, it was fifty, fifty-five kilometres, as the string flies,' he said.

Then he opened the *Birds and Mammals* book. We'd already seen black guillemot, reindeer and great skua, so there were no new ticks today.

'Let's have a look,' I said and flicked through the pages, glancing at the notes in ballpoint pen. By red-throated diver was written 'wow' and by fulmar 'swoops low above the waves'.

'I've never seen a king eider,' I said. 'They've got a yellow crown.'

'Or the Ross's gull,' chimed Shaggy.

'But they don't exist,' I said.

'Yes they do,' he said.

I took off my shirt and fell asleep in the sun. Many hours later I woke up with a headache from the cold.

* * *

The water in Hornsund was steely-blue. The mountains and glaciers surrounding the fjord were dominated by the Hornsundtind peak, which was a fine one. And although a breeze was skidding across the water the waves were easy. The wind was almost across us and we found it was strong enough to drive *Kotick* directly to the next food depot at Isbjørnhamna, Ice Bear Cove, where the Polish research station stood with a blue and white hut and three white flag poles. One flag pole flew the Norwegian blue and white cross on red, another flew white over red, that must be Polish.

There was a man with a flag and he was tying a knot on the string that went up the third pole. He leaned back and looked up, and a Union flag went up the pole. He walked away and then he returned. The flag man took down the last flag and put it up with a Dutch red, white and blue below the Union Jack. We beached.

'You arrived first,' he said, nodding at the familiar profile of the MS *Waterproef* turning in from the open water. He was flying a flag for all of his visitors.

'Are there any Norwegians?' I said, pointing to the Norwegian flag. He nodded and I thought he had understood until he replied.

'Would you like some cornflakes with milk?' He was smiling, and once inside he put cornflakes on the table. He put them slowly and we felt the language barrier.

The cook brought a silver tower with a crown and taps and a chimney. It might have been a table-sized steam engine or a miniature distillery. Shaggy and I looked at it, one of the Poles took a pot and drained clear brown fluid from one of the taps, and he scooped some soggy leaves into the pot.

'You can tell there's a culture barrier if you can't understand their teapot,' said Shaggy.

The Polish cook mixed the concentrated tea with water and sugar in a glass. He had heavy features and watched us quietly as we took up our glasses of tea. We ate two basketfuls of bread and butter and jam. It warmed us and Shaggy took a second glass of tea.

They passed him the milk jug, he tipped it up, there was just a dribble left, and they jumped to find more while Shaggy protested that what he had was fine. After they'd found the milk, they wanted to know more about our trip. What did we wear on the water? Did we see any bears? And then, how close was the bear in the water? Were you afraid? The answer was yes and no. The boss went away and came back with clean towels and soap. We gave him one of our empty fuel containers because he liked the shape and the plastic lid which sealed tight.

We slept for six warm, dry hours. Then we joined the crew for their midnight meal, thick pearl barley soup and coffee. They sat around talking and looking at the boss. One of them explained that they were discussing the tasks and plans for the week ahead. As they talked quietly, looking quickly from one to another inside their own language, there was sensitive humour and laughter that I had not seen before. They were private people. It would have been a privilege to stay and meet them better, but the weather was good so we had to leave.

Shaggy scrawled at the bottom of his current letter, 'Just one hundred and sixty kilometres to go, and the weather is fine. It's going to be a race, this letter versus me. I hope I win.'

It was all so simple for Shaggy. He was powering through to the finish and that would be him, he would move on. But I was reluctant to finish. I wanted to enjoy these closing kilometres. It was a tremendous adventure and we were still in it. In this land of cold coasts, with its freezing water, chaotic winds and treacherous ice, we could cook at sea, navigate in the fog and land in breakers. I wanted to enjoy all of that. And besides I was not very sure what there would be for me at the end of the journey. I had pinned my hopes on this one great adventure, more than I cared to admit, I had looked forward with anticipation for two years, and now – What would success be like? Would anybody care? The worm of doubt was there despite my strength.

Shaggy was urgent, I was happy yet reluctant. We said our goodbyes and walked out into the cold.

18

The narwhal and the Ross's gull

The wind blew out of the fjord, and *Kotick*'s white mainsail and yellow and green jib brimmed and pulled us along so the water crashed out to each side of the gently rocking bow. My feet were dry and I squeezed and lifted my toes so that they would stay warm for as long as possible. I could feel them cooling off already.

Two Poles stood on the beach watching us reach out to sea, and after they waved and walked back to their blue hut we turned and looked towards the headland at the mouth of Hornsund. I rolled two cigarettes, lit them both, and passed one to Shaggy. He was working the rudder bar. He looked away, then spoke.

'If it was a race, what do you think the record would be?' he said.

'What d'you mean, around the island?' His real race was to Anna, but he must mean around the island. Why was he asking? I looked up at the sail, then fore, then aft. The thought of an organised race in Svalbard appalled me, but why not? It was inevitable that access to this magical island would change with the years.

'It would be one hell of a race,' I said. 'The safety cover would cost a fortune.'

'Yes but imagine, it would be the hardest race in the world, you'd need skill to sail and strength to row, and incredible stamina.' He paused. 'And anti-freeze in your feet.'

'And balls,' I said. 'I suppose somebody else will do it.'

I didn't want them to, but I wondered what their time would be.

'Yes, but let's say it was an Olympic sport, rowing and sailing a small boat around Spitsbergen, like us, what do you think the record would be?'

'Well, we lost three days in Ny Ålesund in the blizzard, probably four days in the ice, we didn't have to stop on Edge Island, that was another day. And we should finish inside thirty-five days, or let's say thirty, so by simple arithmetic ...'

'You reckon we could do it in twenty?'

'Yes, then if they are stronger and fitter, Olympic oarsmen and sailors, then they might take another five days off, so let's say fifteen days. That would be the world record,' I said.

'But it wouldn't be so much fun.'

'No, not with safety teams and journalists, they'd ruin it, and imagine the expense and all of those people running around here in their big hot tents.'

'And we've had a lot of extra fun 'cause we've been learning the whole way round,' he said.

'And being the first, I like that.'

'And spotting birds, you'd have to get extra points for each one.'

'How many points for a king eider?' I asked. There was a raft of ducks bobbing close to the shore. We watched a fulmar skimming the surface, both wing tips brushing the waves.

'It wouldn't really work, would it?'

'We've only got two birds left to see.'

I opened the thermos flask and steam warmed my hand which held the cup as I poured. I took a sip, passed the cup to Shaggy, and then I screwed the lid back onto the flask. Shaggy took a sip and looked towards the coast.

'Let's have some positive thinking,' he said. 'I want to see a Ross's gull. Ummm, a Ross's gull being chased by a king eider, no, a Ross's gull chased by a narwhal!'

'Yeah right, you can forget the gull.'

'No, the book says – new to science due to inaccessible habitat – just be positive and think it true.'

The narwhal catches the Ross's gull

He did not convince me. Positive thinking is indispensable for helping a beginner up an extreme rock face, but I didn't think that you could apply that to spotting wildlife.

We rounded the headland and tightened the sails as Shaggy pushed the tiller bar and *Kotick* turned north. The sun was cold and low, and it flashed in the water. The bow was still smashing the waves out to both sides and my watch and the map told us our place and speed. We'd covered twenty kilometres in just three hours when the wind dropped away. So we motor-sailed, then we both paddled. Then we ran aground.

We pushed off and rowed around the shallow ground and then paddled on, finding our way through the numerous skerries that were appearing now that the tide was dropping. We touched a couple more times and felt the brush of thick seaweed on the hull. Then the seaweed dragged at our oars. It was hard to make a good stroke, and hot work. I unzipped, and shed my jacket. Then we ran aground again. It seemed there was deep water just beyond so we pulled harder. *Kotick* edged forward through the weed. We pressed the oars down on the matted brown fronds and *Kotick* eased into the next channel.

The blood was running in my temples and there was sweat under my arms, my jacket was hot, and the keel slid into the bottom again. I stood up and jabbed into the water with an oar. It sank into mud and came up black. As the tide fell more rocks and kelp appeared. There were rocks breaking the calm surface all around.

Shaggy was pulling on the waders.

'Time to push,' he said, and he stepped over the side. It was shallow but he sank deep in the mud. He leaned down and put his hands on the stern post, flexed his knees and pushed up while I poled with an oar to keep us straight. He pushed and the seaweed scraped on the wooden planks, the keel dragged through the mud, a stone scraped along the keel and my oar kept coming up black. He pushed and we moved across the shallow ground. He was pushing and he pursed his lips flat across his teeth. The depth of the water did not change.

'No good,' he said.

'Practically stranded,' I said. 'We could always just wait for the tide to come back in.'

'That'll be hours,' he said.

'We could go and make breakfast on that rock.'

'I'll try to get us over there.'

He rested his palms under the stern post and flexed down on his knees. The mud and weed swished on the keel. After lots more pushing we were close enough, so he took off the waders and we unrolled the kip mats on the wet rock. I made coffee. Then I boiled the beans and bacon and used the water for porridge.

'There you go,' said Shaggy, taking his porridge. 'Could be Sunday afternoon in Poole Harbour.'

'Or a day trip on the Norfolk Broads, may as well enjoy the sun,' I said.

Twenty kilometres was a good start, but running aground was no good. We should have gone outside the islands of Dunøyane and Isøyane, but we were not to know. As the water dropped further more small islands appeared and seaweed broke the surface. We lay back. The tide would not be long.

'Shags, if we get back really quickly, how about going on to Ny Ålesund?'

'What, in *Kotick*? You're kidding, right?'

'Well, it would be fun. Imagine the party.' And it was the

real end of the journey for me, where my idea came, where the real start had been and where I wanted it to finish.

'I don't believe that you just said that,' he said.

We set off again. At dead low we had seen the deepest channel snake between the rocks and weed and mud banks, so we chose a good line and did not run aground again before deeper water. We pulled in time and we covered the ground. The tide kept coming and then we were in deep open water. It was flat enough to row hard and we timed ourselves from headland to headland, watching them disappear into the sea behind us, trying to make each kilometre in ten minutes, over and over, and the hours went and the kilometres stretched in the wake. We were back in the race.

The palms of my hands, and the hard skin on the pads of my fingers, curled around the familiar grain of the oar handles. The finger bones ached with the hours of pulling but my force on the oar did not diminish. Each time I caught a stroke the oar flexed around the wooden rowlock posts, and each time I pulled a finish the blade left a small pool of swirling water.

'Doosh, doosh, doosh,' my blades were jumping in the water.

Shaggy was still digging deep and upsetting the boat.

'Lug-chuck, lug-chuck, lug-chuck,' his blades whipped and stuck behind me.

'Keep the blade shallow, Shags, shallow.'

'I told you, I can pull harder like this,' he said.

After all of these hundreds of kilometres he was still digging deep and tipping the boat. And if I didn't concentrate to keep the rhythm and measure the time then his oars would catch early.

'Slow on the recovery, fast in the water, don't you get it?' I said. He had to learn, how could he not? He's doing it on purpose. He's doing it to annoy me. I should have been more direct at the beginning. I was wrong to think he would learn by practice. Can't he see? He's doing it on purpose.

'For fuck's sake,' I said.

'It's fine Pete, we're going fine.'

Now he's cantankerous. He knows he's close. He doesn't care.

* * *

There were rafts of common eider roosting in the shallow water in the bays, and each time we rounded a headland we saw more of them, lying in the shelter of the low rocks, checking us out with black shiny eyes, waterproof in their eider down, bobbing on the waves. Maybe they were collecting together, preparing to fly south because the summer was ending. I nearly had my journey complete. Then I would fly south too.

'Look, a king eider!' I shouted. 'Two of them, three, swimming in the middle, there.' My arm was raised, pointing into a flock of two hundred common eider. The king eider were there, just the same as the others but with dull yellow crowns, not as yellow as in the book, nor were their beaks so red. But the crowns were there. They were king eiders, there could be no doubt.

'If you say so, that's cool, we've nearly seen them all.'

We rested at the oars and I took a photograph. I knew when I took it the crown would hardly show. It didn't matter, we had the penultimate tick.

'Keep your eyes skinned for that narwhal, it might show us the way to the Ross's gull,' said Shaggy as we dipped the oars in time again.

Kotick ran through the water and ten minutes later we had another kilometre in our wake. That made fifty since the Polish Station and little more than one hundred to go before the Radio Station, the closing of our circle and the end of my dream. How would this journey save me? It was hard to imagine. I'd put so much in. Still, no matter, there was nothing for it but to go for home.

19

Wild goose chase

It was eighteen hours since the Polish hut and the grey light was losing its clarity. The hour hand on my watch crept to six in the evening and we could no longer beat the minute hand to a kilometre in every ten. My arms and shoulders had been holding up but now, after all of these hours, the fatigue was inside me. The flocks of eider showed no interest in us any more. The kilometres trailed in our wake. Shaggy took the map case and refolded the map.

'Just eighty kilometres now, d'you reckon we can make it in one?'

'Let's call six o'clock supper time,' I said.

'Then we go one on, one off? Right?'

Shaggy boiled noodles, then tea. After I'd eaten he made a hollow for his kip mat in the equipment in the bow. He pulled out his bag and settled it, he wriggled his head and rolled onto his side and did not move again. I paddled slowly up the coast, under the mountains. The tide dropped away and the low-tide rocks emerged. I bumped a few. The pulling was easy, it seemed right to pull slowly when the fatigue was inside me. I could pull easily like this for kilometres. And I did.

Four hours later I tugged at his feet, he stirred and looked around, he pulled on his boots and I swapped the oars for the sleeping bag. I took my boots off and made my neck comfortable in the rolled-up down jacket and *Kotick* rocked gently on the inshore water. Just as my eyes closed, Shaggy thumped a rock. I woke and looked sideways at the world.

'Sorry, bit shallow,' he said. Then he thumped another one. I tightened my lips and started falling asleep.

The rocks closed around us. He could not find a way out and he chose the wrong channel countless times. He bumped into every rock. He bumped them sideways and paddled back for space to manoeuvre, and he bumped the rocks behind him. Then he took three strong strokes and we rode up onto a whaleback rock and he had to stand to push back down again. He ground the keel into sand and weed and he rocked to twist the keel free and took one more stroke. Then he hit the end of a headland.

'Watch the rocks,' I yelled. 'I'm trying to sleep.'

I woke up mumbling; we were gliding along in open water.

'What's that?' said Shaggy, 'What 'you dreaming of this time?'

'Errrh, oh,' and my neck relaxed back into the down jacket.

We didn't hit any more rocks and I dreamed of falling with my arms outstretched and never hitting the ground, and some time later we were close to a beach. I twisted up from where my head rested on the jacket and a bell-shaped mountain reached down to the water. There was a small wooden hut and two figures in dirty orange waterproofs with lumpy rucksacks. They were watching us.

'Let's stop here,' I said. I wanted to unroll my sleeping bag, inside the hut, out of the wind and light, and sleep with easy dreams. I wanted to stretch these final kilometres, I wanted to enjoy them. We were close and it was nearly over.

'How far have you come?' shouted a figure on the beach. I sat up and pushed the sleeping bag down to my waist.

'From Isbjørnhamna, from the Polish Station,' I said.

'All the way around the island,' said Shaggy. He stood up in the boat and made a big circle with his arm. 'Nearly all the way.'

The two on the beach were confused. I pulled on rubber boots and held *Kotick* in the shallow water.

'How far have you come?' I said.

'From Russia, from Barentsburg,' they said and smiled.

We lifted *Kotick* out of the waves that lapped on the beach.

The tide was falling so she would be fine resting here. I took the painter and secured it to a grey trunk that was lying far beyond the other driftwood.

The Russians watched us. They didn't seem to be going anywhere and did not seem to have anything else to do.

'I'm Yakov,' said the taller figure. 'What's your name?'

'I'm Peter,' I said.

'Ahhh, Peter, you were here before?' He made me think.

'Yes, last year, at Orustosen.' I indicated the far side. 'I was mapping there.'

'Yes, I thought you were similar. Peter, the geologist.' His memory surprised me and an image, of a hut in the mist on the far side, came back to me. They'd been wearing old red trousers and carried rolling tobacco. We'd made tea together.

'And you, were bird-watching, did you see the birds?' I said.

'Yes, at Camp Bell,' Yakov replied, 'just like we wanted.'

They both smiled and I remembered his story. They'd been going to the bird cliff to see the chicks come down. When the guillemot colonies had chosen the cliffs, many thousands of years ago, it was a short flight to the sea but now with the melting of the ice cap the cliffs have risen out of the sea[41] and stand far back from the safety of the water.

'And the foxes?' I said. They'd told me about foxes.

'Yes, many foxes,' they said, and then 'You want tea?'

'How many came down?' I said.

'A thousand, many thousands, they came down, all in four days.'

'And how many made it?'

'Lots of foxes,' said Yakov. 'And the chicks they don't have chance to practise, it's a long way to fly for them. Lots of them ...' and he flapped his arms then drew fingers across his throat. He smiled again. We all smiled.

'Come to the hut,' he said.

Shaggy shifted his weight onto the other leg and looked across Bellsund, then he looked at the oars that were lying

---

[41] Due to a well-documented tectonic process called 'isostatic rebound'.

down in *Kotick*.

'We can go in this weather, can't we?' he said.

'Let's stop for tea.' I wanted to stop for more.

The roof was complete and windproof and we had to stoop to enter. There was a window across the whole of Bellsund. It was warm and dry and on a shelf there was a primus stove and on the floor a bucket with water. We could stop and sleep, and I wanted my expedition book. What would happen in Mordor? This would be a fine place to find out. Yakov pumped the stove and dipped a round tin until it was half full. The blue flame hissed around it and condensation chilled on the outside of the tin.

Yakov and his friend had come from the coalmine and they were waiting for a Polish field team to pick them up and take them along the coast to look for barnacle geese.

'We will not be back for three days. It's a wonderful hut, you must stay and rest,' said Yakov. Shaggy stood up and stepped to the window.

'Yes, that would be great,' I said.

Shaggy leaned forward. The sound was calm and grey, the sea and the sky fusing in a single line of different shades on the horizon.

'Just sixty kilometres,' he said.

'Let's stay Shags, I need the sleep, and we will finish now, there's no question of that.'

'No way, I want to get there. I'm racing the letter,' he said, 'and who knows when another gale comes in.'

'But we can explore the hills, maybe up the fjord a little.' I felt these last days were going too fast, there was so much to see, so many important details. We were about to complete this tremendous journey but were missing the spirit of it for travelling too fast. All of those details behind us that we had not seen and could never re-live, the fjords running deep into the wild interior. We could stay here and enjoy the solitude. I could finish my book.

'We might see a Ross's gull,' I said. 'And Bellsund is famous for narwhal.' I was smiling, trying to cajole. His mouth smiled but his eyes were steady and with a little pain. He looked away.

The hut with a view of Bellsund

'I want back. You know why, he's coming to Waterloo. I can't miss that.' He was surveying the horizon.

'And anyway, that was the deal: if the weather's good we travel, and the weather's good,' he said, and it was true. We made that deal and so far it had worked well for us. We should travel, if only for Shaggy's sake. He'd been so far and so good with me following this crazy dream. Now he wanted back. I felt I owed him that.

The buzz of a distant outboard cut the air, gently then louder, and a zodiac broke the coastline. We all shook hands, lots of shaking, then we shook hands again to say goodbye and the Russians went with them. It was quiet again. But I so wanted to stay and be here.

'Are you sure?' I said.

'Yes. Let's go,' he said.

So with my reluctance and Shaggy's determination, we turned our backs on that perfect hut. My expedition book would have to wait. I closed the door. We lifted *Kotick* down the pebble beach and clambered aboard.

'It's your turn to row,' said Shaggy. I took the oars and he shook the sleeping bag. We set out, into the grey night-time.

20

Reflections on a wide, wide sea

My knuckles gripped the grain of the oar handles and with muscles that felt like wood I pulled the oars through the still, oily water. *Kotick* jerked from side to side as Shaggy pulled off his boots and unrolled his sleeping mat. There was rustling as he pulled his sleeping bag up to his neck, squashed his red hat over his head and then curled up on his side. The rocking stopped and I sent *Kotick* skimming flat across the water.

'Good-night,' he said.

The blades moved easily but the resilience in my wrists had gone. A gentle ache settled behind my temples and acid hung in my mouth. I pushed my watch up my cuff because it was one in the morning and it was telling me to sleep. I concentrated instead on the light and the space and I tried to think of progress. That would wake me up. There were just sixty kilometres to go and the water slapped on the bow each time I pulled.

Fresh blood reached my chest and my feet stayed cold. I wanted to sleep and I wanted warm feet. I wanted to curl into a dry sleeping bag and hide from the wind and the light. The hut had been such a good place to hide but instead I was making distance away from it. The hut was there, it was shrinking, and I could barely see its dark window, the one I wanted to hide behind, to sleep, to read, to be warm. I wanted to be in there, looking out at this big water with hot soup in my hand, and ten hours' in my sleeping bag ahead of me, not paddle into this grey nowhere at the dead of night. Shaggy was taking slow measured breathes.

The hut shrank by degrees to one tiny brick and the strokes and the minutes stretched into kilometres and hours but I did not measure them because there were twenty slow kilometres of open water ahead and too many hours without landmarks to the far side. Instead I filled the water with whirlpools around the blades, and the time with meandering thought.

We'll finish soon. Just sixty kilometres, *sixty* kilometres, that's twelve hours, if the weather holds. And the sky is settled so this calm should stay. If it stays then we'll finish. The full circle, the first circumnavigation, it might be island history. I wonder what they'll say. Lot's of them said we couldn't. The captain of the *Svalbard*, more scared of me starting than I was, until he scared the life out of me by talking about the fog and the tides and the gales when he didn't know any of them. Then I was scared and scared worse because I thought I was going mad. He told me how to send a distress signal, he told me three times. We never had to send it. This might have been a mad idea but it wasn't, because we did it carefully. Without public announcements. We just did it.

The strokes came easily and my biceps were hot again, I leaned and extended my arms, caught the water with both blades and drove them to the finish, another and another. *Kotick* responded and the water rushed under the bow. In this flat water I could almost make *Kotick* travel like I was rowing for two. I made long sweeps of muscle through wood on the water and the bow wave splashed out from the cutwater. But the fatigue came quickly and I eased off because I had to keep my strength for the twenty kilometres of open water.

I want to tell them the core of the story, without heroics or sensation or understatement, say it how it was: the sea freight and nearly having it half left behind; the rain at the beginning when I'd told Shaggy it never did; how *Kotick* shrank to a matchstick when the whale was underneath; the thunder of the ice and the zoo-elephant smell of a walrus. Can I make it feel like we lived it? The thumping of my heart in the face of an ice bear; the loneliness of Hinlopen; the fear of death in cold water; being afraid too many times and the relief of being alive up a mountain in the sunshine. How to say that in one story? It would be something if I could. I wonder if we'll be in the newspapers. 'Young men defy ice to circumnavigate the end of the world'. I wonder what the headlines will be. What they might be.

The oily grey water reached out to the horizon and the dark mountains rose from the beach. The hut was a spot now and the beach was sinking into the water as I pulled over the curve of the earth. That the beach was disappearing was good. But there was no sign of the coastal plain at Lågneset on the far side, only the mountains beyond, which seemed very close because of their clarity. The pain in my feet gave way to the ache of deep cold. It was diffusing through my ankle and up the shin. There was still no sign of the coastal plain. My tongue turned with acid.

I want my feet back and I want a hot meal and a white linen napkin. I want fresh meat to chew and crisp green vegetables to cut with my teeth, and roast potatoes and gravy, and a glass of red wine. I'll pull for food to chew and gravy and a white linen napkin.

We didn't listen to them that said 'you can't get through'. Perhaps they were still there, back at the islands, waiting for the ice with their kayaks and the big ships. We never listened to 'can't' advice, not even from our own tired, hungry bodies. By not believing in 'can't' we made 'can' come true. That made us strong. Yes, and we argued but it was good arguing, except when Shaggy is cantankerous, or arrogant with maps. And I'm a moody bastard sometimes. But now we have this story, a story worth telling. I wonder if we'll be in the newspapers. 'Men against the ice.' Who knows?

Shaggy so wants to finish. He's rowing for Anna. It's lucky for him to feel so. I wonder if she's the one, I wonder if he already knows, is that what he's going to tell her? I wonder if the copper bob will be in Oslo with her cloud of perfume. She might be. If she is, and I find her, and she remembers that goodbye, and it's easy between us, like last time, then that would be too much luck. It would be a sign. That she's the one. I wonder who will be my One, if there's a one for me. But I have to finish this first.

It's sixty kilometres, less the distance to the hut that's gone over the horizon. Are we halfway across yet? That would be ten kilometres. No, we can't be that far yet. But when we are then it'll be just fifty kilometres to go. Fifty kilometres to post and the telephone and the world of news and fresh coffee and chocolate cake. And Warm Feet. Fifty kilometres, just thirty miles, to the first circumnavigation of Spitsbergen in an un-powered open boat. The dream, it might save me, I'm not sure how. I hope it does. It's lonely out here. I want to get back.

The bell-shaped mountain reached into the open water and disappeared by degrees so that the thin wedge became steeper and shorter until the scarp slope of the mountain cut straight down into the water. I pulled and ignored the pain, I pulled and ignored my desire to see the clock, I ignored the acid in my mouth and I pulled my little amber world of colours – *Kotick*, the tent and food barrels, and the sleeping Shaggy – across the mouth of that great fjord. My brain relaxed into aspic. The water slapped down from the bow in a spray on the water.

Over my shoulder Lågneset appeared, first as the hint of a brushstroke between the two greys of the sea and the sky, then the brushstroke grew dark and it grew towards the higher land above Camp Bell. Another brushstroke appeared and there was a white whisker reaching up from the sea. I rested at the oars. I hung my neck forwards then I arched my back. I tipped my neck from side to side and reached for the thermos. I'm just a pinprick of life in all of this, with my hands and my heart, pulling to make it back to the world.

Mottled oily reflections danced in the water and reached out to a flat horizon. A buzz cut the solitude and I turned to see a skua dropping like a meteor, with short stabs of wingtip zipping the air. At my level he curved away and away. I could only guess what the target had been.

After the drips had fallen from my oars the only sound was the seabird wings, the whistle of a kittiwake's slipstream and the whirr of little auk. Light and dark grey clouds spawned fingers of rain over the fjords inland. Elsewhere horizontal tendrils mingled with the black hills and snowy mountaintops. A low-frequency vibration drifted over miles of silent water and I looked around for the ship. I could see none.

'Are there any interesting rocks around here?' I jumped at the sound of Shaggy speaking quite clearly behind me.

'What, in Bellsund?' I said. It was ten kilometres to the nearest beach and the sea floor was three hundred metres below, through black, freezing water. There were no rocks and I was amazed at the question.

Shaggy was asleep, and the vibration continued. He was snoring and talking to me in his dreams. It was good that he came. We work well together, even if he never learned to row. Lug-chuck, lug-chuck, profanity.

* * *

I was here last year but I'm better now.

Last year there was a full moon and the sun was setting because it was the end of the season. We were going to Camp Bell to see the bird cliffs the Russians told us about. A fellow student, another of the team, was interested to see the birds and I wanted to make distance along the coast as practice for this circumnavigation. A huge silver moon was rising over that bell-shaped mountain and the last of the sun flashed in the crashing spray. There was ice in the shape of an antler catching the last of the brilliant light. It was a warning.

The wind came up and white caps littered the sound. It was onshore, the wind, and it really was dusk and the cold came and the spray was tipping into the boat and I was cold. Then a hut loomed out of the darkness and I took us in on a breaker and up onto the beach. She was a heavy wooden boat and once we were there, in the surf, I couldn't hold her. The backwash was cold and strong and I couldn't hold her and the waves were beating her on the hard stone beach.

I dug three full fuel cans into the shingle with a rope tied around them, and I pulled the boat close and had to cut some line and because I was frantic I cut the rope too short. I was shouting everything in a voice too loud that she could not understand. I could not understand. But I kept shouting all the same. The strength in my arms and back and legs was nothing to the strength of the waves on that hard shingle beach, and when the waves dumped the boat I could hear the timbers split. That boat was not as good as *Kotick* but I loved her too and I couldn't bear to hear her timbers split.

I cut a new rope and tied it to the bow and to the weight buried in the shingle. The wind blew her across and the tide receded, leaving us washed up by the storm. While the tide was down I slept, knowing I'd lost my head and shouted badly and cut the rope in the wrong place at the very moment I had to be clear and cut in the right place.

It was better this year. When *Kotick* went over in Isbukta Shaggy and I were clear and quiet in the moment we had to be and moved against the wind just as we had to. Then the boat came up and although we were muddled and shocked by the cold we did the right thing which was to throw out the water in buckets and take off the mast and collect the important things from overboard, like his kip mat. We made the beach, in control, that was something.

I was up to it this year, not like last year at Camp Bell.

* * *

I hadn't looked over my shoulder for ages, instead I'd been filling the space with meandering thought. The brushstrokes on the horizon, between the greys of the sea and the sky, had been there for hours. They were darker. Now there was a vertical whisker, and a third horizontal brushstroke emerged on the seaward side. As I pulled the brushstrokes grew towards each other and the whisker became a radio mast. I checked my watch and looked at Shaggy. He was still hard asleep.

In that last hour the headache came again and I needed a hot drink. I needed sugar and sleep. I rested on the oars and listened to the air on the birds' wings. The two brushstrokes on the horizon melded with the hours into one long smudge. The coastal plain was dark, long, it was there. There were guy wires holding the beacon vertical. We were near to the far side, almost there. It would not be long before the Radio Station and the closing of our circle. But first, I had to sleep. I shook Shaggy's feet. It was his turn to make the distance.

The brushstrokes grew together

'Hey, five o'clock, we're almost at Kapp Martin.' He tipped his head and looked at his watch. He closed his eyes. When he opened them again he saw the beacon on the coastal plain.

'Huh, hey, we're nearly there.'

'I pulled an extra hour,' I said. And he started to extricate himself from the warmth of the sleeping bag. I laid down the oars and took off my boots. I pulled the socks off, put them under my arms inside my jacket and kneaded the white of my feet until I could feel the skin pulling. Then I tugged new socks over them and tent boots over that.

After coffee, biscuits brown, hazelnut spread and a roll-up, I took a slug of whisky. Then I curled up and fell asleep, hoping that my headache would go.

Forty kilometres to the Radio Station.

21

Full circle

Hours later he woke me. We were in a wide bay and the beacon at Kapp Martin was behind us. I looked around. The water was familiar. The rocks were dark and the light was stronger. My sleep evaporated in waves, leaving a light headache. It was better than before. I rubbed sensation into my hands and legs and pulled on my boots. I tied my laces, thinking, we might make island history today.

'Time for breakfast,' said Shaggy, and I looked at my watch. It was six in the morning. That he was talking about breakfast seemed a nonsense. I counted in my head to thirty hours since the Polish Station and I was happy when his cooker fluttered into a roar and then happy again when his mess tin started steaming. He handed me a cup of light-brown tea. It was sweet and hot, fit for kings. I took another swallow. Shaggy was rustling the foil bags.

'Bacon and beans,' he said. 'No use keeping it.'

I stepped over him and sat down with the oars. I took a slow easy stroke and turned *Kotick* northwards. Then I pulled a little harder and leaned forward to pick up my cup. I took a sip and put it down again. I made another stroke. The bay was familiar. Katrina and I had been here en route for Camp Bell last year. I recognised the headland behind us and the one ahead and the rocky outcrop on the beach, with a stream sweeping down beside it.

The hours I'd sat on that outcrop last year, with my waterproof map case and rock hammer, measuring the dip and strike of the fault plains, marking the different layers, centimetre by centimetre, in my notebook. I was trying to make sense of the shapes and surfaces, trying to see a pattern that might be evidence of folds or faults. Sometimes wishing I'd listened harder to one lecture or another, or remembered more detail from the textbooks on the way rocks cook and crack and how they deform when squeezed up into mountains.

Then while eating my packed lunch I gazed out to sea and imagined a sound boat and a fit crew and I was thinking: can they go all the way? Surely they can. That circumnavigation, is it possible? It must be. Then when it was time to return to the hut I would take off my boots, roll up my trousers, wade over the stream sweeping down the beach and make the hour-long walk back to the camp at Orustosen. And as I walked I hoped that when I plotted the day's work in colour on the white map in the hut, it would fit with the patterns from the days before. Last summer seemed so domestic.

The jet roar of the cooker stopped. I looked over my shoulder. Shaggy was rinsing out the drinking containers.

'How far d'you reckon?'

'Thirty kilometres,' he said, and started to pack his cooker away.

He joined my rhythm and we pulled easily together. The fatigue was deep inside me and the aggression had gone from the lug and the chuck of his pulling. The fatigue was inside him too. We had found a rate driven by determination and controlled by exhaustion that suited us both. We worked our backs and arms and wrists, driving each stroke into the water through the wood in the palms of our hands.

We came through small islands close to the coast and there was the honk and smell of nesting barnacle geese. My friend Oliver had been counting them last year with a powerful telescope, reading the numbers on their leg rings which identified each from another, as birds from Solway on the Scottish borders. It was quite in his character, that he should be chasing wild geese. He always enjoyed long odds.

'He spent hours, crawling around, looking for geese,' I told Shaggy. 'He had this massive telescope but it was only good at night-time, because of the heat haze during the day. Imagine that, an Arctic heat haze in twenty-four-hour daylight. It drove him mad.' In the end he realised he preferred the adrenalin rush of war zones and mountains.

'Sounds like Olly,' Shags replied.

* * *

The water was dancing because the swell kicked up on the shallow ground before smashing up on the rocks into spray that smelled of washed shingle. A headland reached out towards the islands. Beyond that headland there was the bay and the hut at Orustosen.

It was set back from the beach, just as it had been the year before. We'd cooked and slept and plotted colours on the maps in there. And played cards and brewed endless cups of soup and tea. We hosted a party and danced on the beds when four Romanian geologists came through, laden with whisky. They told stories from their revolution. It was here that we kept the heavy wooden boat with the food and equipment from the Radio Station.

Last year this was an outpost in the wilderness. Now it was the first of civilisation. I wanted to show Shaggy so we crunched onto the beach and pulled *Kotick* a little out of the water. I tried the hut door, it swung open and I smelled the dry wood. I put my hands and my weight on the map table and I pointed out the mountain that Olly had climbed. I looked into the food store and I found our signatures in the hut book: 'Great hut, thanks all the parties. Peter, Oliver, Ben, Katrina.'

There were five thousand barley sugars under the bed, right where we left them.

'What a cool place,' said Shaggy.

* * *

After coming so far, doing so much, pushing so hard, and now that we had come so close, I was hungry to finish. I didn't know what it would be like, I was a little afraid to find out, but I knew that we had to finish and soon. It was so close. I couldn't imagine what would stop us now. I knew the water from here to the Radio Station.

227

'Let's go,' I said.

How would it be to finish? I was nervous about that so I put my mind to what I knew, to keeping the rhythm and timing myself to the next break, counting the kilometres along the beach, just twenty left now, and containing my excitement for fear of losing control. Not counting down to the finish. Not anticipating the end of the pain. I was telling myself, keep steady, don't relax, and don't look forward to the wash of relief that must come. Shaggy was counting the strokes again and his counting aloud was more frequent and louder than before.

Not far to Anna, and not far to the first circumnavigation. That worm of doubt wriggled in my belly. Will this really be island history? Will it change my life as I want it to? It has to. I turned to the rowing and Shaggy was reaching three hundred.

* * *

The low clouds on the Van Keulenfjord glaciers which had been claustrophobic through their persistence the year before were overtaken by clearer weather from the south. We pulled and the rhythm stayed with us and the beach was close so we saw it stone by stone and it made us feel the progress.

We were close to the beach to stay out of the tide, which had turned against us. Other days we would have stopped and let the tide run itself out, but now we were feeling the end, hungry for it, and so we continued. Then we saw a vertical pole. It was only just there, but it was there, and it was the Radio Station.

I had to fight the 'nearly-there' feeling. I had to maintain my calm, drive each finish smooth and flat. But we were nearly there. We were level with the last saddle in the ridge before the mountain above the Radio Station. Then the mist came in again and I didn't have to fight that feeling any more because we couldn't see further than the beach embankment. We rowed just like we always did, just like before.

The clouds cleared and the radio masts were there and all the aerials and the guy wires were there. I could see the detail of a satellite dish. There were two large buildings clear in view. One of them was the block where we'd watched the north wind blow itself out thirty days before.

We kept our rhythm because that's what we always did. And we stopped for tea when two hours came up, because that's what we always did and because our routine had worked so far. And we heated water for the thermos flask in case we needed it. But we didn't think we would need it, and when the water was just warm the cooker ran dry and we didn't bother to refill it because the end was so close and we expected to finish.

The clouds were breaking up and the first rain since that long row in Forlandsundet came down from the sky. The clouds washed around the ridge, which was black and dark grey, criss-crossed by snow ramps. We picked a route through the Kapp Linné rocks that were exposed at low tide and bumped quite a few. It didn't give me nightmares like further south.

A figure stood on the headland with binoculars. He lifted one hand and, still looking through them, he waved.

He waved

'Come in number seven, your time is up,' boomed Shaggy.
'Already? Not yet,' I said, trying to keep the joke.

Then there was the final corner, the row around the headland, and the waves stopped rocking because we were inside the bay. The low cliffs reached around us and the concrete of the small dock was there in the rocks. Old tyres hung on steel chains and they smelled of brine and seaweed. The water was clear and dark and cold but it was easy now. Our hands were hard and strong and accustomed to the cold. We were arriving. I gripped the chain and red dust came off in the palm of my hand. I rested my head on the old tyres and smelled the cold rubber.

'Good outing lads,' said Shaggy, as if he were a rowing coach.

'Good outing,' he said again because we were alone.

'Thanks Shags.' I put my hand on his shoulder. I shook it. 'That's something I've wanted to do. For a very long time.'

I lifted my head and looked up the concrete stairs. I wanted somebody to greet us but nobody came. We secured *Kotick* with warps that would let her down as the tide fell, and walked up the steps. It was unusual to be walking on even ground. Beyond the heat-lock the Radio Station was warm and dry, as it had always been. There was the smell of fresh coffee and the Norwegians greeted us, as they always did. Only the Station Chief was smiling. There was chocolate cake, just as there always had been.

'So how far did you go then? The ice was very bad, no?'

'We went through, and around, all the way.'

Their faces were blank. They looked back at me, then at Shaggy, then at each other.

'We've been around, the whole way round,' I said.

They knew that the passage around the north coast was impassable this year, and we were telling them that we'd done it in just thirty days. Impossible.

We told them that yes, we'd been around; about the party in Ny Ålesund and meeting the Polar Institute field team on the far side. I told them about eating polar bear cooked by Heinrich. The chief raised his eyebrows and smiled and nodded. Ah, yes, he'd heard about that polar bear.

'Did you see people?' the chef Gustav wanted to know.

'Yes of course we saw people, they cooked for us,' I said.

'That is a long way in such a small boat,' said the Station Chief.

* * *

I'd imagined what it might be like to finish countless times. It was the pinnacle of my dream, the goal of my life, the end of a rainbow, my salvation. I expected euphoria, intense happiness, maybe gold. I would write a hundred postcards.

'We did it!!'

But no. It felt nothing like that. It hardly caused a ripple at the station. This was not island news. I don't think they even talked about it to each other. I phoned Nick and he was the first to say 'well done'.

We went back to the dock, lifted the barrels and rucksacks onto the dock and took *Kotick* off the old tyres. We beached her for the last time. Shaggy and I took the salty kit up to the barracks. We showered one after the other and planned to celebrate but suddenly his tiredness hit him. Perhaps the relief of winning his race to Anna was too much. He fell asleep.

While he could do nothing but sleep, I could not sleep at all. So with the company of a glass of whisky I read one of my favourite poems, 'The Rime of the Ancient Mariner', and despite my fatigue I did not sleep until I reached the last line. It's a long poem and I was reading slowly, so it was quite some time before the wedding guest went on a sadder and a wiser man.

Scratched in the back of the book was a much shorter Eskimo poem:

And yet there is only
One great thing
To live.
To see in huts and on journeys
The day that dawns
And the light that fills the world.

* * *

In that moment before I slept I was desolate because I knew, without a doubt, that I had been chasing an empty dream. All of that pulling and hoping and hunger and cold was for nothing. Well, no, not quite nothing. We'd seen a bear in the morning light, been scared and held it through. We went beyond ourselves and that was something. Nobody could take that away. As well as the desolation there was a hot coal burning. The journey, not the goal, had been everything. Those thirty days alone on the sea, which gave nothing but hard knocks; that was everything. To live was everything.

I zipped my sleeping bag, wriggled into the unaccustomed comfort of a pillow and closed my eyes. I slept hard and without dreams.

22

The Eskimo

So, we did it: the best part of one thousand two hundred kilometres, as the string flies, in thirty calendar days, two-thirds by oar. We saw three polar bears, three walrus, three king eiders, we survived one capsize and once escaped crushing icebergs by jumping onto a floe and pulling *Kotick* up after us. Shaggy did some water-skiing. There was no narwhal, no Ross's gull, and we didn't make the newspapers. It was not island news.

Shaggy reached Anna. She went to meet the French boyfriend at Waterloo on one day and the boyfriend arrived on another. Shaggy and Anna went to the Mediterranean, they did lots together. They fell in the snow and were scared together. They got married. He survived bloodthirsty rebels in Africa and wrote a best-seller[42] but in the aftershocks and the publicity of that they realised that they'd grown apart and, after many years together, he and Anna broke up. I began to suspect that the French boyfriend never existed. Shaggy had invented him to get us around the island.

Of course I never did find the copper bob in Oslo, but I did go skiing with another Norwegian in Antarctica. Then my life changed and I worked as an engineer for seven years in Patagonia and in what is called 'La Gran Colombia', until my hair grew dark and I spoke Spanish with no accent. I climbed the highest mountain and descended the longest river of that

---

[42] *Unscathed*, by Major Phil Ashby. Macmillan, London, 2002.

great continent and I fell in love many times. I almost disappeared there. Then I came home via Fontainebleau in France and now I do what I always dreaded.

I live in London and catch the tube to a big company office. Sometimes I think of the ice, or that extraordinary light. But not so much, because I have a house and a mortgage, and you know what? It's not so bad. In fact, I like it.

The Eskimo was right. The important thing is to Live.

Maps

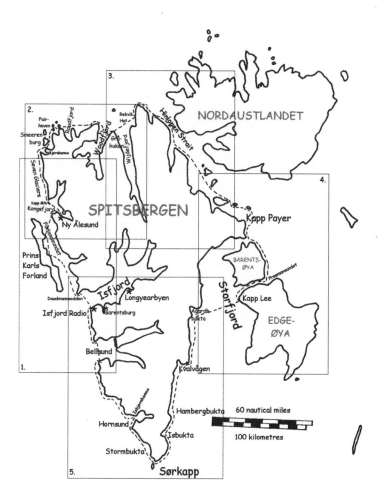

Full circumnavigation, with key to detailed maps

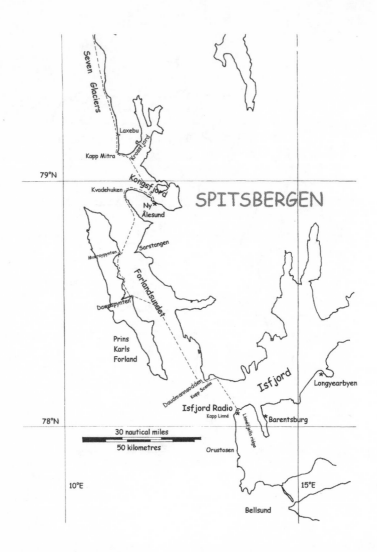

1. Isfjord to Ny Ålesund

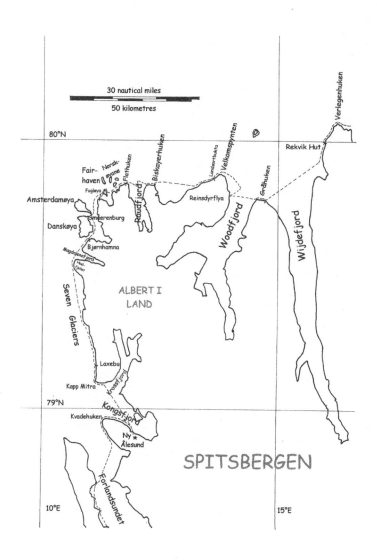

2. The north coast

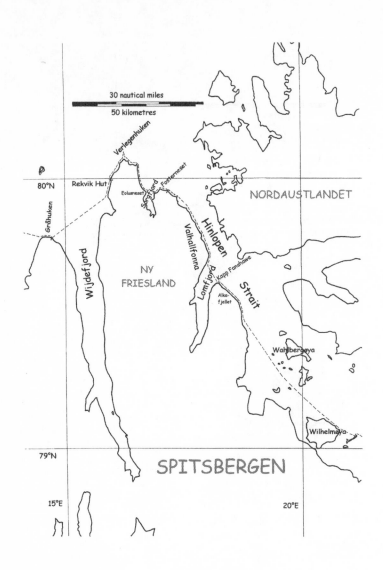

3. Hinlopen Strait

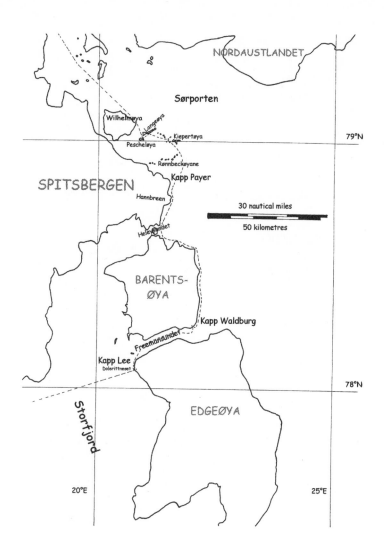

4. Kapp Payer and Kapp Lee

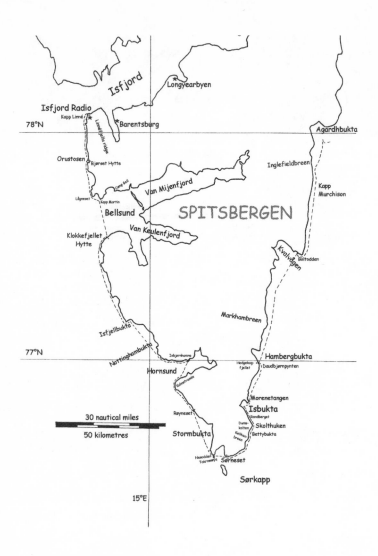

5. South Spitsbergen

Dates and distances

Transcript from field diary.
Distances shown are from the last waypoint.

Isfjord Radio, Kapp Linné		start 7 p.m., 9 July
Kapp Scania	21 km; sail	
Daudmannsodden	3 km; oar	row into wind through rocks
Dawespynten	55 km; sail	ashore; night-stop; gravel and grit
Murraypynten	21 km; oar	ashore
Kvadehuken	27 km; oar	aches: arms, hands, back, bum; snow later
Ny Ålesund	14 km; sail	ashore; 3 night-stops; 2 parties
near Kapp Mitra	23 km; sail	
Laxebu	17 km; oar	ashore; night-stop; camp with NPI arctic char project
Bjørnhamna	56 km; sail	ashore; night-stop; walrus
Smeerenburg	12 km; sail	ashore; night-stop; food depot; first serious ice
Fairhaven	10 km; sail	radio contact with Rudolph
Fuglefjorden	3 km; oar	ashore; night-stop; 3 kayakists; test firing
Fugløya	4.5 km; oar	ashore
Svenskegattet	10.5 km; oar	ashore
Flathuken		ashore; night-stop; exposed rocky beach; ledge bivouac

Biskayerhuken	11.5 km; oar	ashore; hytte? what hytte? bad ice
Landsortbukta	26 km; oar	ashore; night-stop; beach bivouac & barbecue
north of Mullerneset	13 km; m/sail	ashore; fog cleared
Gråhuken	13 km; m/sail	ashore; night-stop; camp; next day beautiful
Rekvik Hut (80° N)	38 km; oar	ashore; night-stop; hut; ice bear and 80° N celebrations
north of Eolusneset	26 km; oar	ashore; walrus in mist; aground at Verlegenhuken
south of Fosterneset	9.5 km; oar	ashore; night-stop; wild
south of Holmboeodden	12 km; oar	ashore; sunburn
Bordtoppen (Kapp Fanshawe)	34 km; oar	ice cliffs; Valhallfonna; streaky clear sky; no wind
off Wilhelmøya	67 km; sail	wind strengthens and gets cold
Pescheløya	7 km; oar	ashore; night-stop; barren; arctic tern; hungry
Langeøya	4 km; oar	ashore to study ice ahead
near Kiepertøya	9 km; sail	ashore; lunch on wet salty rock
in Rønnbeckøyane	8 km; m/sail	ashore
south of Hannbreen	20 km; oar	Shaggy's café revue bar
Kapp Waldburg	60 km; oar	ashore; ice bears and belugas en route
Kapp Lee	33 km; sail	radio contact with *Lance*
Dolerittneset	4 km; oar	ashore; 2 night-stops; chilli con polar bear, water-skiing, post

Dates and distances

0200 hrs fix	35 km; sail	dreamy!
off Inglefieldbreen	18 km; oar	swell roars on huge bergs
south of Kapp Murchison	16 km; sail	she pointed to windward!
Boltodden	35 km; oar	ashore; night-stop; one rowing; rock falls; sheltered swells
Hedgehogfjellet	63 km; 70% sail, 30% m/sail/oar	ashore; night-stop; winds off glaciers; wheezy; swamped at Daudbjørnpynten
Morenetangen	16 km; m/sail	ashore; hot chocolate on Kotickøya
near Randberget	8 km; sail	knocked down by katabatic
near Skolthuken	4.5 km; oar	ashore; 2 night-stops; hairy ride; walk up Dumskolten
across Bettybukta	8 km; oar	ashore; nearly to Hopen
Keilhaubreen	2 km; walk	ashore; night-stop; gulls walking
Sørneset Hytte	17 km; oar	ashore; calm; Peter, Shaggy on edge!
Nesodden	7 km; sail	following wind and fog
northwest of Tokrossøya	1 km; oar	through sound in fog; out to 'Atlantic' swell
'Copius Rock' (Stormbukta)	20.5 km; sail	wind veers to following 3 or 4; view of Hilmarfjellet
south of Røysneset	5 km; oar	ashore; night-stop; egg noodles and burger chunks
Kulmstranda	24 km; oar	king eider; 1 hour firm pressure on the oars
Wilczekodden / Isbjørnhamna	8 km; sail	ashore; night-stop; 'close' reach; arrive with *Waterproef*; Polish welcome

below Torbjørnsenfjellet	12 km; sail	fjord breeze and falling tide
Nottinghambukta	6 km; oar	ashore; aground
Island in Isfjellbukta	13 km; oar	rowing lesson!
Olsholmen (bird reserve)	16 km; sail	Shaggy's noodles
Klokkefjellet Hytte	38 km; oar	ashore; half-on, half-off for 7 hours; snags a problem
Bjørset Hytte (Osodden)	40 km; oar	ashore; night routine across Bellsund; breakfast off Gravsjøen
Isfjord Radio, Kapp Linné	23 km; oar	both rowing; finish 7 p.m., 8 August
Total	1120 km	
	618 km rowing	23 of our days, i.e. 23 'night-stops' (30 calendar days)
	500 km sailing	
	2 km walking	

The Oselvar

The boat used was a seventeen-foot Oselvar, built at Os, near Bergen, Norway. These excerpts from the Oselvar Foundation website are reproduced with permission.

2000 years of boat building history

Our oldest documentation of Norwegian boat building is portrayed in ancient rock carvings from 1800–500 BC, whilst finds of ancient boats and boat-remains can be dated back to the beginning of the Christian era and onwards. The Vikings were renowned as seamen, and their reputation was based on a fully developed boat building culture. The techniques, tools and materials chosen and developed by craftsmen over a thousand years ago have remained in use along the coast for many centuries. The craft of boat building was handed down from generation to generation, maintaining its ancient traditions and ensuring some form of gradual development.

The 'Strile' boats

The Oselvar boat was named after the most important building site for this type of boat during the 18th century: at the mouth of the River Os. The boat builders were renowned for building light, swift and elegant wooden boats. And this kind of boat was just perfect for the 'striler' (pronounced streeler). This is the originally insulting, but now somewhat affectionate term given to the people who lived on the islands and coastal regions outside Bergen. The striler used these boats as transport. They were dependent on boats to transport fish and crops to Bergen. The market in Bergen lies on the quay, and Strile boats would huddle together, their wooden sides bumping into each other, whilst their owners stood unsteadily bargaining to sell their goods. The Strile boats were both a form of transport and a market place.

Variety of design

The main form of transport, for both travellers and cargo, along the Norwegian coast was by boat. A large number of boat types were developed, varying from district to district, but all connected to the same traditions of pre-Viking boat building crafts. Boats were built for different purposes. This meant that the one type of boat could be built in many different styles and sizes. The models were often named after the number of oars, for example the 'færing' (four-oared) was one boat with two pairs of oars.

Within the West Norwegian area, the boats could be classed as such: south-western boats from the area between Agder and Bergen; mid-western boats from the area between Bergen and Møre; north-western boats in the county of Møre og Romsdal; and the northern boats from Trøndelag and Northern Norway. The Oselvar is the most renowned West Norwegian boat, a light, swift and smooth sailer, with its three broad planks being one of its distinctive features.

Working boat

The Oselvar was, of course, built initially as a working boat for fishermen – and as a means of transport. Boats were built both to be used and to last. No attention was paid to small details, and the boats were rough and robust. Their exteriors were painted with a thick coat of tar. The most attractive Oselvar boats are those built during this century; with surfaces polished with oil or varnish to show the natural beauty of the wood.

Traditional timber

The Oselvar is a clinker built boat with thin, very wide planks. First the planks are sewn together between the stems and the keel. Then the ribs (joists) are inserted. A four-oared boat would have three planks on each side. Oak was used for the keel, stems, rowlocks and the bent piece of wood that connected the keel and stem. The rest of the boat was built in pine. The work of every boat builder begins in the forest. He has to find pine trees suited to boat building (large trees) and wood the correct and natural shape for use as ribs, rowlocks etc. One essential element of the boat's construction is the 'halsane', the corkscrew shaped, practically triangular planks which gave the boat bottom its form towards the stems. The planks were traditionally shaped with an axe, but they have also been shaped by using a technique of steam and weights.

Sport and leisure

Initially the Oselvar was rigged with a square sail. Towards the end of the 19th century the 'striler' began using sprit sails. Other forms of rigging are the gaff sail and the Bermuda sail.

Although initially a working boat, the Oselvar also has a long tradition as a leisure craft. A boat which could achieve such grace and speed was perfect for sailing and rowing competitions. The first regatta was arranged by the Bergen Sailing Association on Midsummer's Day in 1871. Interest in the Oselvar as a racing boat has played a major role in its survival to this day. Today several clubs and sailing associations are engaged in promoting the traditions of the Oselvar – also as a sports and leisure boat. In competitions the Oselvar is classified as: 8 square metre sprit sail, 8 square metre, 10 square metre and 15 square metre Bermuda sail.

Buying an Oselvar

You can order your boat from the **Oselvar Boatyard**.

The færing – the four-oared boat – is the most common size being built, but the Boatyard will be glad to build a seksæring – a six-oared boat – now and then. Even bigger boats can be built.

Delivery time is two or three years.

www.oselvarverkstaden.no

Peter Webb

Peter Webb learned to sail on the east coast of England in his father's Folkboat, and learned Arctic survival when he served with the British Royal Marines on a winter deployment near Narvik, at the age of eighteen.

When he went to Cambridge to study, Peter was drawn back to the higher latitudes and elected to do his geological fieldwork in Spitsbergen. He organised a mapping expedition that was patronised by the Norwegian adventurer and glaciologist Monica Kristensen, and on leaving university in 1991 he undertook the journey described in *Ice Bears and Kotick*.

Since then he has been to Antarctica with the Aurora Expedition, and he returned to Spitsbergen with the Pole-to-Pole team as a snow-scooter driver. He then went to Patagonia to live and work as a rig engineer, and other travels and expeditions followed.

Peter Webb lives in London, and this is his first book.

DIVER

TONY GROOM

An honest, moving and sometimes hilarious account of a
hair-raisingly exciting career, both in the Royal Navy and in
commercial deep-sea diving – training the most unlikely of raw
recruits ... handling unexploded bombs while under air attack ...
living for months in a pressurised bottle with a voice like Donald
Duck ... commuting to work through a hole in the floor in the
freezing, black depths of the North Sea. Tony Groom joined the
Royal Navy at the age of seventeen, determined to become a
diver. As a member of the Fleet Clearance Diving Team, he found
himself diving for mines, dealing with unexploded bombs and
being shot at in the Falklands War. He left the Navy in 1985, and
has since travelled the world as a commercial diver.

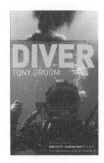

'**The Royal Navy Clearance Divers, not the SAS, are the
British mystery unit of the Falklands War**'
     Major General Julian Thompson

'**Wide-ranging, illuminating and sympathetic ... This tale fills
a massive gap and is long overdue**'
     Commodore Michael C Clapp

'**Epitomises the *esprit de corps* of the Royal Navy's Clearance
Diving branch, as well as the close-knit camaraderie of the
commercial offshore diver**'
     Mick Fellows

Illustrated · UK ISBN 978-1-906266-06-6 pbk
USA ISBN 978-1-57409-269-1 pbk

SKELETONS FOR SADNESS

A novel

EWEN SOUTHBY-TAILYOUR

It is September 1980. Edward Casement, sailing with his crew
towards Cape Horn and the Pacific in his ketch *Nomad*, calls in at
the Falklands. Things do not go according to plan, and, having lost
his crew, he ends up spending longer in the islands than he had
intended, sailing on charter for the Governor in the company of
an English nurse. In an atmosphere of growing intrigue, not all
is as it seems, and then comes the Argentine invasion. A story of
love, espionage, a yacht, and a war in the South Atlantic.

Illustrated · ISBN 978-1-906266-02-8 pbk
USA ISBN 978-1-57409-260-8 pbk

SALVAGE – A personal odyssey

CAPTAIN IAN TEW

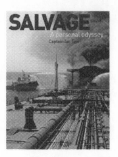

'No cure, no pay' is the rule. If a salvor is defeated by the elements, he receives nothing. Salvage is not a business for the faint-hearted. Ian Tew joined Selco of Singapore in 1974. As tug captain and salvage master, he roamed the world, from the coast of Cornwall to the Southern Ocean, from the Gulf of Suez to the South China Sea. Here he tells of the challenges of ten tough years – a barge adrift in a hurricane – a freighter aground on a reef – a tanker hit by a missile in the Gulf. This gripping account of drama at sea is a tribute to the seamanship, courage and resourcefulness of the salvor.

'The often heroic work, sterling seamanship and amazing professionalism of salvage vessel crews often goes unnoticed and unsung by the wider world ... a vivid and insightful account ...'
> Andrew Linington, Head of Communications, Nautilus UK

Illustrated • UK ISBN 978-0-9550243-9-9 pbk
UK ISBN 978-1-906266-00-4 hbk, signed limited edition
USA ISBN 978-1-57409-256-1 pbk

JOSEPH CONRAD: MASTER MARINER

PETER VILLIERS

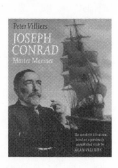

Before he published his first novel in 1895, Joseph Conrad spent 20 years in the merchant navy, eventually obtaining his master's ticket and commanding the barque *Otago*. This book, superbly illustrated with paintings by Mark Myers, traces his

sea-career and shows how Konrad Korzeniowski, master mariner, became Joseph Conrad, master novelist. Alan Villiers, world-renowned author and master mariner under sail, was uniquely qualified to comment on Conrad's life at sea, and the study he began has been completed by his son, Peter Villiers.

'A book that finally does justice to Conrad's time at sea'
Traditional Boats and Tall Ships

Illustrated with 12 paintings in full colour by Mark Myers RSMA F/ASMA
UK ISBN 0-9547062-9-3 pbk
USA ISBN 1-57409-244-8 pbk